THE DIVINE DOCTOR
HEALING BEYOND MEDICINE

THE DIVINE DOCTOR
HEALING BEYOND MEDICINE

JOSEPH MICHAEL LEVRY

Rootlight, Inc.
NEW YORK, NY

Copyright ©2003 Joseph Michael Levry.
Second edition 2004. Third edition 2005.

Rootlight, Inc.
15 Park Avenue, Suite 7C
New York, NY 10016
www.rootlight.com

All rights reserved. This book is protected under the copyright laws of the United States of America. This book may not be copied or reprinted for commercial gain or profit. This book may not be reproduced in whole or in part, or by any means electronic, mechanical, photocopying, recording, or other, without express written permission from the publisher, except by a reviewer who may use brief passages in a review.

COVER AND BOOK DESIGN: Renée Skuba
PHOTOGRAPHY: Fedric Eschew, Mark Finne, Marni Lustig
MODELS: Taunya Black, Alyssa Gaustad,
Jane Ohmes, Renata Spironello

Printed in the United States of America
For Worldwide Distribution
ISBN 978-1-885562-99-9
Library of Congress # 2003112183

Printed on recycled paper

CONTENTS

Preface ix
Introduction 1
CHAPTER ONE: The Healing Power of Love, Faith and Hope . . . 7
CHAPTER TWO: The Seven Karmic Influences 11
CHAPTER THREE: Meditation and the Subconscious 23
CHAPTER FOUR: Breath 27
    Exercise to Raise the Vibratory Rate 34
CHAPTER FIVE: The Nervous System 41
CHAPTER SIX: Healing Sounds 51
    The Healing Mantra: Ra Ma Da Sa Sa Say So Hung 52
    Sacred Music 64
CHAPTER SEVEN: Healing and Your Feet 69
    Footbath for Relaxation and Renewal 73
CHAPTER EIGHT: Healing Through the Light of the Sun 75
CHAPTER NINE: The Law of Nature and the Seven Planets . . . 87
    The Seven Periods 89
    The Moon 97
    The Sun 99
CHAPTER TEN: Planetary Influence 101
    Finding Your Primary and Secondary Planets 103
    Helpful Planetary Influence 105
CHAPTER ELEVEN: Vital Foods for Health 113
CHAPTER TWELVE: Healing Cancer 127
    Exercises to Overcome Health Challenges 136
CHAPTER THIRTEEN: Healing Heart Disease 147
CHAPTER FOURTEEN: Spirituality and Depression 155
CHAPTER FIFTEEN: Spirituality and Stress 161
CHAPTER SIXTEEN: Harmonyum 167
CHAPTER SEVENTEEN: The Healing Power of Magnets 177
CHAPTER EIGHTEEN: Healing Remedies and Yogic 181
    Practice for Specific Conditions
CHAPTER NINETEEN: Daily Exercise for Overall Health 235
    Kundalini Yoga "Stress Away" Series 236
    The Five Tibetans 243
CHAPTER TWENTY: The Three Lines of Defense 249
CHAPTER TWENTY-ONE: Transition 257
    A Mantra for Departing Ones 264
Conclusion 267

Other books by Joseph Michael Levry:

*Lifting the Veil: The Divine Code
Practical Kabbalah with Kundalini Yoga*

Alchemy of Love Relationships

*The Healing Fire of Heaven:
Mastering the Invisible Sunlight Fluid
for Healing and Spiritual Growth*
(formerly titled *The Splendor of the Sun*)

ACKNOWLEDGEMENTS

THIS BOOK IS DEDICATED with love to my family; my mother, a constant source of strength; my sisters for their loving support; and especially Yannick for his healing optimism and support.

I wish to express my love and gratitude to Yogi Bhajan, master of White Tantric and Kundalini yoga. Some of the meditations included in this book originate from his teachings.

My deepest gratitude goes to those who have helped me organize, edit and produce *The Divine Doctor*. Without their labors of love, this book would not have come together with such ease.

It is my sincere desire that this work brings light, healing, and joy to many.

—Joseph Michael Levry
New York, 2003

Disclaimer:
Always consult your physician before beginning this or any other exercise program. Nothing in this book is to be construed as medical advice. The benefits attributed to the practice of Kundalini yoga come from the centuries-old yogic tradition. Results will vary with individuals.

PREFACE

AFTER THREE DECADES of extensive work with the sacred sciences of Kabbalah and Kundalini yoga, as well as comprehensive study of the connection between physical, emotional and mental health, the time has come for me to share the wisdom with which I have been so richly blessed. I have found the healing truths I am passing on to be enormously helpful techniques, as well as extremely accurate, for self-healing and greater spiritual comprehension. Working with this sacred science will release new healing energies throughout your body, while treating the root of health problems. The wisdom you gain will tap into the source of light and infinite power and attract wonderful blessings. I reveal these priceless teachings to you with the hope and prayer that you will truly embrace them and heal yourself and others. This book contains the culminating wisdom of decades of intensive study; I have devoted my life to the principles contained within and witnessed the extraordinary transformative results in thousands of lives.

I invite you to delve deeply into these healing truths, which will enable you to understand the essence of their sacred wisdom, and how they can be employed to relieve specific health issues, negative thought patterns and detrimental habits. Most of the principles in *The Divine Doctor* are derived from the Harmonyum healing system—a transcendental healing system born out of Universal Kabbalah that raises the vibratory frequency of the whole spiritual body, thus neutralizing negative karmic influences and energy blocks from the past. It helps release the life force in the body, thereby activating the body's innate healing mechanism. I assure you that the teachings contained within this book are of the greatest practical utility to every person who desires to heal unhealthy patterns and cure energetic disturbances that exist on the mental, emotional and physical level. When you work with this timeless wisdom, you automatically will be attuned to heavenly vibrations and receive the blessings of the universe.

If we realize that Man is an encapsulation, an expression of infinite life, substance and intelligence, it naturally follows that if he abuses or neglects the life principle, he invites illness or disease to enter into his spiritual body and take root in his physical body. All disease, pain and suffering result from a lack of harmony experienced by the spiritual body. While the medical community is beginning to acknowledge that there is more to an individual than his physical body, there are still many well-meaning doctors and healers who do not fully understand that in order to initiate permanent healing, one must first address the disharmony within the spiritual body. By focusing on the physical body alone, one fails to deal with the whole person.

What we witness on the physical level is in fact the manifestation of spiritual disfunction. Treating the physical body alone is similar to pulling up the head of a dandelion without addressing the root; therefore, any initiating causes of illness remain and are likely to resurface. Thus, human beings quickly become trapped in a cycle of injury and repair that cannot truly be rectified. However, if we redirect our conscious efforts to the spiritual body, and the root causes of all hardship, blocks in the subconscious are eliminated. The body is then free to heal itself; the individual who was once trapped alone in his pain is reunited with a healthy existence and is reintegrated within the wholeness of his personal health and within the universal idea of health shared by all. I humbly submit to you that *The Divine Doctor* is a complete and thorough treatise on the art and science of self-healing.

Most people do not understand that human beings are both physical and spiritual. The great spiritual masters and ancient students of nature discovered that spiritual ailments actually create imprints on the physical body. This secret key to the healing of disease means that we must address the spiritual sickness—the birth of the cause of the symptoms—in order to affect the body on the most profound level. History tells us that in the past, the great men who uncovered these truths and recorded them in writings, were ordered to remain silent so that the information would not reach the masses. Vast libraries of priceless healing knowledge were burned, so that the writings of these wise spiritual masters could not be accessed and man would not know the truth about himself. It is recorded that the early fathers of the church vigorously attacked all manuscripts or books that dealt in any way with divine spiritual wisdom. This book gives you the key to hundreds of mysteries in medicine and healing completely unknown within ordinary medical practices, giving you access to timeless healing technologies. It reveals the precise methods of working with the spiritual body to achieve self-healing and maintain vibrant health.

Make the wisdom in this book your healing companion, and it will nurture your energy. *The Divine Doctor* will guide you through techniques for working with the spiritual body, so that you may recover more quickly from illnesses and become healthy while tapping into the wonder of self-healing; ultimately, it will connect you with infinity.

Those who were brought to the knowledge and use of the truths revealed in this book, found themselves healed and call their healing a miracle. Working with *The Divine Doctor* will cause the mysterious and beneficial forces of heaven to come to your aid, so that you may heal yourself and manifest your highest destiny.

This book is of inestimable importance, as it reveals the keys necessary to unlock the knowledge of self-healing, for self-knowledge and awareness are the keys to self-healing. When we are able to see our unhealthy patterns and understand ourselves with emotional clarity, free of judgment, we are able to face and cure our weaknesses with loving kindness, as well as recognize and amplify our strengths.

I believe whole-heartedly in this transcendental healing system, and in the healing and blessing that it bestows. Behind the simple presentation of this sacred wisdom lies a profound sacred science and vast catacombs of knowledge; I have endeavored here to explain the psychotherapeutic applications of the divine spiritual wisdom for your greatest benefit.

As I wrote in my book *Lifting the Veil*, we are living in a world where more and more people will be drawn to this path, choosing to teach others about the depth and efficacy of the truths contained in these books. These are the teachings for this age and beyond. *The Divine Doctor* is for all yogis, Kabbalists, doctors, serious health practitioners, vegetarians, non-vegetarians, and anyone who desires to achieve self-healing and help others heal through the application of profound meditations and practical techniques. By reading and practicing these truths, you will expand your consciousness, purify your mind, and renew yourself. Share them with your loved ones, friends and patients, and you will be multiplying their effect throughout the planet, sharing the sacred gift of expanded consciousness and vibrant health.

INTRODUCTION

Although traditional medicine has made wonderful advances toward eliminating various kinds of health disorders, and even prolonging life, there is one thing it cannot do: It cannot clean your mind—and the mind is where all illnesses begin. Medical science is unable to remove the unhealthy mental attitudes and negative speech patterns that are at the root of disease and adversity. Our bodies literally get sick when fed a diet of negative speech, toxic emotions, dark thoughts or unhealthy mental attitudes. A stressful life coupled with toxic thought patterns held in the deep recesses of our consciousness can cause general disease and a complete breakdown of our entire system. The principle of causality states that for every action there is an equal and opposite reaction. This principle is true even for genetically related illnesses and problems that have existed since birth. It is important to keep in mind that all sickness follows the Law of Emanation, which is based upon the Principle of Causality. The fact is, we seldom realize that our thoughts, feelings and words create—and they create according to their kind. Thoughts and words of worry, fear and criticism create disease, while thoughts of love, light and joy create health.

Before any physical symptoms manifest in the body, they are created first in the mind. It takes only a few bad thoughts to accumulate clouds of negativity in our heads, much like tempests gather in the sky above us. Negative thought patterns can undermine our entire being; they can make us mentally depressed and physically ill. However, by altering our thoughts, we can change everything for the better. Black and degrading thoughts can create disease, and this can be undone by thoughts of light and enrichment. The universe in which we live is a universe of thought. That which we experience is nothing but a manifestation of our thoughts and beliefs. Constructive thoughts produce harmonious conditions; unhealthy thoughts produce limitations. By controlling our thinking, we shall control our lives.

Sickness is a symptom of deviation from the perfect pattern of life and is the natural consequence of breaking the basic laws of harmony of this universe. Not only are we an expression of God, but also, there is a whole self that has power and capacities beyond anything we have ever known. Our true self never knows sickness, fear or failure, because it is one with God. This book will elucidate some of the laws of nature that bring us in harmony with the universe. Knowing those universal laws and abiding and working with them brings grace and divinity into our lives, making self-healing possible.

Many people who have sickness will say that it is not spiritual because they have been given a diagnosis by a doctor such as the presence of a bacteria or virus, or pain caused by misalignment of the bone structure, the presence of a tumor or cancer, or the existence of an allergy to a substance. These may be symptoms or even "physical root causes" but they are not the ultimate reason for their existence in the body. A person with a low energy vibration, stemming from unhealthy mental, emotional and behavioral patterns, allows these things to develop in the body. For example: A mental thought pattern, such as guilt leading to mentally tearing oneself down, may cause the physical immune system to attack itself, as is the case in autoimmune disorders. The brain cannot instruct the immune cells to discontinue this behavior so long as the mental pattern continues. In another example, a woman's frustrated desire to have a child can lead to the creation by the uterus of fibroids. A person who has a problem setting boundaries may have a weak immune system whereby every opportune pathogen penetrates and develops colds or flu.

As is the case in foot reflexology, where every organ in the body has a nerve flow to a specific location in the foot, so does every part of the body correlate to a specific aspect of our lives. For example, key issues surrounding love relationships and children will have an effect on the breasts and reproductive system. And problems with communication may create thyroid gland disorders.

The truth is, no one can cure you but yourself, and the only way to generate a permanent cure is through self-healing. Healing oneself is a peace-giving and nurturing act that fills the heart with true happiness; at the same time, it causes you to develop a relationship with your expanded identity, the infinite. Self-healing makes the heart warm like the sun and the head peaceful and clear like a crystal. It causes you to be at peace with yourself and your environment. No one can know their capacities and potentials until they know themselves. Knowing oneself opens up a new dimension of life. When a human truly experiences the self-healing that comes from an expansion of self and life, they no longer have a taste for anything other than awareness. All other kinds of healing are not only temporary, but they also encourage you to have a limited definition of self and reality.

By learning the laws of the universe, developing our spiritual nature and putting God first, we attract the good grace of the universe, causing self-healing to occur. (Throughout this book the word God is used to signify the source of creation, universal intelligence, Light, Love, and the Generating/Organizing/Destroying principles. If you are uncomfortable with the word God, you may substitute it with your own terminology.) Self-healing is possible only when you recognize and remove the negative mental attitudes and speech patterns that are at the root of all health troubles, for the greatest of all remedies is found in how you think, how you feel and how you act. Every day, every hour, every waking second we are either creating health or disease with our thoughts, emotions, speech and actions. Thus, it is of supreme importance to be aware and in control of our every word and deed. When awareness is practiced, every act becomes a spiritual and healing one. If you raise your awareness and keep in your mind constructive, positive and loving thoughts, you will find yourself speaking constructively and acting in loving ways. Consequently, your whole outlook will be positive and your life will be filled with love, joy, happiness, health, success and harmony. Everything that takes place in life happens because of our consciousness. By raising our consciousness, we raise our whole being, our whole outlook on life, and we start to live the full and glorious life which is our true heritage.

The axis of the earth has shifted and a new era is upon us. Time and space have changed. A new universe is presently birthing, bringing back a high vibrational energy—not only to earth, but to every particle of existence, every parallel universe and every life form in this realm and all others. Our civilization is in a state of terrific hurry and of life lived on superficial levels; it is one that is in constant need of excitement. This is causing alienation, separateness and a dispersal of consciousness that hasn't previously existed on the earth. As a result, people are experiencing stress mentally, emotionally and physically. Health is being affected as well as relationships with friends, loved ones and ourselves. Many people are feeling empty. Emptiness is the feeling of powerlessness to do anything effective about one's life or the world in which we live. Many people find they don't know what they want or even what they need. There is a craving for more and more sensation and diversion.

With the stress caused by these rapid changes, we are growing away from the natural self-regulation system of the body and its self-healing wisdom. We subject these regulating centers to all kinds of disturbances that disrupt their natural rhythm. As a result, we become exposed to various emotional infections such as insecurity, anger, resentment, fear, dislike, worry, envy, jealousy and irritation, which burn up our precious nervous force far faster than any human equipment can replace it. This can cause us, sooner or later, to run down in all departments. This is the main cause of all the diseases we see today: the neuroses, the cancers, ulcers, etc...

This transition from the 20th to the 21st century is harsh, stressful and challenging. People are not ready to face the consequence of the shift. As a result, the enormous stress is creating loss of energy, increased irritability, feelings of fatigue, and feelings of hopelessness. There is a decreased level of activity in some people, and a lack of interest in the usual activities and pastimes for others. Some people are experiencing an inability to think and concentrate normally, while others are undergoing weight loss or weight gain. Trouble falling asleep or staying asleep is quite common in this age. It is important to get enough sleep, because it is during sleep that the nervous force or psychic energy is replenished in the fullest quantities.

We cut ourselves off from the helpful influences of heaven by wasting our lives in the pursuit of all kinds of things that are less important than our relationship with our spirit. More and more persons have exaggerated feelings of guilt and worthlessness. We hear of impaired job performance from those who do not do what they like, nor like what they do. Certain people go so far as having thoughts of harming themselves. All the above, and especially our anxieties, insecurities, fear of pain and death, and fear of loss of power and influence, may break out in an illness which manifests pathological changes in the body. They may cause a person to break out in a rash or to exhibit gross physical changes in the body.

Eczema and asthma, nausea and vomiting, indigestion and stomach or duodenal ulcers, high blood pressure and heart disease, arthritis and crippling body deformities, sterility and miscarriages, and a score of other illnesses can be directly attributed to one's mental state.

For example, in duodenal ulcers or stomach ulcers, emotional tension will start the glands in the stomach to secrete more acid than is normally required for digestion. This excessive amount of acid will then start digesting or burning the delicate lining of the stomach. Prolonged burning or irritation will eventually produce an ulcer formation, which can eventually end in cancer. Remove the emotional strain and the ulcer will clear up.

The body's functions are disturbed when the mind works all the time. Intellectual or physical overwork provokes excessive dispersion of the life force and sometimes prevents it from moving freely. Anger makes the life force climb toward the upper part of the body, whereas joy procures tranquility, helping the life force to circulate easily, causing one to be peaceful. Anxiety provokes constriction of the heart and dilation of the lungs. As a result, the energy of the triple burner no longer circulates, preventing the life force from circulating freely.

Fear provokes closing of the upper triple burner, causing a lack of flow in the energy of the organism.

The stressful life, along with emotional infections, disturb our electromagnetic field and weaken our nervous system. We get nervous, irritable, and eventually become prey to disease.

This book will reveal to you the psychotherapeutic application of the divine spiritual wisdom for a permanent cure. It will show you how to raise the rate of vibratory energy functioning throughout your entire physical body to such a superior frequency that further disease cannot attack it, nor can any form of illness continue to exist in it. Since the physical appearance of disease is only the result of some broken laws of nature, we must learn to direct our free will to obey the laws of the universe. These laws govern human conduct and well-being. By learning these laws and bringing our lives into harmony with them, we become healthy. Disobeying these laws will create difficulties for ourselves and others. By not learning the laws of nature, we become our own worst enemies.

The study of the divine spiritual wisdom will fill the mind with healing and higher truths. Learning about the blueprint of the universe, the movement of the planets, and the nature of the soul expands the mind and fights disease. The key is to develop a relationship with our expanded identity, raise our frequency, and serve others. Let us utilize the healing principles that our sages have discovered and tested. We must bring our lives into harmony with the laws that govern this universe. No matter how sick you may be, or regardless of your loved one's health challenge, keep in mind at all times that no disease is impossible to cure—for the forces of nature, the rejuvenating capacity of constructive thoughts, and the healing power of faith and prayer, will support anyone who is determined to become well.

CHAPTER ONE

THE HEALING POWER OF LOVE, FAITH AND HOPE

It is through prayer, or the realization of spiritual truth, that we overcome challenges in health, love and life. We have to realize that God or light is always present where trouble or darkness seems to be. The link to God is the secret of life; it keeps life moving gracefully and smoothly. For we can not cut ourselves off from that which created us and breathes through us, but we can deny the existence of our divine connection, and in turn are thrown into limitation and trouble of all kinds.

We are all created and designed to be physically, mentally, and spiritually in harmony with the healing and regenerating forces of heaven. We must maintain our communion with God. To cease our communion with God would, in itself, be to slip out of heaven and back into limitations. Prayer is the simplest way to connect with God. No matter what your experience or condition may be, the potential for good, healing or light is always at hand. Prayer is an opportunity to connect with the limitless reserves of spirit within us, so that we may come out of darkness, or rise from any crossroads. It is the simplest act that connects us to the abundant, free-flowing, healing energy of the universe. Prayer is a gift from heaven, a powerful spiritual weapon against darkness, and a grace that is given to us by God. It is the great mystery that causes the action of divine law to move quickly and resolve any challenges into a progression of circumstances that lead to good. Prayer opens our minds and hearts to God's light and enables us to receive the highest influences in action from heaven. As one mystic says, prayer is an ineffable act, because it does not claim to be anything, yet it can do everything. Prayer transforms all misfortune into delight, it works for your highest good. When our prayers are not answered, we must remember that heaven knows better than we do about what we need, or what is best for the person for whom we pray.

The secret of demonstration or salvation lies in the application of love, faith and hope.

With the use of love, faith and hope we can heal ourselves by getting in touch with the three great cosmic forces known as Fire, Air and Water. This trinity of elements, Air, Fire and Water, are the primal makers of the material world. The whole material system would perish if they were thrown out of balance. And the same trinity of these three elements in the body maintains the breath, the body's temperature, and so on. They build and nourish the body with the help of blood, secretions, and other fluids produced in the body. If these are thrown out of balance, we ultimately fall prey to disease and an untimely, painful death.

Those great forces are represented in humanity by the head, the chest, and the stomach. Our head, chest and abdomen relate to the three faculties of thought, feeling and action. By bringing love, faith and hope into our lives, we can condition our minds to attune with the harmonious and healing forces of heaven. This attunement brings with it a greater supply of vital life force, which infuses our bodies, thus using and activating the body's built-in repair mechanisms. Love corresponds to our head, faith to our chest, and hope to our abdomen. Love, faith and hope are spiritual weapons we can use to fight challenges. They destroy fear and anger, and transform negativity into positivity, while releasing our hidden powers. They cause life to be a continuous experience of growth and change.

Love influences the head, especially the brain. The head gives birth to thought, which it manifests. It is upon thought that we depend for our understanding of the mystery of the triad of Nature, Humanity, and God, as well as of the character of the absolute omneity. In the head of man is found his intelligence, whose job is to control and direct all his lower faculties according to their particular laws. The head represents the intelligent nature. If we want a vast and deep meaning to our life, love must flow in us like a source. Without love, life loses its whole meaning, in spite of any knowledge and riches we may acquire.

Love is the first cause. It is the point of light beyond all light and darkness, it is truly the cohesive power of the universe. Love is the key to every closed door. The easiest and direct way to experience God's presence is through the use of the principle of love. At any moment of the day, direct thoughts of love to those you know, not only to those you already love, but to those you may not even like. It will return to you and cleanse your mind of all evil and negative thoughts. There should be no discrimination in love, for divine love embraces all alike, no matter what color, race, sex, creed, or religion.

If someone has said or done something to hurt you, direct thoughts of love to him or her. True love excludes self-polluting energies such as fear of failure, fear of truth, fear of life, and fear to be loved. True love is always understanding, although not necessarily always understood.

Service through uplifting others is one aspect of love that can work miracles in our health condition. When your health is being challenged, start serving in some capacity in a place like a church, temple or synagogue. The key is to expand, to serve and to uplift. The practice of gratefulness, kindness and forgiveness will put you in touch with the energy of love. God is love. You cannot enjoy the reality of love until you can forgive. Even from Christ's heart of true love come the words "Father, forgive them for they know not what they do."

When you experience true love, it fills your heart with such joy and gratitude that you cannot contain it, and it has to bubble over and out to all those souls around you. It is a glorious feeling of well-being and of being at one with all life.

Where there is true love, all unhealthy energies such as fear, hatred, jealousy, envy, and greed disappear.

When your heart is cold, and you feel no love, look around and find something you can love.

Let your love and compassion be extended to all; not just to those souls who love you, but even to those souls who hate you.

Love enfolds, penetrates, and transmutes negativity into positivity. Love is forgiveness, understanding, wisdom and strength.

Love of the real self regenerates man's faith in the inherent good of all, and teaches him, even while admitting the possibilities of human error, that error is no part of the real self.

The success of our prayer or any undertaking depends above all on our sincerity in our faith. Prayer is also an act of absolute faith.

Faith influences the chest and especially the lungs. The chest gives birth to life, which it preserves within it. The heart in the chest is the seat of the emotions and sentiments of humanity and further, it pumps the life blood through the body. We must cultivate faith if we want to be full of energy and fulfilled in our lives.

Without faith it is impossible to please God. Without faith in love it is impossible for us to be pleased with ourselves or with any of our relationships. You must be willing to hold on, no matter how dark or gloomy the situation appears to be. It may even be necessary to see it get worse before it gets better. Simply know that all will work out in true perfection at the right time. You must have faith and your faith must be strong and rock-like to be able to live this life. Faith grows stronger when it is put into practice. Faith is not something to be talked about. It has to be lived. Faith is the key into the world of transcendence, the heavenly kingdom. Your faith must be strong and unshakable. A weak faith creates doubt, and doubt weakens our electromagnetic field. A lack of faith weakens the chest and specially the lungs.

Hope affects the stomach or digestive line of defense. When hope is strong, it has a favorable influence on the stomach and the whole digestive system. The stomach gives birth to the body, which it renews. It is in the stomach, the lower part of the body of man, that the material functions of vegetation and reproduction take place, and the separation of the most impure parts. Weak hope creates weakness in the stomach, causing the digestive system as well as the beauty of the body to be affected. Therefore, always hope for the best, always hope to find the best. Hope leads to power. As long as a human breathes, there is always hope in life.

CHAPTER TWO

THE SEVEN KARMIC INFLUENCES

OUR PAST, including all the many incarnations we've had, not only shapes what we are now, but also determines in large part exactly where we'll be in the future. Our mental attitude is shaped from many experiences we have encountered in this life, as well as those experiences with which we've had to deal in previous lives.

Everything that happens to us is recorded and becomes part of our memory, whether we consciously remember it or not. There are two types of memory: psychological memory, which is a combination of old impressions, likes, dislikes and prejudices. And then there is what can be referred to as technical memory, which is the "know-how" of things, such as scientific knowledge. Technical memory is not a detriment, in fact it is essential to practical daily life. On the other hand, our psychological memory can be an enormous obstacle to our health, relationships and our lives in general.

Our psychological memory can color our perceptions of reality. As a matter of fact, our psychological memory is responsible for much of the impulsive behavior that ultimately leads to pain, disease and suffering. This is due to the fact that we have a tendency to identify with old, stale memories, believing they are us and compulsively repeating and recreating them in our lives. They form our bad habits and constitute our greatest enemies. They follow us from incarnation to incarnation, until we overcome them. Each habit born from our psychological memory creates a pattern in the brain, and these patterns make us behave in a healthy or unhealthy way. It is because of our psychological memory that our perception of reality is often distorted by an identification with old, false images that no longer serve us.

Our psychological memory originates from what we will refer to in this book as the seven karmic influences. Our goal is to identify these karmic influences and recognize their effects on our being. With that knowledge, we can raise our level of consciousness and achieve self-healing. It's important to keep in mind that these karmic influences determine our mental attitude and the way we react to life's happenings. These mental outlooks cannot be changed overnight. It has taken years, probably even centuries to mold our thought patterns, and it is only through the strictest discipline that we can outgrow them and establish new trends. Our karmic influences and the negative patterns they perpetuate are two reasons why so many people spend years in therapy trying to heal themselves. It is also why we meditate. Meditation can help us understand and resolve these patterns, so that we may disconnect from the unhealthy genetic and negative influences caused by some of them. Doing this releases us from all the unhealthy and undesirable situations they have created during our lives.

As mentioned earlier, there are seven karmic influences that contribute to our psychological conditioning, establishing psychic patterns that determine everything from how our physical body will manifest in this lifetime to our mental and emotional inclinations and inhibitions. Housed in our bodies are lifetimes of experiences, both traumatic and strengthening, and our physical being reflects how we have faced the challenges of time and space. Therefore, all our positive and negative experiences are stored in our muscles, in our nervous system, and in our brain.

These psychic patterns come from seven specific karmic sources. The truth is, since the time of our first incarnation from our fall from paradise as individual cells, we have had numerous earthly experiences in different physical bodies as different personalities. Throughout these experiences our inner self has been the same, and through the cycle of earthly existences, the separate lessons and experiences of each lifetime has accumulated as added wisdom. In each of those lives, we've done some good and we've done some bad. Therefore, the first source of our karmic debt is from past lives, which we carry into this physical world at birth. Some of these debts have a connection with the second and third psychic sources, the mother and father.

Since the soul must be contained within a vessel to live on Earth, it must inhabit a body. When a soul decides to return to Earth, it chooses two parents it believes will be a perfect match in terms of carrying out its mission of karmic obligations or responsibilities. In other words, parents are chosen by virtue of the child's karma. That is why we are born in a certain area under particular conditions: We pick longitude and latitude, we pick parents, we pick environment. If your karma is such that you are meant to suffer, the parent you choose will provide the basic ground root of these sufferings.

Scientifically speaking, when the father's sperm unites with the mother's ovum to form the first cell, or zygote, both of their individual gene pools combine to create an entirely new combination of genes imprinted with the parents' genetic patterns. Just as a new genetic combination is created, so, too, there is a new karmic inheritance that carries factors from our ancestors' individual karma, with particularly strong elements from our parents.

In other words, it's not just our mother and father whose karmic influences are transferred onto us. It is also the millions of people—our forefathers—involved in our genetic past who died, but still have some of their positive or challenging patterns living through our current conditions of health, relationships, career, etc. It is important to realize that genetic karmic influences are a major factor in the patterns of our lives. Thus, many of our challenges in health, love, and life are often transmitted through the genes of our ancestors.

As you can see, most of the inherited challenges come through the primal cell or zygote. Each zygote holds within it the sum of genetic sequences that make up the 23 pairs of chromosomes in each human cell. Half of each pair of chromosomes is donated by the man or woman; however, the genetic information is not evenly divided in the chromosomes, which results in a remarkably uneven landscape. In essence, these pairs of chromosomes are the building blocks of the genome, considered the map of the human gene. The genome is the very guidebook to the formation of our species.

Each human being's genomes carry the residue of an evolution that spans millions of years. In fact, there are three billion letters that make up the human genetic code, which constantly fluctuates in response to new human developments. Interestingly, only a few genes actually build and maintain an organism as complex as a human being with its 90,000 to 300,000 proteins and 100 trillion highly specialized cells. The human genome is a living text that continually edits and rewrites itself, continually creating new metaphoric alphabets that spell out biological messages necessary for survival. As our world continually changes, so does the genome in response to each new genetic challenge. This extraordinary and beautiful process is a never-ending story that drives the evolution of our species. Just as researchers study abnormal genetic patterns to learn how to treat and prevent disease, so, too may these patterns be observed to neutralize negative karma and encourage positive karma.

The fourth source of psychic patterns originates in the environment of the womb, the true beginning of life. It is there, where all the idiosyncratic likes, dislikes, hopes, fears and anxieties of your mother become an intrinsic part of your psyche. Everything the mother eats becomes the body of the baby. Everything the mother thinks becomes the mind of the baby. The way the mother feels about God becomes the brightness of the soul of the baby to be born. In addition, the joys and stresses of pregnancy are transferred to the child in the womb and they will impact the child's karma in a positive or challenging way. For this reason, it is highly advisable for pregnant women to listen to spiritual music, read holy books and stay away from negativity. As a pregnant woman, your food and life style must be suited to the child that you are expecting. You should avoid food that is difficult to digest, such as spicy food, and eat small, frequent meals.

The fifth source is the Kabbalistic planetary body that rules the day of your birth. These planets are seven in number and the days of the week have been named after them. In their order from Sunday through Saturday they stand for the Sun, Moon, Mars, Mercury, Jupiter, Venus, and Saturn. Each planet will have a positive and negative impact on you. Its vibration will affect you from the cradle to the grave. For example, if you were born on Tuesday, you should know it is the day ruled by the planet Mars, and anger is one of the aspects governed by Mars. You'll find people born on Tuesday have a tendency to draw experiences or circumstances to them that bring out anger. Every time they go through those situations, the anger generated pollutes their blood, eventually leading to diseases of the blood or cancer. In other words, illnesses that typically end up in surgery—or going under the knife—which, by the way, is one of the instruments ruled by Mars. The way to circumvent some of the karmic adversities is knowing the planet under which you were born. In the case of Tuesday-born people, the knowledge that anger is a weakness should cause them to avoid anger-driven situations. Controlling anger will allow them to manage their health. So knowledge here is power. Conversely, by accessing some of the positive aspects of Mars, such as determination, loyalty and stamina, Tuesday's children can improve their health and enhance their lives. The quality of determination, for example, will allow them to turn the impossible into possible. Loyalty will attract very helpful friends. Stamina could make exercising easier, thus contributing to overall health.

The sixth source of karma is your environment. The environment in which we are born dominates our patterns of thinking to a high degree. In this case, the environment encompasses the continent, the country, the city, the neighborhood and the house in which you live. The environment can be poor or rich, polluted or clean, loving or abusive. For example, those who are born in a poor environment find it very difficult to break out of the loop of poverty. Another example: Some of us who were raised in an abusive environment may grow up thinking that abuse is acceptable.

A loving and supportive environment contributes to healthy growth. This is how the environment becomes a part of the pattern.

The seventh source is our upbringing. Every detail of an individual's life from the age of one to eleven will be permanently etched in his/her psyche, forming the core of his/her karmic burden. Thus, those people who guide and teach the child from the earliest days contribute the most to his/her emotional karma. Each word, deed, and belief expressed will be automatically recorded in the conscious and subconscious mind of the child. I need to add here that at eight years of age the pineal gland begins to degenerate. This decay corresponds to the beginning of sexual maturation precipitated by the release of hormones from the pituitary gland. Many children do not cope well during this transitional period, when sexual awareness is developing. The high level of these hormones in their blood causes an imbalance between their mental and pranic body. The pranic and mental body are unable to coordinate with each other. Moreover, the adrenal and thyroid glands do not function in a coordinated manner. Parents should be aware that as children become more sexually aware they might experience difficulties. Disruptive behaviors such as anger, resentment and violence often manifest. Avoid burdening children with inappropriate sexual impulses during this transitional period. This can be achieved by maintaining a balance between the sympathetic (pingala) and parasympathetic (ida) nervous systems.

This seventh phase is about the way your parents raised you, most specifically between the ages of one to eleven. The first three years of your life in terms of development and growth belong to the mother. If at all possible, the child should be nursed by the mother. Before nursing, the mother should wash her breast. Habits begin to form around age three. From age three to age seven, you are aligned with your father, who serves as your teacher. From seven to eleven you belong to the immediate environment, such as your extended family or social circle as well as the school. After age eleven, your essential character has been molded. You are what you are. If the first three teachers did not do their job, you will need a mentor or a strict spiritual discipline to steer the course of your life in a healthy direction.

All those old familiar patterns of frustration, fear, wounds, embarrassment and anger that plague us as adults happened during those crucial years. The way our parents speak to us and interact with us becomes our karma. All the guilt, fears, positive and negative emotions they elicit in us will be recorded in our psychological memory. And it's not just our parents; it is also our teachers. Many of the challenges we encounter in our lives are created by the doctrinal patterns of the way in which we have been educated. Some of these patterns are helpful and constructive; other patterns create a feeling of guilt, failure and wrongfulness in us. These can be religious, ethical, lawful. They have to do with the way we feel.

Many patterns of thought, belief, conviction, and our religion originate from those who raised and taught us. For example, love as we know it; hatred and violence; war and control; our sexual patterns—both the natural and the deviations; our psychological neuroses, and physical illnesses are often delivered to us in the first eleven years of life by those who brought us up. These factors determine whether we will undergo suffering or happiness. In the most literal sense, the negative results from the emotions stirred by the karmic influences can create negative vibrations in our spiritual body that cause the eventual breakdown of our physical cells. For example, our reactions of anger, depression, and hatred, which come in part from these patterns, can put into motion certain negative vibrations, which eventually build in our spiritual body and bring about the gradual breakdown of our physical cells.

In essence, it is these seven karmic influences, from past lives up to the age of eleven, that determine the course of personality development in the individual.

Furthermore, the mind is like a computer: all it knows is what has been programmed into its memory. Therefore, when the mind is confronted with a new situation, it retrieves the data necessary to process the commands from the program of our past experiences.

Consequently, all relationships subsequent to our primary ones and those we formed long ago with family members will always engender similar reactions. That is because the mind, a creature of habit, tends to attach itself to old, familiar patterns. Therefore, our subconscious urges keep us forever in a loop consisting of the past experiences of our conscious mind, which are the real obstacles to self-healing. When we believe we are conscious of experiences as they occur in our lives, our so-called awareness is only an identification with the false images that are projected by unconscious instincts and impulses. These images are in truth our greatest enemies, encouraging our bad habits and following us from incarnation to incarnation until we overcome them.

Thus, every single experience we undergo during the formative years leaves an imprint on our psyche. The intensity of each experience, whether it is joy, sadness or pain will determine the force of the imprint, forming memories that will affect every area of our lives. These imprints are seedbeds in which our thoughts and actions bloom and grow, becoming the complex garden of our present and future experiences.

In reality, we are not as free as we may think. We are victims of patterns that we genetically inherited, as well as those we directly or indirectly created. Self-healing is possible when we understand and neutralize both the genetically inherited challenges and the self-created ones that have an influence on our lives. These undesirable karmas are stored in the deep recesses of consciousness in the brain. They constitute part of a large area of the unconscious mind which we have yet to explore. The negative aspects of the seven karmic influences inhabit the deeper strata of unconsciousness and become the dominant spirits of the underworld. They roam the lower astral world and disrupt our conscious life, block our intuition and cloud our perception.

As previously mentioned, the seven karmic influences are the experiences that we have collected, both traumatic and strengthening. The difficulties that we have experienced, the darkness, the bitterness, the betrayal, the hurt, the vengeance, the sadness and sorrow; as well as the longing, and desire, the love and the purity of emotion that has at times seemed so uncontrollable that it was a river that would wash over us and sweep us away, comes from our patterns.

The reason our body is what it is, and has the shape it has, is because of our seven karmic influences. We have developed our physical nature by the way we have used it in the past, and the manner with which we have faced the challenges of time and space. Therefore, some of our traumatic experiences are stored in our muscles, in our nervous system, and in our brain. It is in this manner of recording our every thought, word, deed and experience that all the negative and positive conditioning inserts itself in our body and remains active today. That is why during mental strain, emotional challenges, and health problems, or under stress, it is healthy to work out, run, practice yoga or exercise the physical body. Through the use of meditation, chanting, yoga, or exercising our physical body as well as taking a morning or nightly walk, we can allow ourselves to work through things, heal faster, and find solutions to our problems.

Also, it is important to acknowledge that anyone who experiences situations, in some way has invited them into their life for their own personal learning processes. These circumstances enable you to transcend or overcome the difficulties in your personality caused by the karmic influences. As a result, we progress and learn what we have agreed to learn in this particular lifetime. In essence then, blaming and shaming other individuals in a challenging situation is irrelevant. It would be more beneficial to examine our circumstance from a neutral perspective. Taking personal responsibility by acknowledging, owning and honoring our part within a given circumstance ultimately leads to healing.

These negative karmic influences are not only part of our psychic personality, but are also the cause of mental diseases. The human mind has a natural tendency to personalize these negative karmic influences, or in spiritual terms *dominant spirits*. These negative karmic influences are devastating to our way of thinking. They exercise a freezing effect on our personality. Impulsive behavior, emotional commotion, doubt, uncertainty, incapacitation of memory, numbing of feeling and senses, neuroses and phobias, in addition to a host of physical and emotional problems, are the result of these negative karmic influences. Sometimes in our dreams, negative karmic influences symbolically take some human or animal form. We are so completely at the mercy of irrational behavior born from these karmic influences, that in order to restore one to wholeness, or to experience self-healing, the afflictions stemming from these dominant influences must be eliminated from our consciousness.

To eliminate these negative karmic influences, it is first necessary to identify them. We could heal ourselves if we would stop and analyze our thoughts and emotional patterns, as opposed to going from doctor to doctor. One of the greatest problems we are faced with is that when we analyze our seven karmic influences, it can reveal self-deception, hypocrisy and small-mindedness.

As long as these subconscious knots of emotional patterns, caused by the seven karmic influences, are unknown and uncontrolled, we are unable to direct them to our best advantage, to examine them thoroughly, to accept the good ones and neutralize and transmute the destructive ones. Through meditation, we bring to awareness some of the karmic experiences that are holding us back, so we may neutralize or transmute them positively. Otherwise, as long as they remain intangible and unseen by the ego, they cannot be healed.

If we can transcend the mistakes of this life as well as those of former lifetimes that have not been so beneficent, then we may have the capacity to access new energies that may allow the divine presence to operate through us in perfect and healing manifestation.

This is what meditation can help us achieve. Meditation enables us to transmute the ego. Since negative karmic influences have strongly shaped our mental attitudes and beliefs, the work at hand cannot be accomplished overnight. As aforementioned, it has taken years, possibly even centuries, to mold our thought patterns, and it is only through a committed spiritual discipline that we can neutralize them and establish new trends. By disconnecting ourselves from these unhealthy genetic and negative karmic patterns, we will release their powerful grip upon our psyches and be allowed to flourish in this and other lifetimes. The seven negative karmic influences are essentially the dominant spirits that dwell in the lower astral world and disrupt our conscious life. Identifying, understanding, and neutralizing them not only allows us to heal ourselves but also by recognizing how they manifest in our own character and in others, they assist us in becoming compassionate, neutral and nonjudgmental with others. Let us study ourselves, our lives, and our environment. Whatever we cannot personally change, we must gracefully accept. If changes can be made through the study of the divine spiritual wisdom, let's do it. We may not be able to change other people, but we can change ourselves. We can improve our personality and expand our circle of friends.

Therefore, we must stop blaming others and have the courage to face our destructive patterns and positively transmute them so that we may become free of negative karma. No one is perfect; the seven karmic influences are the cross that everyone carries. The expression, "everyone has a skeleton in the closet," applies here. Your skeleton is your seven negative karmic influences. It is impossible to go beyond our conscious mind as long as we remain slaves of our unconscious urges that are influenced by these seven unhealthy karmic patterns. And since every one of us is unique, our freedom cannot be obtained from external sources, but rather, it can only come from our own realization, and through meditation. We need to meditate in order to ease our mental unrest caused by these unhealthy patterns. By easing the mental agitation, we can go beyond our conscious mind and experience true self-healing. Meditation allows us to move from duality to divinity, leading to self-healing and cosmic consciousness.

If we can transcend the mistakes of this life as well as those of former lifetimes… then we may have the capacity to access new energies that may allow the divine presence to operate through us in perfect and healing manifestation.

CHAPTER THREE

MEDITATION AND THE SUBCONSCIOUS

OUR UNHEALTHY PATTERNS create various mental and emotional conflicts in us, and can disrupt our lives and become an obstruction to self-healing. Some people spend a lot of money on many years of therapy trying to deal with their negative karmic influences. Some therapists mistakenly attribute the cause of their patients' problems to the father or mother. This results in family division and more disharmony. No one can heal you but yourself. For anyone to heal you, they have to clean your mind. As I said in the introduction, even a doctor cannot clean your mind. All people can do is either coach you or show you the way. The truth is, only self-healing can achieve a permanent cure. In that regard, the time-proven science of meditation has been known to be a catalyst in self-healing. Through meditation we gain the lost capacity to express and resolve these conflicts, so that we may experience self-liberation and self-healing.

Meditation allows us to bring out the negative karmic experiences and unhealthy patterns inhabiting the deep recesses of our consciousness. Then through mantra, coupled with the power of breath, they can be neutralized and constructively assimilated into consciousness. They no longer become the chaotic energies dwelling in the unconscious and disrupting our conscious life. Through meditation, we neutralize and transmute these energies from negative to positive. Then they are brought back once more into our personality, as beneficial and integral parts of our psyche.

During the process of meditation, you will be caused to occasionally revisit some early experiences in relation to your loved ones, including traumatic experiences. This process allows you to see how you emotionally react as you are reliving them. As you analyze your feelings towards them, you will uncover the source of your unconscious reactions to the various situations in your life. Those emotional reactions actually modify your conscious outlook on life. Meditation and the awakening of the conscious allows you to objectively realize the nature of your negative karmic influences, so that you may detach yourselves from them. It is the critical examination of these experiences, the understanding of their nature and the means whereby they came into being, that allows you to gradually, and with the passage of time, free yourself from their grip.

For example, a particular experience can give the uncomfortable feeling of knots in the stomach, pain in a particular body part, or fear. Often that memory gets recorded in us, and every time we relive the experience, the pain comes back in those same body locations. By meditating we gain the capacity to understand and resolve the experience, so that we may be free from the pain. We meditate to obtain peace and joy. Meditation allows us to discover and realize the self, for through knowledge of the self, we heal the self, and by healing of self, we improve humankind.

Everything we do is permanently recorded in our subconscious mind by a cosmic device that is located within us, and whose job it is to observe us day and night. It sees and records all good and negative actions. We are completely transparent to that intelligence. During our sleep, while we are unconscious, this internal mechanism releases parts of this record through our dreams. During sleep, our breathing pattern causes carbon dioxide to accumulate in the blood, which, in turn, allows a release of the subconscious mind. That release is perceived by us as dreams. For us to maintain our sanity, eight out of 24 hours in a day should be respectively allocated to our conscious mind, unconscious mind, and subconscious mind. A lack of sleep can prevent our subconscious from releasing its garbage, leading to mental breakdown. Sleep is necessary, and next to it is meditation.

Meditation is a means whereby we can process and cleanse our subconscious mind. When we neglect meditation, the full and often overflowing subconscious gets released all at once at the moment of death. The observance of this final life recording is the person's opportunity to judge their actions. The nature of their judgment determines the condition of the next incarnation.

Meditation gives you a chance to burn your destructive patterns, while cleaning your subconscious mind makes you more aware of those patterns, so that you may become clean and clear and experience that deep connection with yourself.

We each have a depth or potential that is waiting to be unfolded, once we neutralize the seven karmic influences. By the use of meditation, we can neutralize the seven karmic influences and unfold our potential, while enjoying the total awareness and intuitive wisdom that it brings. It allows us to ease our mental activity and break down the psychological complications, so that we may experience serenity. It is an opportunity to turn inside and observe our negative karmic patterns without emotional involvement in them. Thus it awakens our spiritual wisdom, which will help us be one with divinity. The practice of meditation helps us develop our divine faculties.

True self-healing bestows clarity of vision and awareness through which it is possible to see the timeless moment, so that we may deepen our understanding in the discovery of our reality and totality.

Meditation allows us to develop our talents and gives us the courage to rise above the limitations of our environment. It improves the function of the mind and protects us from the destructive impact of negative criticism and disapproval. It gives us the fortitude to ignore those who undermine our confidence and faith. We are no longer at the mercy of people who like to discourage those who are working at getting better. Meditation gives the awareness of peace, linking us with the Absolute Reality, through which we experience both the joy of bliss, and also the capacity to resolve problems gracefully. We must neutralize our negative patterns and transform our mind, so as to bring peace to our consciousness and enjoy the reality of self-healing. In order to enjoy the reality and fullness of healing, we must aspire to reach our primal state of divinity.

Meditation is really an art of surrendering oneself to the inner power, which restores the mental stability and provides renewed energy to face the challenges of time and space with divine grace. Not only does it turn life into a creative enterprise, but also, it causes us to concentrate on the present. We start to live in the here and now. Our life becomes the material we have to work with in order to perform the alchemy. We become the creative artists in the living of our lives. No matter how humble our lot is, or how limited our environment may be, we start to make our life a sanctuary of joy and sunshine. Meditation along with breath enables us to merge with the harmonious flow of divine grace, stilling the sense organs and the mind, so that we may face our own true self and experience ultra-consciousness.

CHAPTER FOUR

BREATH

THERE IS A MYSTERIOUS and invisible energy that vitalizes the body, and it is by far more important than any other form of nourishment. This unseen and vital cosmic vibratory energy that is omnipresent in the universe, structuring and sustaining all things, is known to yogis as *Prana*. Science teaches that the air we breathe contains nitrogen, oxygen and water. But prana, which is unknown to science, is in the air we breathe as well. Prana, which is extracted through breathing, is the primal breath of life, the source of all energy in the universe, and an essence existing in the universe that serves to connect us directly with the phases and manifestations of the universal forces. It is the primal source of all vitality. Bacteria, epidemic pathogens, misalignment of the bones and plaque deposits are merely results of a declining or poor circulation of prana.

Metaphysics teaches that human beings are dual by nature: There is the physical body which is visible, and there is the spiritual body, which is invisible to normal eyes. These two bodies have the same shape. The physical body, which comes from matter, is only the negative half of man. Health and happiness lie in the positive half of man, the spiritual body, the body that has a bond with the soul, the universe and to God Himself. The way to health cannot be found through matter or the physical body. Although it may appear to us that ill health begins in the physical body, more often it stems from neglect or mistreatment of the constituent essences and pranic energy that make up the spiritual body. The root of all disease lies in the vibratory nature of the spiritual body, and before a permanent cure can take place, one must take care of that spiritual body. In fact, the master key to true and lasting health lies in changing the rate of vibratory energy that runs throughout the entire physical body, via the spiritual body. One of the ways to accomplish this is through breath, because the quality of health we enjoy is directly linked to the quantity of prana in the body. Prana may be extracted by the body from a few sources, but primarily from inhaled air.

Oxygen is fuel for the physical body, or the negative half of man, whereas prana is fuel for our spiritual body, or positive half. As oxygen is essential for our blood, so is prana essential for the nervous system. Every nerve impulse requires prana; it is food for the nerves. Prana has a double polarity, containing both solar and lunar aspects. The solar prana enters the body through the right nostril, and the lunar through the left nostril. By the left nostril, we receive the magnetic or negative current, which is linked to our solar plexus. By the right nostril we receive the electric and positive current that affects the brain. The left nostril current is linked to the heart and the right nostril current is linked to the intellect.

When one of these currents is predominant, it creates disharmony; either in the heart or the intellect.

When we inhale with the left nostril and exhale through the right nostril, we work on the emotional plane and increase the development of our heart. By inhaling with the right nostril and exhaling through the left nostril, one works on the mental plane and develops the intellect. Alternate nostril breathing is a means by which one can balance the two hemispheres of the brain, and also achieve equilibrium between the heart and the intellect. This is how we harmonize our heart and intellect, our feelings and thoughts, our magnetic and electric currents.

Generally, in the morning, it is best to inhale with the left nostril and exhale through the right nostril. During the afternoon and night time, it is beneficial to inhale with the right nostril and exhale through the left nostril.

It will be of interest to know that inhaling with the left nostril, holding the breath and exhaling through the right nostril calms the nerves, helps the brain, and develops the memory. This breathing exercise is best for those who are studying. People who are living in a stressful environment, as well as those who want to heal themselves, should inhale with the left nostril and exhale through the right nostril. Inhaling with the left nostril and exhaling through the right opens one to the inflow of love and light. It opens up the door to your heart and allows nothing to stop the flow of healing. Practice inhaling with the left nostril and exhaling through the right nostril, in order to keep the doors of the heart wide open so that love, light and healing may flow freely in and through you, bringing vibrant health and grace. When the door of your heart is closed and the flow of light and love is interrupted, your whole life becomes stagnant and nothing works properly. That is why it is very important to consciously keep this door open for you to come close to God, the source of all life, so that your heart may never become empty.

Breath is vital; it is our connection with life. Therefore, every human being must learn how to breathe correctly. In fact, this simple process is a brilliantly composed mechanism endemic to humanity that can be utilized to extract prana from the atmosphere. Hidden within every human is a God-given capacity to raise the spiritual and cosmic energy to such a superior frequency that disease cannot penetrate the body, nor can any form of illness continue to exist in it. In other words, by the proper use of breath and sound, we can raise the rate of vibration and level of vital energy or prana in the body for our self-protection and healing. This is something that no amount of pharmaceutical medications and surgery can accomplish. Additionally, the ancient masters of Chinese medicine stated that acupuncture alone will not directly increase the prana level in the body. This, they stated, is done through "cultivation." Because our level of health and happiness is directly related to the level of prana in our body, we must make breath a major part of our daily health routine.

Most of us are conscious of breathing, yet seldom do we direct our attention to the process. Through proper breathing we can eliminate neuromuscular tension and increase energy and vitality, for the air we breathe is charged with vitality. By breathing deeply, we cause the life-giving oxygen to penetrate the body and clean the blood of deadly carbon dioxide. Many people breathe only with the upper portion of the lungs. The most beneficial breath is called diaphragmatic breathing: On the inhalation, the abdomen expands or becomes larger; while on the exhalation the abdomen contracts and becomes smaller. This is how babies breathe. All sorts of disorders arise from improper breathing. Conversely, disorders such as severe emotional problems can cause one to breathe improperly, resulting in massive muscular tension, which hampers the entire breathing process. Ultimately, this causes poor oxygenation, which in turn leads to low vitality. Since life absolutely depends upon air, it might be well for us to consider its value. The body depends upon prana. Prana can be defined as life force or energy. Air, one medium for prana, enters the body through the breath; when the body's allotment of prana has been exhausted, the spirit leaves the body.

When we change the way we breathe, we change the way we think, feel and act, for our mind, body, and spirit are influenced by the vital life force, or prana, contained in the breath. When one is experiencing fiery conditions, such as being angry, upset, or nervous, one must inhale deeply and hold the breath for a count of 100 and exhale in order to calm oneself. You can observe that people with good energy breathe correctly, whereas those with unsettled and negative energies breathe improperly. Through the breath, you let the peace which exceeds all understanding fill you and enfold you. When you are at peace within, you reflect peace without. Therefore, let nothing distress or disturb you.

Normal breathing draws a certain amount of prana into the lungs with the air. But when the breath is methodically controlled and consciously regulated, a great deal of prana can be brought into the spiritual body and transferred to the nervous system. The seat of prana is said to be in the heart. It is stored in the brain and nervous centers and distributed by our solar plexus throughout the physical body. Prana has a very exceptional property, that of being extremely sensitive to suggestions of the will.

By focusing the mind on the breathing process, we can consciously absorb a great amount of prana. The conscious absorption and the storage of this energy can benefit us physically, mentally and emotionally, causing us to gain happiness, self-control, clear thinking and spiritual growth. Above all, it awakens and develops our divine faculties.

An abundance of prana in the body harmonizes a person with the universe, strengthens the psycho-electromagnetic field and eliminates diseases. It flows through the subtle nerve channels, through the blood vessels and energizes the blood stream. As a matter of fact, prana strengthens the metabolism and circulation by purifying the blood, and animates the life process of the whole system while removing all unhealthy emotions. With every breath you take, you are renewing the essence of life itself.

Those with a completely balanced flow of prana are perfectly healthy. A surplus of stored prana, whether used consciously or unconsciously is not only a producer of radiant vitality and power, but also, has the capacity to renew our cells to the vigor of our youth. It helps in the renewal of both the mind and body. Those with a surplus of prana are not only magnetic and radiant, but also, they can perform wonderful healing and/or send positive thoughts to others. The practice of yoga enhances general vitality because it increases the flow of prana throughout the body by bathing and massaging the internal organs.

The relationship between you and God depends upon the rhythm of the breath. By controlling the breath, we can do everything from calming the nerves to obtaining a consciousness of ecstacy. Proper breathing allows one to have a relationship with the soul. The reason is, yogic science teaches that the soul is in the ribcage, the prison of the body. Through breath we can cause the body and mind to flow with the soul, thereby enhancing every aspect of our lives. If the body does not flow with the soul and the soul cannot command the body, then life becomes empty, without meaning and purpose.

God gave us two lungs, and it is no mistake that they are the biggest organs in the body. For in His infinite wisdom He knew that without the development of breath, which brings total purity of blood and complete oxygenation of the brain, you can neither meditate nor live a serene life. With every breath we fill our bodies with the sacred and omnipresent life force, which is essential to our very existence. The spiritual art of breathing involves the control of this all-pervading energy, and it is in breath work that one is able to generate the will power to gain mastery of the body.

The proper use of breath and sound can assist the natural healing forces of the body. When the vital powers or divine cosmic powers within the human body are functioning to the proper degree, there is no necessity for herbal extracts or medicines. The efficacy of medicine, herbal extracts, and drugs is strictly limited to the physical and material composition of an individual's body. It is the spiritual body that creates the so-called white blood cells, whose job it is to purge the body of undesirable and abnormal conditions. Those white blood cells are created and maintained by prana or the vital force that is taken into the body by the breath. These white blood cells have a bigger job than the ordinary red blood cells, which merely nourish and take a certain amount of energy through the capillaries to all parts of the body. The white blood cells must preserve their integrity to function as separate living bodies. They must be able to identify and analyze all that they come into contact with and determine what is destructive, what is dangerous, what is unnecessary and what should be destroyed. Additionally, they are responsible for the eradication of the remaining refuse. All of this requires a supreme and divine intelligence that is not possessed by all cells in the body. Cellular, as well as mental, intelligence enters the body by way of the breath.

As we can see, for any treatment to be successful and effective, it must raise the vibratory state of the entire body. By bringing fresh prana into the body with proper breathing, not only is the frequency of our spiritual body raised, but also our individual cells are prompted to regenerate themselves and work together harmoniously.

By breathing properly and consciously, one can become strong and healthy. Holding the air in the lungs for a long time makes us patient. Therefore, when you breathe, hold the breath in so that you may extract the prana that it contains. Also keep constructive thoughts in your mind while breathing. Remember that by breathing slowly, we purify the nervous system. Therefore, breathe slowly and consciously, thinking of all the wonderful elements that each fresh breath brings to benefit your health, strengthen your body and calm your mind. Use the breath to take care of yourself before you get sick. Through the proper use of breath, you create perfect peace within yourself and it is reflected without. As a result, peace, tranquillity and serenity emanate from you. You create the right atmosphere wherever you go. You are a blessing, a help, and an uplifting angel to all people who cross your path. You create peace and harmony in the world around you. Therefore, breathe deeply and slowly, so that the peace and love of the divine can fill you and enfold you. Lift up your heart and give eternal thanks for the use of the breath of life.

The three-part exercise starting on the following page is a supreme method for raising the vibratory state of the body.

Exercise To Raise the Vibratory State

PART I:
- First, ensure that you are relaxed and begin with this healing breath: Sit comfortably in a chair with your back straight, your head erect and hands resting on your lap.
- Focus the eyes, slightly closed, at the tip of your nose.
- Then let the breath flow in as you inhale, while mentally counting very slowly to 20. In other words, make the inhalation last 20 counts. Hold the breath to the count of 20. Then slowly relax and let the breath out to the count of 20. Repeat this for a minimum of 11 minutes.

Gradually, as the mind accustoms itself to this pattern, the lungs will automatically take up this healing rhythm. As the lungs take up the rhythm of inhaling for 20, holding for 20 and exhaling for 20, they communicate and gradually impart a sense of peace and well-being to all the surrounding cells and tissues. In a few minutes, the whole body will vibrate sympathetically. Very soon, the entire organism comes to feel as if it were an inexhaustible storage battery of power. During the practice of the 20-20-20 breath all effort should be gentle and easy. There should be no unnecessary forcing of the mind, no overtaxing of the will. If 20 counts is too challenging, start with a lower number like 10-count intervals. Those who have high blood pressure or who are pregnant should go at their own pace, especially avoiding strain while holding the breath. With practice, the whole process will become extremely simple and pleasurable. It is in the tranquility and calmness developed by the breath that the mind and body opens up and receives the healing light.

This meditation expands the lung capacity. The greater the lung capacity, the greater the intake of oxygen. This breath also enables the blood to be more effectively cleansed, allowing for a greater resistance to disease. In addition, this breath will clean and purify the lungs and other organs. It will bring more oxygen to the brain, leading to greater calm and clarity of thought.

Breath allows one to maintain the balance between the sympathetic (Pingala) and the parasympathetic (Ida) nervous systems.

Ida and pingala are the negative and positive currents, that respectively correspond to the left and right nostrils. These subtle nerves intertwine around the spine. By focusing the eyes on the tip of the nose during your breath work, the ida and pingala are stimulated. This in turn stimulates the shushmana at the third-eye point where the pathway of the three meet. (Refer to *Alchemy of Love Relationships* for further details.)

Inhaling large quantities of oxygen has a strong effect on the endocrine glands because of the tremendous stimulation they receive. It also improves blood circulation due to the rhythmic movement of the diaphragm.

There are three natural postures that can be used to do breath work. They are lying down, sitting or standing. Each posture has a particular effect upon us. Doing breath work while lying down connects us with earthly forces. By practicing while sitting, we are in touch with the spiritual world, and our sympathetic nervous system is more involved. Doing breath work while standing affects the brain and connects us with the divine world.

For positive results, one must work with the breath three times a day: morning, noon, and night. The most important time is during sunrise or in the early morning hours. During those times, the back must be straight to connect with the solar forces, causing our breathing exercises to be more effective. All breathing exercises must be practiced with joy and confidence. Why not make every day a glorious one by starting off with breath work, so that you may get in touch with the beneficial forces of the heavens as soon you wake up. Just breathe slowly and deeply and fill your heart with love and gratitude for a day filled with expectation of the very best and the highest, and you'll find that joy and peace will follow you throughout the day. Breathe so that you may develop the perfect peace of heart and mind that comes when you raise your vibration.

The three-point breath strengthens and stimulates the will into a most formidable instrument of power. By causing the cells in the body to vibrate in unison, as they do during this three-point breath, a powerful electric current of will or spiritual energy is crystallized in the body and mind. This breath develops will power by calling for the exertion of the utmost determination to continue.

After finishing the three-point breath for 11 minutes, move on to the relaxation phase of the exercise.

PART II:
Bring your awareness to every part of the body, starting from your feet and ending at the top of your head. Focus on your body; be aware of it. Be aware of what you are doing. This relaxation exercise will allow you to develop powers of concentration; therefore, do not allow your mind to wander from what you are doing, or, more importantly, from the area you are relaxing. If your mind wanders, gently bring it back. Your power of concentration will improve each day as you practice.

Preparation:
Start by placing the feet heavily on the floor; think of them as stabilizers, giving steadiness. Feel the muscular heaviness in the legs and the relaxation in the ankles and knees. Sit back in your seat with your spine supported. Release the muscles in the back so that they hold you erect without rigidity.

Make sure that the diaphragm is high so that the solar plexus is free and breathing easy. Let your shoulders drop back, leaving the neck muscles free to hold the head easily without strain. Now ease your throat and relax your jaw. Soften the lips and let the tongue lie comfortably curved on the bottom of the mouth.

As you breathe, deeply flare the nostrils so that you have a wide, light, unobstructed feeling at the top of the nose and through the sinuses. Let the eyes tip back in perfect release, giving the inner eye a chance to have a broader vision, a glimpse of the plan of life as a whole, rather than the small part that looms so large at the moment.

Relax the abdominal and diaphragm muscles in order to loosen up the greater part of the musculature and the other tissues supplied by the involuntary or vegetative nervous system.

Now empty the lungs, releasing the breath completely. Do not strain, just let it drain away, then take a deep breath gently and easily. If you are holding on in some part of the body, you are also holding some emotional or mental attitude. If you let go in the body, you will find that the other strains drop away as well. You will feel the love flow through you as all resentments, fears, and doubts drain away. At this point many people fall asleep. Try to remain conscious and aware.

1. Bring your attention to the soles of your feet. Concentrate on them in your mind. Feel the blood moving through the veins, arteries, and capillaries just below and in the skin.
2. Move your attention to your toes, including the toenails, then to your instep, heel, ankle, etc. You may choose to focus on one at a time or all at once. Focus on the bones, muscles and flesh inside your feet. Use your imagination to extend the boundaries of your awareness. By concentrating on any part of the body you can increase the flow of blood to it. This relaxed form of imaginative suggestion can actually serve to remove tension in any internal organ or body part as it stimulates the vasodilation fibers that relax blood vessels, enabling the blood to flow there in large quantities.
3. Gradually work up the legs to your knees, thighs, hips, groin.
4. Move up the torso. Work thoroughly on the abdomen—the more you relax this middle area of the torso, the more likely it is that the whole body will respond massively with letting go. The abdomen part of the body is the seat of instincts, feelings, passion, and all the dynamic forces inherited from the past that we attribute to the unconscious. Do not forget the internal organs (intestines, reproductive organs, stomach, kidneys, adrenal glands, liver, gall bladder, spleen, lungs, heart). Concentrate on the bones in the torso as well (the spine from the tail bone to the nape of the neck, the ribs, scapula and collarbone). Mentally scan the muscles surrounding all those bones and organs. Work easily through all these areas of the abdomen until you reach the shoulders and the arm areas.
5. Now move your attention to the fingers, hands, wrists, forearms, elbows, arms, shoulders, neck, throat, esophagus and thyroid. Continue this same system of concentration on the various parts of your head. Keep visualizing the warm blood flowing through widened blood vessels to the temples, the ears, the cheekbones, then to the nose, mouth, lips, tongue, jaws and chin. In much the same way, after having made mental constructs, you will feel warmth and tingling build up in the area being imagined, gradually giving way to feelings of relaxation. Move on to your left outer and inner ear, right outer and inner ear, nostrils, sinuses, eyelids. Then focus on the eyes and optic

nerves, imagining that these are like two balls, each hanging from four tiny muscular chains. By building an imaginative picture, you bring more prana and blood to those areas, which warms and heals the surrounding musculature, causing them all to relax, giving you a sensation of the eyeballs sinking back into their sockets. Work on your jaw, mouth, tongue, cheeks, forehead, scalp, pituitary and pineal glands and the brain. Hold the picture of your brain firmly in your mind until you begin to sense a warm feeling spreading out from the center of the skull or a gentle tingling sensation.

By consciously scanning the body this way, you will begin to feel your whole body vibrating harmoniously.

PART III:

6. Now concentrate on the entire body. Imagine that you are floating far above the Earth. Look at the Earth revolving in space, filled with humanity and other life forms.

7. From the point between and slightly above the brows (the third eye) project rays of light towards the Earth. Send vibrations of love and light to everyone, without exception or discrimination.

8. Now bring yourself back down to Earth, and visualize yourself in a lake. Feel its harmony, peace, and tranquility. Feel completely relaxed. Dwell in this state of ecstasy for a moment.

9. Inhale, hold your breath (still imagining yourself in the lake) and exhale. Project this picture of yourself into the Universe, saying: *"It is done."* At the end of the exercise, record your feelings. Permit the sense of real pleasure, enjoyment and freedom to make an indelible impression upon your mind. If the memory of this experience is well-recorded, it can be evoked at any moment from your storehouse of memories. It does not matter if you are riding in a subway or driving a car. All you have to do is remember the pleasure of relaxation and the memory is summoned from your psyche and will once again create an impact upon all the tissues and fibers of the body. Relaxation then follows.

10. To end, relax deeply on your back in corpse pose, arms at your sides, palms facing up.

Enjoy this feeling of relaxation. Impress it upon your mind. Get the feel of complete relaxation as vividly and as strongly as you can, because from now on, when you need to relax, you can restore this state of calmness, serenity and complete ease merely by thinking of it. Anytime you want to relax, all you have to do is take a deep breath and as you exhale, think of the word relax and remember this wonderful serene feeling of complete relaxation, and once again it will be restored to you.

Do not take this exercise lightly, for it is extremely potent. It stimulates the psychic consciousness on many levels and develops concentration and body awareness. Concentrating on the different parts of the body greatly stimulates the natural healing process. This particular exercise has even been known to cure cancer and other so-called incurable diseases. In cases such as cancer, see or feel that the blood is sweeping through the cancerous growth, breaking down the malignancy in order to sweep it away for elimination elsewhere. If there is a weak spot or organ in your body, concentrate on it and feel vitality centering there. See additional blood coming there and feel healing prana active in that region, restoring health and harmony. Or imagine a host of knights in shining armor bearing down and slashing the tumor to bits. By focusing our thoughts to any part of the body, we can increase circulation of blood there, causing the life force to remove diseases and restore healing. This exercise can be a support to traditional medical treatments.

Devote 30 minutes a day to this practice, concentrating on the formation of the conditioned reflex that eventually can produce the relaxed state without having to spend so much time on the actual exercise. You may find you'll have to practice several times before being able to call up the conditioned reflex at will, but don't give up for it will not be long before you will notice fruitful results. Ideally, it should be performed once a day. The more you do it, the healthier you will become. It becomes easy to do once you grasp the process. If you find it difficult to do this self-guided visualization, you can make a cassette recording with your voice leading you through the meditation.

The whole thing should take 30 minutes at the most, although you can take more time if you wish. As you master it, you will be able to perform it in a very short time.

*The spiritual art of breathing involves
the control of this all-pervading energy (prana),
and it is in breath-work that one is able to generate
the will power to gain mastery of the body.*

CHAPTER FIVE

THE NERVOUS SYSTEM

As mentioned earlier, the life force runs through our nervous system, which consists of millions of cells. Our health depends upon the quality and smooth flow of our life force. Therefore, a strong nervous system can benefit our health, happiness and success in life. The fact is, each day we not only use up our nervous fluid through worry, fear, anger and insecurity, but also in facing our various daily challenges. Mental and emotional strains deplete our nervous fluid and weaken our nervous system, thereby destroying health, youthfulness, and life itself. A weak nervous system with a low circulation of life force in the body causes one to become vulnerable to mental, emotional and physical challenges, whereas a strong nervous system both protects our health and allows us to gracefully face the various challenges of life.

Metaphysics presents the great principle of the dualistic nature of man: We are both physical and spiritual. The physical aspect is only the negative half of man; it comes from matter. This is the biological part of man. The material body has been found by the ancient students of nature to be the physical reflection of the spiritual body.

Likewise, we are governed by two main nervous systems: On one hand we have the *cerebrospinal nervous system*, or central nervous system, which is associated with the cortex and cerebration. This is the nervous system of the physical body. The chemical, biological and physiological composition of the physical body must be neglected for a long period of time before real disease begins to manifest. The cerebrospinal nervous system deals exclusively with the physical body, the functions of the five senses, and the voluntary or objective functions of the body.

On the other hand, we have the *autonomic nervous system*, connected with the viscera and inner centers of the brain. This is the nervous system of the spiritual or astral body. As we mentioned before, the real secret key to health or the healing of disease cannot be found in matter, it is in the divine part of humans. The answer to health problems can be found in the spiritual body.

The autonomic nervous system is made up of the *parasympathetic nervous system* and the *sympathetic nervous system*. It deals with the involuntary, subjective, or psychosomatic aspect of man. This is the nervous system of the spiritual body. The autonomic nervous system controls and activates our biological functions, those that regulate and affect temperature, metabolism, endocrine gland secretion, digestion and sleep. It transmits psychic impressions, which is the divine intelligence, to our physical body. All conditions originate in the spiritual body and are transmitted to the physical body through the autonomic nervous system. It is difficult to give a conscious order to the autonomic nervous system. Although it is affected by what happens in the cerebrospinal nervous system, it acts independently of our conscious.

Disease occurs when the essential vital and pranic energies of the spiritual body are neglected or abused. One great key in achieving a permanent cure and self-healing is the spiritual body, which is ruled by the autonomic nervous system. Happiness lies in the positive half of man or the actual source of man which is the spiritual part, the soul and its affinity to the universe or God Himself.

This mysterious power that humans have very little understanding of, and which vitalizes the entire body, is more important than that which strengthens the material body. When the pranic and vital energies are performing at their highest levels, the body does not need either herbal or pharmaceutical interventions. Both traditional drugs and herbal supplements are limited in their capacity to heal, as they work solely on the physical, or material, composition of the human body. *In order to effect permanent change in one's health status, one must address the needs of the spiritual body, for the physical bodily functions are ruled by the spiritual body.*

The immune system offers a perfect example of the importance of maintaining our vital and pranic energies in order to avoid illness. White blood cells are the warriors of the immune system. They travel throughout the blood stream fighting bacteria and other germs. The amazing ability to perform this function is not solely reliant upon body chemistry or the physical nourishment of food, drink and oxygen. The white blood cells have real intelligence. These cells have to do more than ordinary red blood cells, which merely nourish and take a certain amount of energy through the capillaries to all parts of the body. White blood cells have to maintain their own integrity, their own existence, and they have to maintain a consciousness and condition that is typical of an individual living body. In addition to this, they must be able to definitely analyze all that they come into contact with and decide what is destructive, what is dangerous, what is unnecessary and what should be destroyed. Then, they must get rid of the destroyed and remaining refuse. All of this requires a supreme and divine intelligence that is not possessed by all of the cells in the body. It is the autonomic nervous system, which is governed by the spiritual body, that is responsible for the vital force. The vital force in the human body, extracted through breath and inherent in the soul, creates the white blood cells and maintains their integrity. These white blood cells may be fueled by proper nutrition, but they are guided by our intelligent spiritual body via the autonomic nervous system. When this intelligence goes awry, they may remain very physically strong yet they attack the wrong particles, causing in many cases autoimmune disorders (in the case of white blood cells attacking the body).

The activities of the immune system can be compared to an entire cleaning crew. People who are cleaning a house should not just throw away everything they see; they have to systematically remove waste while preserving the precious furnishings of a home. An enthusiastic crew may have a lot of vigor, but without intelligence and the ability to discern the waste from the person's belongings, they will produce ruinous effects.

The autonomic nervous system controls everything in the organism, from the most delicate of the arteries to the intestines. During sleep, the functioning of the cerebrospinal nervous system ceases, but the autonomic nervous system continues; it stimulates the digestive system and the assimilation of nutrients and the creation of chyle and lymph; it causes the blood to circulate and distribute forces and nutrients everywhere. The autonomic nervous system also is in charge of the defense of the organism by conveying the leucocytes to the locations of trauma, healing the flesh of wounds and preventing infection.

The human body is a vast chemical machine, creating and recreating new matter out of what we eat and drink. There is an intelligence directing this chemistry that is not well-understood by the average person. The spiritual body, through which that intelligence manifests, carries out the function of the autonomic nervous system, and preserves the form of the material body that it keeps alive and in a state of perpetual renewal. It intelligently maintains functional harmony, in spite of normal die-off and regeneration of every cell in the body, as well as illness, stress, frequent imprudence and indiscretions.

Certain people believe that intuition comes from the voluntary nervous system. But in humans, the true source of intuition lies in the autonomic nervous system and in the totality of the cells of the body's nerves, which are connected to the old, inner brain—the part of the brain that is active when receiving a Harmonyum healing treatment. *(See chapter on Harmonyum)*

In a normal healthy body, this additional high-level vibratory, vital cosmic energy is not needed, because strong bodies have energy in reserve to deal with illness, injuries or temporary stress. Each hour of the day, whether we are awake or asleep, laboring, exercising, working, or resting, a certain number of cells throughout the body break down and disintegrate and are discarded. An equivalent number must be rebuilt to take their place. People who have been chronically ill or who have weakened bodies have often used up their energy reserves and are less able to replenish the naturally deceased cells.

Most people are fascinated with externally based solutions to health such as diet, medication, surgery and/or other alternative approaches. They are unaware of the vital importance of the spiritual body of man and its bridge between the physical body and the autonomic nervous system in the restoration and maintenance of vibrant health. *The key to removing disease is to raise the vibratory state of the entire body.*

Illness starts in the mental world or mind. Karmic patterns are written in the deep recesses of the mind. In fact, a karmic pattern behaves like an astral tree whose seed is in the mental plane, with its fruit in the physical body. If you want to achieve self-healing, you must understand that the mental seed of a negative thought pattern grows into a tree in the astral body, and eventually reaps fruits. Negative fruits can be a particular disease or any other life challenge. In other words, when we allow reoccurring thoughts of anxiety, doubt, hatred, anger and fear to invade the mind, our mental body directly impacts our astral body. The astral body, in turn, transmits—via our sympathetic nervous system—unhealthy or disturbing nerve impulses to our physical body, thereby creating disease with clear pathological changes. Just remember that if you nurture an unhealthy thought or speech pattern, the negative mental energy or seed will send unhealthy nerve impulses through the parasympathetic nervous system into the astral world. As you keep on nurturing that thought with repetition, the sympathetic nervous system will keep sending negative nerve impulses to the physical body. The result will either be health challenges, misfortune or adversity.

Nature has a safety mechanism, which can only be bypassed by the act of repetition. The minimum time to bypass can be anywhere from 40 to 120 days, based upon your level of consciousness. For instance, if in an effort to improve yourself, you play a cassette tape that repeats, *"Every day in every way, I am getting better and better, God and me, me and God are one,"* after a while your psyche will override the old and now ineffective safety mechanism put in place by nature to protect us, and begin to assume that the desire of that person is what this person really wants. It will then change from its previous pattern to the new suggested one.

On the other hand, the negative seeds of a thought such as those produced by fear, anger, animosity, or vengeance will grow into a negative astral tree. If you constantly keep that thought in mind, the tree will create unhealthy fruits by making your thought a reality. These fruits manifest themselves as illness or the person attracting or creating other unfortunate life circumstances.

Destructive energy patterns or negative karmic influences written in the deep recesses of our consciousness will produce a blueprint in the astral body for reoccurring illness in the physical body or adversity in one's life. These patterns act like a "negative" from which photographs are reproduced. If you destroy the photograph, you do not eliminate the negative. Many curative methods from modern medicine mostly eliminate the photo but not the negative, which is the underlying cause of the illness. For example, a person with back pain may have a slipped disc in his vertebrae. The surgeon may fuse the two surrounding vertebrae, rendering them more stable and possibly even eliminating the pain. This could be seen as removing the photograph but not the photo negative, which would be the root cause of the slipped disc. As a result, the likelihood of developing more back pain is very likely because the photo negative can still produce pictures.

In another example, a person who is addicted to alcohol might, through the help of a drug rehabilitation facility, be able to stop drinking. He will often replace that behavior with smoking cigarettes and eating sugar. Although it is highly commendable that he discontinued the most destructive habit, which in our analogy will be considered the photograph, he did not yet destroy the "negative." Until the root cause behind the behavior is resolved, the addictive behavior will continue to manifest in one way or another and the potential to restart the alcohol will be there. The continued presence of the destructive energy pattern capable of reproducing the illness explains why some illnesses reappear during times of stress and others are deemed "incurable." What is crucial to permanent healing is the elimination of the negatives of these energy patterns.

Doctors, who don't see the unseen, approach health by attempting to remove the fruit of the disease without healing at the level of the tree or the original seed that produced the tree. Some people can feel sickness from the mental and astral world before it hits the physical body. This explains why a patient goes to see a doctor complaining or feeling sick, even before any sickness manifests physically. The doctor will be perplexed, because at this point, the problem is still in the mental and astral worlds and the doctor is unable to see that world. Months later, the tree bears fruit in the form of an illness and the doctor is still more perplexed as to how the patient knew a problem was developing before it actually existed.

The key to this phenomenon is in the astral body. As humans, it is easier to work on the astral body, because it is right above the physical world. The astral world will immediately affect the physical body for it emanates into the physical body. The mental plane is the world of thoughts and ideas, whereas the astral plane is the world of feelings. To manifest an idea or mental picture on the physical plane, you must attach feelings to it. A mental thought must go through the astral plane or world of feelings, before it can manifest physically. This explains why feelings or emotions are so powerful. They are right above the physical plane. Therefore, it is important to remember that we can chose to grow positive seeds, which will grow positive trees and bear nice flowers and sweet fruits, such as good health, good fortune, prosperity, love and success.

Since habitual mental tapes are very difficult, but not impossible to change, it is easier to work with the astral body because it is midway between the mental and the physical levels. In fact, there are three worlds; in descending order, they are the mental, astral and physical worlds. The mental body creates the astral body, and the astral body gives birth to the physical body. By purifying the astral body, you can create positive changes in the mind. The astral body, which unites the physical body with the mind by dual polarization, is supported by the autonomic nervous system.

Technically, if you experience aches, pain or disease, it means that your astral body is transmitting from the mind, through the sympathetic nervous system, unhealthy vibrations to your physical body.

The way we think, feel, speak, and act influences our spiritual body. The autonomic nervous system then transmits positive or negative vibrations to our physical body, causing well-being or pain and disease. Our anxiety, insecurities, fear, and anger do not create good fruits. Therefore, we must take responsibility and focus on reaping the best possible fruit in order to heal ourselves and uplift humankind.

We are surrounded by a magnetic field with our own attracting and repelling effect based upon the way we think, feel, speak, and act, which accounts for our feelings of sympathy and antipathy. Each of us is responsible for shaping our life. As such, we attract whatever corresponds to our own magnetic field and repel whatever is in disharmony with it. Everything that is felt and thought is present in the tenuous material spheres, either polluting or purifying the world. What we send out, we get back. That is why, as was previously mentioned, the greatest of all remedies is found in how you think, how you feel and how you act. Every day, every hour, every waking second we are either creating health or dis-ease with our thoughts, emotions, speech and actions. Thus, it is of supreme importance to be aware and in control of our every word and deed, in order to cause our spiritual body to transmit positive and healing nerve impulses to our physical body. When awareness is practiced, every act becomes a spiritual and healing one. Therefore, the key is to cleanse the spiritual body so as to balance the mind, body and spirit and transmit through the autonomic nervous system positive nerve impulses to our physical body. As a result, all our cells will vibrate with pranic light and new life. This, in turn, strengthens the entire body and promotes longevity. It frees our whole being from energy blocks to make room for more creative purposes.

As you can see, it is vital to regulate the autonomic nervous system; the equilibrium of which determines the health of the body and mind. The sympathetic nervous system (SNS), which stimulates excitement, works mainly by day, actively affecting our cells from sunrise to sunset. The parasympathetic nervous system (PNS), on the other hand, which promotes relaxation, works primarily at night and during our resting hours. It affects our body from sunset to sunrise.

These two systems must be in harmony for our health to be strong, because the two aspects coordinate the workings of our organs. The typical stressful modern lifestyle tends to overstimulate the sympathetic nervous system; most modern music, news, movies, stimulant beverages, and stressful work conditions promote a state of hyper-alertness. As a result, the parasympathetic nervous system becomes less active than it should be, and the person has a difficult time relaxing. The bodily functions that it is supposed to support become weak. These functions are digestion and assimilation of nutrients, general repair, rejuvenation and, most importantly, sleep. When the sympathetic nervous system is dominant over a long period of time, the body becomes weak and open to disease development. The answer to diseases rooted in this cause is to strengthen the parasympathetic nervous system and promote autonomic nervous system equilibrium. Modern medicine places little emphasis on this approach to healing.

Interestingly, our sympathetic nervous system is ruled by the principle of light, whereas our parasympathetic nervous system is ruled by the principle of sound. Sound, which is the highest principle in spirituality, has been known to have the ability to fix the parasympathetic nervous system, so that all nerve impulses originating from the mental plane may be transmuted into positivity for our well-being. This explains the miraculous cures obtained by prayers, chanting, listening to sacred music and other methods of sound therapy. The deeper you explore the mysteries of life, the more you will find that its whole secret is hidden in words. Everything comes from words. That is why St. John revealed that, *"In the beginning was the Word, and the Word was with God, and the Word was God...,"* The power of words has been known to yogis, Kabbalists and occult philosophers down through the ages. Words have been vibrated audibly and silently to achieve certain mystical results. In fact, the destiny of a person is written in the word. All spiritual practices are based upon the science of the word or sound.

It is by sound, in sound, and through sound that all things seen and unseen, have been created. Sound is not only the mother of Light, but it also creates life.

Through sound the world stands. Sound can be used to move the life force and achieve perfect healing. When everything else fails, man can be saved by the proper use of mantra or words of power. The ancient Egyptians had a method of concentration and repetition of words for the various parts of the body. This practice released a great deal of power from the stored-up energies in the physical body. It improved the health, affected the astral body, and had a profound effect on the spiritual and moral life of the person who used it. These ancient Egyptians taught as well that the physical universe was brought out of chaos by rhythmic sound. Planets, people, and everything else was projected into physical manifestation by the power of sound. He who knows the science of making sound the vehicle of thought, and synchronizing it with other forms of vibrations, has at his disposal a mighty tool to effect extraordinary changes in his body and life. Great energies and talents can be aroused within the individual himself by his or her own proper use of sound. Sound allows us to merge with our soul. By not establishing a connection with our soul energy, we depend exclusively upon external sources of energy, with its various limitations. One limitless supply of energy and healing is the soul, our internal source of prana. Sound enables us to go in and merge with our limitless source of pranic energy, our soul, our totality. Through the use of sound, chanting, prayers, sacred music or the power of the word, one can cause the spiritual body to transmit positive nerve impulses to the physical body.

Mantra or sound current, for example, is a love that flows, a divine shield that protects us like a spiritual immune system. It is a link between us and the divine. Those who perfect their mantras can break down physical confines and allow the mind, body and spirit to become one. Through listening or chanting mantras, you can move from darkness to light, from negativity to positivity, and from sickness to health.

CHAPTER SIX

HEALING SOUNDS

As humans, our greatest power lies in our frontal lobe and upper palate. Our total personality is governed by the frontal lobe, and in order to face time and space with happiness, we must control our frontal lobe through mantra. Control of the frontal lobe stops impulsive behavior and creates a meditative mind. All brain activity is controlled by the neurological system, the mastery of which, through chanting, can free anyone from disease. Most importantly, in the nucleus of the magnetic psyche, there is a central nucleus that is the pivot point of life. Taking care of that pivot point of life can give humans inner peace and balance. This leads to external balance. Words can be used through mantra and prayers to bring health and harmony into a person's life.

Certain sounds can be used to benefit our health. There are reflex points all around the mouth, but above all, there are 84 energy points inside the palate. The hypothalamus sits on the palate. When you chant or vibrate a mantra, the tongue, which represents the male organ or solar force, goes in intercourse with the upper palate, which stands for the feminine or lunar force. As a result, the hypothalamus is stimulated, and in exchange, the pituitary and pineal glands are also stimulated. These glands regulate the autonomic nervous system, which, in turn, protects us from negativity. Through this process, the neuron patterns in the brain are realigned with the past, present and future. Once this is achieved, the molecular frequency of the brain changes, thereby affecting the whole molecular structure of the body, improving our health and life. As a result, one receives the blessing of intuitional intelligence. The most direct way to move from darkness to light, from negativity to positivity, from disease to health, is through sound and breath.

Chanting meditation is an advanced form of prayer that directs the sunlight fluid to empower us, nurture us and bring out our true reality, which is divinity. In essence, mantra is the art of using the science of sound to direct the sunlight fluid to heal the mind, body and spirit. Words, through chanting and prayer, can be used to move the life force in any desired direction. Chanting and prayer moves you into the heart in order for you to merge with the center of the cosmic wheel. By chanting, you erase bad luck and experience the ecstasy of the power of the word, which was in the beginning, which is now and which shall ever be. By praying or chanting we absorb more prana, and this enlivens our whole being.

THE HEALING MANTRA:
RA MA DA SA SA SAY SO HUNG

After almost thirty years of teaching, healing and working with thousands of individuals of every race, gender, religion, and class, I realized that I needed to formulate a universal and elegant mantra especially for those plagued with health problems. I wanted to find a sacred sound that would work for anyone, in any situation, in any country, without the limitations that constant ritual and overly formalized structures often bring, especially for those restricted physically with ill health. When I first began reaching out to those with health and spiritual challenges, finding the most efficient and effective way to help and heal proved challenging at times. For each person, in each situation, I had to sift through the most vital and important of the sacred teachings and make them accessible and compatible with their own religious beliefs, cultural customs, as well as their individual challenge in order to help them immediately.

In my restless desire to find a solution for my students, friends, and those who came for my help, I began to petition the cosmic energy source for guidance. This is how *Ra Ma Da Sa Sa*

Say So Hung in this form was revealed to me. *Ra Ma Da Sa* is one of the most powerful mantras known and is extraordinarily effective in dealing with health challenges. It is powerful. It is universal. It works on many levels: the mental, spiritual, emotional, and physical.

Ra Ma Da Sa is called the *Shushmana Mantra*. It contains the eight sounds that stimulate the Kundalini to flow in the central channel of the spine and in the spiritual centers. This sound balances the five zones of the left and right hemispheres of the brain to activate the neutral mind. As this happens, the hypothalamus pulsates in rhythm with the divine gland, causing the pituitary master gland to tune the entire glandular system. Then the sympathetic, parasympathetic and active nervous systems match the timing of the glandular system. As a result, the muscular system and cells in the blood work in conjunction to receive this healing vibration, and the rebuilding process of one's health is triggered.

This mantra, which is set to a healing classical tune, can purify the aura and consolidate your mental projection into a one-pointed positivity towards yourself and your health. Listening to it helps rebalance the entire auric circulation and gives you a sense of security that activates your self-healing capacities. A consistent listening or chanting practice becomes impressive enough to permeate the subconscious, which, in turn, automatically influences the conscious mind. Then it becomes a part of one's deep intuitional conviction.

Ra Ma Da Sa is like a rare diamond, which connects you with the pure healing energy of the universe. You can instill the health trend in your consciousness by injecting this strong healing vibration into your mind. Then your actions and whole being will obey that thought. In order to change health troubles, we must alter the process of thought that brings the crystallization of consciousness into different forms of matter and action. This recording helps you develop the pattern of health.

RA—the fire principle—symbolizes the Sun. There would be no life on Earth if it were not for the Sun showering us with the pranic life force. Working with the Sun is the highest practice of

Kabbalah. The Sun is a source of energy, life and warmth. In other words, the Sun is the heart of our universe. It purifies and energizes.

MA—the water principle—is the energy of the Moon. MA calls on the cosmos through the sound of compassion, causing the universe to become the mother and you the child, and this brings you help and healing. It is cooling and nurturing.

DA—the Earth principle—provides the ground of action.

SA—the air principle—is the impersonal infinity. When sound takes place in the external plane, it becomes "A", which represents manifestation.

The first part of the mantra expands toward heaven. By repeating the sound *SA* as a turning point, it causes the spirit to descend from above into matter in order to animate and vitalize it with healing and life. In other words, the second part of the mantra brings the healing qualities of the superior world back down to the Earth. The last stanza of the emerald tablet from the great Hermes Trismegistus, which reveals the secret of healing and order in the material plane, is followed in this mantra. It reads, "Ascend with great sagacity from Earth to Heaven, and then again descend to Earth, and unite together the powers of things superior and inferior. Thus you will obtain the glory of the whole world and obscurity will fly away from you. The secret is adaptation, transforming one thing into another thing." *Ra Ma Da Sa Sa Say So Hung* transforms an imbalanced and unhealthy body into a harmonious, healthy one. As in the Star of David—a symbol of two interlaced triangles—this mantra interlinks spirit with matter.

After *SA* comes *SAY*, which is the totality of experience. *SO* is the personal sense of identity. *HUNG* is the infinite, vibrating and real. *Hung* suggests *Hu*, which is the life of God in every thing and every being. The *ng* causes the sound in *Hung* to stimulate the divine glands. The sound of the breath is *So Hung*. The inhale is *So* and the exhale is *Hung*. The two qualities of *So Hung* together mean "I am Thou." As you chant this mantra, you expand toward the infinite and merge back with the finite. Most people have forgotten that their essence is with the infinite, unlimited creative power of the cosmos. When a person goes within himself and consciously experiences his own beauty, he touches his divinity. Then he can reunite his destiny to his highest potential. A regular listening practice is not only good for practical, preventative self-healthcare, but it will also aid in the assurance of a healthier life. It can help preserve the body and pave the way toward a positive mental projection. Chanting or listening to this mantra set to this classical tune will drive out depression and revibrate your life. It is timeless and cannot be outdated. It has worked in the past, it works now, and it will work in the future. There is no time, no place, no space and no condition attached to this mantra. It burns the seed of disease. Use it every day. Offer it to anyone. If you work with it, it will work for you. In moments of anxiety, despair, fear or worry, let it be your safeguard. It will give you a strong sense of your own centeredness.

This mantra is a pure divine thought. When you think pure thoughts and are mentally strong, you cannot suffer the painful effects of bad karma or disease. A regular practice of listening to the CD recording or chanting along with it is like praying unceasingly. When you continuously pray and meditate, you go into the land of light, where all troubles disappear.

MANTRA	MEANING
Ra	*Sun*
Ma	*Moon*
Da	*Receiver of SAA*
Sa	*Totality*
Sa	*Totality*
Say	*Spirit, energy*
So	*Manifestation*
Hung	*Experience of Thou*

Use *Ra Ma Da Sa* to heal and/or maintain balance and health. Chant with the Rootlight CD *Ra Ma Da Sa (see end of book for order information)* for 11 minutes in the morning and/or at night. For very challenging conditions, chant for a maximum of 31 minutes morning and night if you can. For surgery, see page 232.

Meditation for Healing Self and Others

Position:
- Sit in easy pose with the legs crossed or in any comfortable meditative sitting posture with a straight spine. The eyes are closed.
- Bend the elbows. Palms are open at the sides of the body, facing up to receive healing energy.

Mantra:
RA-MA-DA-SA
SA-SAY-SO-HUNG

Ra Ma Da Sa Sa Say So Hung

Time:
Continue 11 to 31 minutes.

Meditation for Self-Healing

Position:
- Sit in easy pose with the legs crossed or in any comfortable meditative sitting posture with a straight spine. The eyes are closed.
- Palms are pressed together at the chest, fingers pointing up, known as prayer pose.

Mantra:
RA-MA-DA-SA
SA-SAY-SO-HUNG

Time:
1. Sing mantra aloud for 11 minutes.
2. Whisper the mantra for 5 minutes.
3. Listen in silence to the mantra inside you for 1 minute.

To End:
To end, breathe in deeply, hold the breath to extract the healing prana, exhale and relax in stillness.

Elevation of Body, Heart and Mind

Position:

- Sit in easy pose with the legs crossed or in any comfortable meditative sitting posture with a straight spine.
- Arm and Hand Position: Raise arms straight out to the side parallel to the floor and bend the elbows so that the hands are in front of your heart. Interlock the index fingers maintaining a medium pressure while resting the thumb on the middle fingers.
- The eyes are closed.

Mantra:

Chant from your navel for 31 minutes.

RA-MA-DA-SA
SA-SAY-SO-HUNG

To End:

Inhale deeply, hold the breath, straighten the spine and pull on the index fingers. Exhale.

Inhale deeply, hold the breath and squeeze your entire body. Exhale.

Inhale deeply and stick the tongue out from its base as far as possible. Exhale and relax.

Comments:

Chant from the navel—it will heal you. Chant from the heart—it will take away calamities. Chant from the throat—it will quiet a busy mind.

Meditation To Send Healing Energy To Those Who Are Suffering

Position:
- Sit in easy pose with the legs crossed or in any comfortable meditative sitting posture with a straight spine. The eyes are closed.
- Tightly interlock the fingers (Venus lock) in front of the chest or heart chakra.

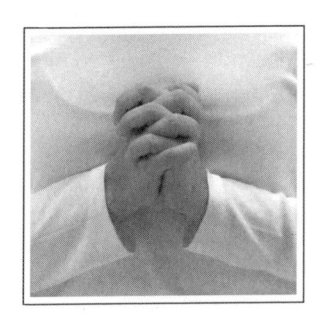

Mantra:
Chant aloud for 5 1/2 to 11 minutes. You may chant along with a CD recording of this mantra.

RA-MA-DA-SA
SA-SAY-SO-HUNG

To End:
Inhale and hold the breath in prayer. Exhale, then inhale deeply and hold this breath of life. Meditate on the universe. Exhale. Inhale again, hold it tight with your prayer in mind. Exhale. Inhale deeply, hold the breath in prayer, directing it for healing of the person in need. Release your prayer and relax.

THE ART OF ABSENT HEALING

All who embrace light and walk the path of divinity will find that they are led to spaces and times where they will need to access their power and truth in order to send healing energy to others. Not only is this a requirement of those who seek enlightenment, it is a desire.

The best way to help oneself is through helping others, temporarily forgetting one's problems and giving oneself over to help others where it is needed.

Healing can be directed toward a loved one, a stranger, a country in turmoil or the planet in general. RA MA DA SA is the mantra we invoke to project our healing strength to others. By chanting RA MA DA SA, we help to rid our environment of negative, unhealthy energy. Comfort is given to the sorrowful, courage to the fearful, moral support to the weak. The seeds of goodness that will restore the planet to its original state of beauty are sown.

Employ this mantra of healing transformation. Know that within you lies the key that will open the door to salvation and vitality. Each act of healing we undertake will be returned a hundredfold. When we commit to using RA MA DA SA to impart healing energy, our spirituality is heightened and we find the joy that comes with living in a less troubled world.

The purpose of the following technique is to render metaphysical healing to a person you know who is in distress. It may be a member of your family, a friend, a neighbor, or anyone who is afflicted by a physical, mental or material problem.

Preparation:
When you have selected the person in need of healing, close your eyes and take a few deep breaths to quiet your mind and go within. Now say the following prayer:

> ***Divine Intelligence, purify my whole being so I may be
> a perfect channel for healing energy. So be it.***

Step One:
Start with the three-point breath to bring the entire nervous and glandular system into balance. The beauty of life is based on the breath. It is the link between God and you.

Position:
- Sit in a meditative position with the spine straight.
- Hands are in prayer pose (palms pressed together, fingers pointing upwards, placed at the level of the sternum).
- Eyes are closed and focused between the mid-brow point.

Breath:
Inhale for 20 counts, hold 20 and exhale 20.

Repeat breath cycle for 3-11 minutes.

Step Two: Meditation for Self-Healing
This mantra heals all imbalances and sickness. Place palms facing each other 6 inches apart at the level of the heart in the Tree of Life hand symbol. Eyes are closed. Vibrate this powerful healing mantra for a minimum of 11 times, or a maximum of 31 minutes. Inhale, hold the breath for a few seconds, and chant the mantra up the major scale (as in Do, Re, Mi, Fa . . .) as you exhale: **RA-MA-DA-SA SA-SAY-SO-HUNG**

To end, inhale, hold the breath, and surround yourself with the healing light of the sun. Then exhale. Do this three times. *(Pause for approximately one minute before continuing to the next step.)*

Step Three: Send Healing
- Visualize as vividly as possible the person who needs your help. Then imagine the person sitting completely receptive. *(Pause)*
- While in this receptive state, picture a light that slowly beams down from the sun and surrounds the person. *(Pause)*
- As the light intensifies around the person, feel their entire being gradually becoming charged and vibrating with strength, health and harmony. *(Pause)*

- ⋄ Visualize the person happy, smiling, laughing, joking, being their best, and vibrating with health. *(Pause)*
- ⋄ While maintaining this visualization, inhale, hold the breath and mentally say, *"It is done."* Exhale.
- ⋄ Now forget the face of the person and say, **"Divine Intelligence, bless my work. So be it."** *(Pause)*
- ⋄ Go back to your daily activities.

Your may draw your inspiration from this simple ritual, performing it any time of the day, shaping it to your liking, and adding any other elements you may deem necessary. RA MA DA SA will carry you through every test. It combines the energy of earth and ether. The first four syllables comprise the earth mantra and the second four syllables make up the ether mantra. RA is the sun. MA is the moon. DA is the earth. SA is the infinity. SAY is Thou. SO HUNG is I am THOU. This mantra is used to channel healing energy. Use it to heal yourself and others.

HEALING WATER: A Technique for Revitalization

Here is a method to revitalize yourself:

Position:
Take a glass of water. Hold it in both hands at the level of the solar plexus or heart center.

Mantra:
RA-MA-DA-SA
SA-SAY-SO-HUNG
Chant up the major scale in one breath. Do this 11 times or for 11 minutes, depending on whether or not you are pressed for time. Then drink the water.

Comments:
This meditation has the power to create the condition for health to be restored in the body. The water will be charged with the energy of the healing mantra RA MA DA SA. Similarly, after completing the chant, you can drink it or give it to a sick person to drink, and it will have tremendous beneficial impacts on their health. Your hands become like a magnet, the right hand being the positive pole and the left hand being the negative. In a magnet there is a perfect expression of the basic principle governing life: electricity and magnetism. In other words, life, which is vibration—meaning up and down—is the result of magnetic and electric forces. These two principles rule everything. You will even find them in the atom as protons and electrons, and in the world as electricity and magnetism. Giving and taking also displays respectively electric and magnetic forces. When you take a glass of fresh water, wrap both hands around it and put it at the level of your navel, which is the root of your 72,000 nerves. That water in turn becomes charged with healing properties. It will enhance your aura, improve your health and help anything from chronic fatigue to digestive problems.

SACRED MUSIC

There are a number of ways of inviting the blessings of light, but by far the most effective is simply by chanting mantras or listening to sacred music. We exercise for the physical body, we breathe for the mind and we chant for the soul. Certain music heals and uplifts the spirit. Certain music is beneficial, while other kinds of music can actually be quite harmful. Chanting mantra or listening to sacred music in times of illness is like meditating on divine truths that exist on a far higher plan. As a result, something in the depths of our being stirs into life.

Just as slow and deep breathing can quiet the mind, so can beautiful sacred music feed and heal the soul and awaken the spirit. The sage and initiate of the past recognized that music was the fastest way to reach illumination. The soul works with music and manifests itself by way of inspiration or miraculous cures from illness. Initiates who understood the potency of sacred music have only one desire: that is to bring healing warmth to frozen hearts, restore peace where it is gone and turn on the light to remove darkness.

By listening to sacred music, you are coming closer to your soul. We need music that engages the soul. We need music that penetrates the depths of our being and touches the soul with soothing and uplifting energy. Chanting or listening to sacred music is the fastest way to merge with the soul and get closer to God. Sacred music provides new energy, life and hope to suffering and afflicted souls.

When sacred words of power are merged with music during the most positive phase of the moon under the influence of beneficial planetary energies, and when sacred words of power are chanted from the heart while being merged with a melody that engages the soul, they are able to penetrate the heart and heal.

In moments of anxiety or despair, fear or worry, let sacred music be your grand safeguard and defender. The very act of prayer is the activity of God. Prayer is simply letting God be God in us. We must discipline ourselves to put the heart first and never allow ourselves to become preoccupied with trivia, so that we miss the finer and more important things in life. We must discipline ourselves in right thinking, right speaking, and right action. We must chant in order to liberate our own imprisoned splendor.

Over the years we have used the sacred science of Kabbalah and Kundalini yoga to guide people from all walks of life, including yogis and Kabbalists. We are now bringing these teachings out through music into the open so that everyone, without exception, may reap the many benefits that are associated with these divine teachings.

It takes time, dedication, knowledge, and great skill to create sacred music that has an impact on the soul. All music on the Rootlight label is especially created to bring the listener a host of benefits and blessings. They are created in accord with the natural and healing laws of the universe. It is the birthright of everyone to experience all the many benefits and blessings associated with these once highly secret words of power. They are being made available for the full benefit of the general public through refined music and soul melody.

Rootlight has formulated and compiled the most effective and proven words of power in its *Healing Beyond Medicine Series*. When properly used, these CDs make it possible for you to connect with the healing energy of the Sun and open yourself to receive its pranic light. All music on the Rootlight label has been created during the most positive and healing phase of the moon to magnify the beneficial impact upon the listener.

HEAVEN'S TOUCH

The first mantra on this CD is excellent for realigning the body's master control system to facilitate recovery from chronic physical dysfunction, or spiritual imbalance. The first track on *Heaven's Touch* intermixes the infinite and the finite. The first part (*Guru Guru Wahe Guru*) is a *Nirgun* mantra, which vibrates to the cosmic, and projects the mind to the source of knowledge and ecstasy. Whereas the second part (*Guru Ram Das Guru*), is a *Sirgun* mantra, which represents form and calls upon the wisdom that comes as a servant of the infinite. This mantra projects the mind to infinity so as to allow a guiding relationship to come into your practical activities. This is a mantra of humility that brings emergency saving grace and spiritual guiding light.

This meditation can be done with your hands in prayer pose. Prayer pose neutralizes the energy flow within the body and keeps you centered.

A note on how the recording of this mantra came about may be of interest: When I went into the recording studio, my intention that day was to record a completely different sacred sound. Frustratingly, no matter how much we tried to produce that sound, nothing sounded right. After a long while, I took a deep breath and unexpectedly, seemingly out of nowhere, the mantra Guru Ram Das came out of me. And at the very same moment we decided, okay let's try it, everything flowed together with effortless ease and grace. In fact, it was recorded in just one take. I am convinced that heaven had a different plan for me that day, not allowing my planned choice to materialize, rather providing me with something better than I could imagine. It was a touch from heaven: that's why I called the CD *Heaven's Touch*.

It is not by chance that the mantra in track one is repeated five times per breath. The number 5 conceals the most profound arcana. All those captivated by the mystical and noble secret science will be familiar with the beauty and power of the mantra's rhythm. From the high science we know that five is the number of the human that has fallen from his high estate because of disobedience to the laws of God. Five is also the number of the will, the instrument of reintegration. It can cause a human to enter into his glory, taking with him his regenerated human nature. Five is the great redemptive force of the will. For the full effect, try, if you can, to do each of the five repetitions in one breath.

The benefits of this mantra also encompass the healing and protective energy represented by Guru Ram Das, who was known for universal service. This meditation brings protection and healing of any physical, mental or circumstantial situations. In the midst of trial and danger, this mantra can rescue you. It has a very soothing effect on the personality. This meditation brings the mind, body and spirit under control, and enables you to meditate on your own divine force, your own fiber. If the fiber of the being is not right, the being itself cannot be right. It is very important to be centered. When you're centered, you are not susceptible to upsetting and unsettling circumstances. This mantra will invoke and develop in you the values that will be unbeatable in the times to come. Guru Ram Das synchronizes your energies and hypnotizes your pituitary, which is your control center, so that it may serve your power of prayer.

Please see our other books for more mantras and their explanations: Lifting the Veil, Alchemy of Love Relationships, and The Healing Fire of Heaven (previously titled The Splendor of the Sun).

*There is no illness that will not be healed
by working with the feet.*

*The condition of your feet determines
your health, strength and vitality.*

CHAPTER SEVEN

HEALING AND YOUR FEET

THERE IS NO ILLNESS that cannot be healed by working with the feet. If you know someone who is sick, you may start the healing process by massaging their feet. In fact, it is important to take care of the feet on a daily basis. By working on the feet, we cause the nervous fluid to circulate smoothly throughout the body, giving strength and healing, so that we may gracefully face the challenges of time and space. The condition of your feet determines your health, strength and vitality. Healing through the feet relaxes, calms and soothes our nerves, allowing the nervous system to rebuild itself, which in turn promotes mental and physical fitness. By working on the feet you can relax the entire nervous system.

A human foot has 26 bones that compose the structure, 72,000 nerves that end at the feet and through which the life force flows. Every organ in the body has a nerve ending in the foot. In order for a disease to take over, calcium deposits must choke the nerves to prevent the earthly nurturing energy to feed the organs. Before you get sick, the nerve ending center must be jammed with calcium or acid deposits. A buildup of crystallizations at the end of these nerve endings often precedes weakness of the organs. In other words, when there is a problem in any organ or area of the body, there is a crystallization of calcium and acid deposits in the corresponding foot area. With 20 pounds of pressure applied in a circular motion with the thumbs on the foot, one can break up these crystal deposits. Working on the feet prevents the depletion of the life force, helping our organs to get a normal supply of the nervous fluid. Nervous depletion can lead to constipation, poor circulation, extreme tension, and sluggishness of the vital organs. Pain in the feet indicates weakness and abnormal functioning of the organs. Proper work on the feet helps the life force flow smoothly, giving you a surplus of power and vitality. The life force runs through our nervous system, which consists of millions of cells. Our health depends upon the smooth flow of life force as well as its quality. A strong nervous system can benefit your health, happiness and success in life. Every day we use up that force not only through worries, fears, angers, and insecurities, but also, in facing the various daily challenges. Fear, anger and worries weaken the nervous system by depleting the nervous fluid, thereby destroying health, youthfulness, and life itself. A weak nervous system, with a low circulation of life force in the body, causes us to be mentally and physically tired.

This is what attracts people to the use of coffee, alcohol and other stimulants, which actually further exhaust the nerves and speeds the process of complete breakdown of our nervous system. Fear, anger or worries can especially impair the function of our sympathetic nervous system, which governs the vital organs.

By working on the feet, we recharge our solar plexus, affect the pneumo-gastric nerve, help our nervous system and heal our vital organs. Proper foot therapy can ease the nervous system, help our digestion and breathing. Problems with breathing and the digestive system come from a disturbance in the pneumo-gastric nerve. This nerve, which is a major branch of the sympathetic nervous system, governs our breathing and digestion. The solar plexus is its center, causing it to affect the function of vital organs. Working on the feet opens the solar plexus, and assists the pneumo-gastric nerve in its healing function. Because our nervous system is bombarded on a daily basis by all kinds of stresses, it is vitally important to help our nervous system by working on the feet. For most people, trying to earn a living can often become a chronic drain to the life force. A bombarded nervous system, not properly attended to, can result in nervous indigestion leading to conditions such as gas, fermentation, heartburn, sour stomach, hyperacidity, and dilatation of the stomach, resulting in shortness of breath and pressure in the heart. This can create heart irregularity, palpitations and heart failure.

The greatest thing about the foot center is that it has contact with the earth, and that means that the destiny of man is basically influenced by the condition of the feet. The feet are the foundation of a human. The forces of heaven which enter into a human being through the top of the body, combined with the earthly energies that we receive through the feet, will determine our health, life and destiny. For us to live on the earth, we must continue to receive earthly energies through our feet. The expression *"death comes through the feet,"* originates from the fact that, when a person is about to expire, and the life force is dying in the body, the feet become very cold. Therefore, when someone is sick, it is very important to work on their feet, for by working properly on the feet, we keep receiving the earthly forces in the body and prolong our life. In other words, working on the feet keeps death away. In truth, as one grows older, the quantity of earthly energy entering the body through the feet starts decreasing, causing all types of problems, such as bad circulation, swelling, aches and pain in the feet. All this is due to nature, progressively detaching us from the earthly forces, so that we may be prepared for death. Therefore, the older one grows, the more one should walk to maintain body and brain health. As a matter of fact, you will find that old people who take long daily walks remain alert, maintain good memory, and are in better health.

We often get callouses by wearing tight shoes for fashion and design. Because of the importance of the health of the feet, wear comfortable shoes and rub the calluses off regularly. It is important not to let callouses develop on the bottom of the feet. A build-up of dead skin on the feet makes it difficult to stimulate the important nerve endings that access and nourish the organs. A 30-minute massage with around 20 pounds of pressure morning and evening will help regenerate the nerves and break up the crystallizations. This is important for healing purposes. You can use both feet to massage each other. We have to take special care of the circulation in the feet, because the feet are the body part farthest from the heart. You can massage the feet with a coarse towel and wash them in cold and hot water. In case of dizziness and high fever, cut an onion in half and use it to massage the feet. If the nerves are weak, put garlic juice on the feet and massage it in. Garlic and onion on the feet help to remove poison from the body and combat paralysis. Any oil or cream we put on the body is absorbed by the pores into the bloodstream. Our skin behaves like an additional lung, for as the breath takes the vital life force or prana in the body, so does our skin. For headaches with feelings of too much heat in the body, massage the feet in cold water and mentholated eucalyptus.

If the toenail has no reddish shine in it, the blood is impure and thick. It is important to keep the feet clean and best to wear comfortable shoes that do not pinch, bind or cause pain. If the feet have started hurting, it is an indication that the physical structure of the body is being damaged. Before one dies, the life force starts leaking from the sides of the feet. Cold feet are a direct indication of a weak life force and bad circulation in the body. If one does not take care of it at the proper time, it can end up as a disease. These symptoms serve as useful warnings for the betterment of the body.

The easiest way to regulate the function of the organs is through foot massage. Massage is best done by the individual himself. It is also helpful to massage the foot reflexology locations associated with the corresponding weakened or diseased organs. In reality, nerves carry the functions of the organs and feed the organs, so that they may thrive. Any type of sickness of the feet must be taken very seriously. Almond or grapeseed oil massage keeps the feet healthy and soft. When the nails stop growing, it is a sign of weakening bones. Walking on a sandy beach is a very therapeutic massage for the feet. Walking on dew-filled grass is the best energizing exercise, because the dew gives the water and the grass provides soft friction.

Foot baths in warm water, for about 11 to 20 minutes is another effective method of opening the solar plexus and allowing healing energy to circulate. Unbeknownst to most people, working on the feet is a practical healing application rooted in the Kabbalah.

Footbath for Relaxation and Renewal

Here is a simple and powerful method to calm and revitalize the nerves, open blocked channels, and strengthen the spleen, liver and glands. We have 72,000 nerves, which are the transporters of prana. These nerves end in our feet and hands. Every organ has a corresponding spot on the soles of the feet. Therefore, massaging the feet relaxes the nerves and creates a healing effect on the body. You can prevent many health disorders, heal vital organs, and strengthen the immune system by doing the following:

The items you will need are:
- hot water
- sea salt (optional)
- eucalyptus oil (optional)

1. Fill the bathtub or a bucket with enough hot water (not scalding) to at least cover your ankles.
2. Add sea salt (to draw out impurities) and eucalyptus oil (to calm and soothe the nerves).
3. Sit down on a chair and place feet into the water. For the first 3 minutes, massage your feet with your hands. Then sit back and relax for an additional 15 minutes or more.
4. Remove feet and dry them. Optional: Massage feet with oil or lotion.
5. If you so desire, this is a good time to go to your meditation place and do Sitali Pranayam for a minimum of 11 minutes. *(Directions for Sitali Pranayam are on page 139.)*

This healing footbath, followed by Sitali Pranayam, is best done at the end of the day. However, you may do it anytime you choose.

*Becoming connected to the light of the Sun
nourishes and cleanses both body and mind...
It will help you experience the radiance of
your heart center and your boundlessness.
You will feel yourself expand beyond time and space
into a realm of total peace and joy.*

CHAPTER EIGHT

HEALING THROUGH THE LIGHT OF THE SUN

MANY OF US LONG FOR THE SUSTAINING HEAT and brightness of the Sun's rays, yet years of dismal warnings about the dangers of Sun exposure have led many people to believe that sunlight must be avoided. Dermatologists warn that too much Sun exposure increases our risk of developing skin cancer. The American Academy of Dermatology's sun protection guidelines include avoiding all outdoor activities between the hours of 10AM and 4PM when the Sun's rays are strongest, and the use of sunscreen with a Sun Protection Factor of 15 or higher on the body every two hours. However, there is a bright side to Sun exposure. Indeed, there is evidence that too little sunshine can increase an older person's susceptibility to a range of serious diseases. The key to maximizing the benefits of Sun exposure, and minimizing its risks, is knowing when and how to take advantage of the Sun's healing rays.

THE SUN'S HEALING RAYS & THE CURE OF DISEASE

One of sunshine's most pleasant and obvious effects is its ability to cheer people up and make them more alert. This is evident as we examine how our mood fluctuates during the changing seasons. As light from the Sun's rays travel via the optic nerve to the brain, it stimulates serotonin production. Serotonin is one of the body's "feel good" chemicals. Many people feel brighter and more optimistic during the spring and summer months when the Sun is ever-present. Conversely, depression can set in as winter approaches with its shorter, darker days.

An intriguing new finding related to sunlight's effect on mood suggests that it might ease post-surgical pain. Bruce Rabin, medical director of the Lifestyle Program at the University of Pittsburgh Medical Center, found that patients who were placed in sunlit rooms after surgery reported less pain and took less pain medication than those in darker rooms. Sunlight has also been found to dampen pain perception from other conditions, such as arthritis.

In addition to the role sunlight plays in regulating our moods, there is evidence to suggest that sunlight is important in maintaining good health, and may actually help prevent the onset of disease as it is directly linked to Vitamin D production. Indeed, sunlight is a critical component in the body's ability to change Vitamin D into a usable form. Studies show that Vitamin D not only helps the body absorb calcium in order to build stronger bones, but also protects it against a host of ailments, including heart disease, rheumatoid arthritis, multiple sclerosis, Type 1 diabetes, and cancers of the breast, prostate and colon. The risk of disease increases in individuals over the age of 50 who get little exposure to sunlight. This is due to the fact that over the age of 50, the skin produces less Vitamin D. Vitamin D deficiency has also been linked to an increased risk of falls among people over 65, as well as persistent, unexplained bone and joint pain.

Experts note that many people are not receiving adequate amounts of Vitamin D. A National Institute of Health conference recently reported an "alarming prevalence" of Vitamin D deficiency in the United States. About 40 percent of otherwise healthy adults between the ages of 49 and 65, along with half of all people over 65, are Vitamin D deficient. In addition, breast-fed babies who get little sun exposure also are at risk, because human milk doesn't contain much Vitamin D. The easiest way to heighten the body's production of Vitamin D is to expose the skin to direct sunlight.

Getting a little more Sun will get you more Vitamin D. Let's clarify that a "little" means just that. Basking in the Sun for hours every day is not necessary, nor is it recommended. The American

Cancer Society claims that exposing the face and arms to sunlight for five minutes a day, a few times per week produces sufficient levels of Vitamin D. While the American Academy of Dermatology states, unequivocally, that unprotected sun exposure is never safe because of the risk of skin cancer. Many experts believe that excessive sun exposure and sunburn cause skin cancer. I believe this to be true only after 12 noon, when the black or negative tides start coming on the Earth. In reality, one needs 15 to 30 minutes of daily sun exposure. Thirty minutes of sunscreen-free exposure several times a week before noon allows your body to create plenty of Vitamin D, and it won't increase your chances of developing skin cancer. People with dark complexions may need a little more sun. It must be emphasized that the safest sun exposure occurs between sun-up and noon. Sunscreen must be used after 12 noon if your exposure exceeds 10 to 15 minutes.

If the Sun doesn't shine much where you live, sufficient amounts of Vitamin D can be obtained from foods such as cod liver oil, salmon and mackerel, as well as fortified dairy products and breakfast cereals, and multivitamins. Current guidelines recommend 200 International Units (IU) daily for people under age 50; 400 IUs for those 50-70; and 600 IUs for older people. Some experts think adults need 1,000 IUs a day for the best health. One cup of fortified milk contains 100 IU; fortified dry breakfast cereal has about 40 to 50 IU per serving, and multivitamins usually contain 400 IU.

THE HEALING TIDES OF THE SUN AND SEASONS

Every day the Sun's energy is separated into two distinct periods. From midnight to noon there is a high tide of energy. This high tide is the most powerful and invigorating, and reaches its peak at sunrise. After sunrise the high tide gradually diminishes until noon, when the low tide begins. The low tide lasts from noon until midnight, and is at its most powerful at sunset.

The Sun and Earth energies behave like the Star of David. From noon to midnight the Earth radiates positive energy into space, which gradually becomes negative. Then, from midnight to noon the Earth radiates negative energy into space, and absorbs positive energy from the Sun. Therefore, the Earth is at its most negative at sunrise. This is when it absorbs the largest quantity of positive sun energy. During sunrise, then, there is a great amount of positive energy flooding the Earth. At the same time this is occurring, the Earth is sending the greatest amount of negative energy into space. This process of energy exchange is a replication of a perfect Star of David. This is why it is so important to perform your meditative practice at sunrise. At this time the rays that are refracted by the atmosphere have a great influence on the brain and nervous system. The brain, as we know, behaves like a battery, giving birth to thoughts that it then manifests. Via meditation, we can align our brains to give birth to positive thoughts. Moreover, we depend upon thought for our understanding of the mystery of the triad of Nature, Humanity, and God, as well as of the character of the absolute Omneity. Intelligence, whose job is to control and direct all lower faculties according to their particular laws, is found within the head. The head, then, represents the intelligent nature. The spine is our supply center. It distributes energy to all the organs of the body.

In addition to your meditative practice, sunbaths can help your brain battery absorb the healing and beneficial rays of the Sun so that it can initiate healing later by distributing this energy to all parts of the body. One way to perform a sunbath is by exposing the entire body, specifically the backbone, lungs and brain, to the Sun's rays each morning between 8 and 10 AM.

The Sun's rays affect different areas of the body at different times. Therefore, the healing effect of the Sun is different depending on the time of day. At sunrise, the rays descend in a straight line, influencing the respiratory organs and our sensibility. With the approach of noon the same rays influence our digestive system. It is important to point out that individuals who can endure staying in the Sun from the morning to noon are in good health, while those who cannot endure staying in the Sun for a long time, are not in good health. The more energy you absorb into your body during the beneficial hours of the day, the greater softness and magnetism you will develop.

After 12 noon, the healing effects of the Sun's rays are quite insignificant. This is due to the different absorption capacity of the Earth, as well as the human system. In other words, the Sun's rays are so potent after 12 noon that they are no longer beneficial to the human system. In fact, they can be detrimental, as these hours are the time of the black, or negative, rays. If you expose your body to the Sun's rays during these hours, you must take care to concentrate your spirit on positive things. This will ensure that you continue to absorb only the most positive rays. Moreover, if you do choose to stay in the Sun all day long, you can protect yourself from its harmful rays by wearing a hat whose shape will refract the harmful rays. In addition, be sure not to fall asleep in the Sun during this time. Along with the black, or negative, rays of the Sun, there are also waves radiating from the Earth as well. They too are harmful to the human system.

With its negative rays, the second period of the day (12 noon to midnight) is a time of weakness when negativity can easily triumph. Until you learn how to shield yourself from these waves of negativity, it is recommended that you stay in the Sun only during the early hours of the day, up to noon at the latest. Again, after noon, you must strengthen your electromagnetic field to protect yourself from the Sun's rays. Mantra meditations can help draw out negativity and eliminate it. Indeed, sunset is a beneficial time to chant for balance and protection.

In general, take advantage of the changing tides of sunrise and sunset to bolster your life force and strengthen your aura, or magnetic field. At sunrise you will attract all manner of health and well being, while at sunset you will create a shield that protects you until the following morning. Make it your guiding rule to know those hours of the days that are most beneficial for the absorption of the healing rays of the Sun.

It is also important to know that the Sun's rays do not act in the same way during the four seasons. During the spring and summer there is a high tide of healing energy flowing toward the

Earth. Conversely, during the fall and winter there is a low tide of healing energy flowing toward the Earth. That is why the Sunrays of spring (from March 21st to June 22nd) possess the strongest healing effect. From March 21st onward the Earth gradually becomes positive. As we move into summer, the rays of the Sun have a healing influence, but it is less than that of spring. During the spring and summer it is recommended that you go to bed and get up early in order to welcome the Sun and gather its healing, strengthening, and uplifting energy.

SPECIFIC APPLICATIONS OF THE SUN'S HEALING ENERGY

Before I outline the specific applications of the Sun's healing energy, it is important to note that while working with the Sun your consciousness must be focused. Do not allow yourself to think of anything other than healing. Unless otherwise indicated, recite the *Prayer of Love, Peace, and Light* during each particular practice.

PRAYER OF LOVE, PEACE, AND LIGHT

Love before me	*Peace before me*	*Light before me*
Love behind me	*Peace behind me*	*Light behind me*
Love at my left	*Peace at my left*	*Light at my left*
Love at my right	*Peace at my right*	*Light at my right*
Love above me	*Peace above me*	*Light above me*
Love below me	*Peace below me*	*Light below me*
Love unto me	*Peace unto me*	*Light unto me*
Love in my surroundings	*Peace in my surroundings*	*Light in my surroundings*
Love to all	*Peace to all*	*Light to all*
Love to the universe	*Peace to the universe*	*Light to the universe*

The healing energies of the Sun can be accessed in a variety of ways. For general healing, expose yourself to the rays of the Sun every morning between 7 and 8 AM. First, turn your back to the East where the Sun rises. Next, turn to the North for a while. Finally, turn back to the East again. Stay in this position. Those who are healthy will also benefit from this practice, as it strengthens the nervous system. Remember that your spine is your supply center. It distributes energy to all the organs of your body.

Perhaps the easiest way to access the healing energies of the Sun is to allow the sunlight force to enter your body through the pores of the skin. As we have discussed, the first rays of the Sun are the most active and, therefore, the most beneficial. This is due to the fact that these rays contain more vital energy, or prana, than the rays shining later in the day. The following method of absorption is particularly helpful to those who are experiencing health challenges. Lie on a patch of grass, sandy beach, or floor of a sun-drenched room in such a way that the Sun's rays are able to penetrate the skin's entire surface. Be sure to allow the sunlight to shine on your solar plexus. Fifteen minutes of daily exposure will greatly benefit the spiritual centers of the body, boosting their healing properties so that the body is strengthened and health improves.

One of the most effective ways of using the Sun as a tool of healing is to take a sunbath. Remove your shirt so that you are naked to the waist. Next, lie down on a bed with your head pointing north and your legs pointing south. Face your chest toward the Sun's rays while protecting your head. When you have held this position for 30 minutes, turn your back toward the Sun for an additional 30 minutes. Continue to alternate your body position in this way, holding each position for 30 minutes, until you begin to perspire profusely. Perspiration is the most important aspect of this healing ritual. During a sunbath it is recommended that you dress in either white or light green clothes. Concentrate your thoughts on the healing power of Mother Nature. In turn, she will lend her forces to your healing efforts.

Those who suffer from chest problems should turn their back to the rays of the Sun, and then turn their chest to the rays of the

Sun. During exposure, they should pray that the light of the Sun will heal and strengthen them so that they may work for the glory of God on this planet Earth. This practice should be repeated consistently for at least 120 days. The chest gives birth to the life that it preserves within it. The heart is the seat of the emotions and sentiments, and it pumps the lifeblood throughout the body. By working on the chest in the manner described, the Sun will produce a beneficial and healing change in the body.

In a previous section we discussed the benefits of sunlight in relation to Vitamin D production. To reiterate, low levels of Vitamin D have been linked to a whole host of ailments including cancer, hypertension, diabetes and osteoporosis. Mystics have known for thousands of years that there is a connection between the Sun and the bones. Human bones are highly concentrated light of the Sun. The quality of life-force concentrated in our bones is superior to that of the flesh and fluid, because of their enduring strength. That explains why, after one passes on, what remains through time are the bones. The bones are crucial to our structure and support as a human being. Trees, like bones, are full of prana or lifeforce. This explains why trees can have a lifespan of 300 hundred years or more. Human bones outlive trees by several thousand years. There is evidence of some bones from early humans, *Australopithecus,* that have survived over a million years.

Vitamin D is the physical connection, in that it is a vital substance to the bones. Moreover, when we work with the Sun in the ways we have described, a D-related hormone found in the skin soaks up the Sun's ultraviolet rays and travels to the liver and kidneys, where it picks up extra molecules of oxygen and hydrogen. This process transforms the pre-vitamin D into a potent hormone called calcitriol. Scientists are beginning to think that, along with the liver and kidneys, many bodily tissues can convert the pre-vitamin D, thereby making their own disease-fighting calcitriol. For example, prostate cells produce the hormone calcitriol, which can then act as a break on cell growth. When the cells cannot get enough of Vitamin D's precursor to make calcitriol, they start to multiply uncontrollably creating a platform for prostate cancer.

Sunlight, then, not only provides us with the Vitamin D that is so crucial, it also strengthens our health and helps us heal. Allowing the Sun to warm your unprotected arms and face for a few minutes each morning (the early morning hours are the best) will allow your body to make all the Vitamin D you need. As previously stated, it is essential that your arms and face be left unprotected, as sunscreen reduces Vitamin D absorption to nothing.

Exercise is also extremely important, as a lack of exercise leads to a deficiency of heat. Heat is a major element in the body. It propels all physical movements in the body apart from the enzymatic reactions. In a heated area, blood flow is increased. When blood flow is increased, the body receives a richer supply of nutrients, its repair functions are faster, and waste and toxin removal is quicker. Exercise increases various metabolic reactions in the body. The heat produced during the increase in metabolic reactions during exercise drives circulation, indirectly aiding in the removal of toxins and waste materials from the cells. In addition to an increase in blood circulation and heat circulation, exercise promotes air and energy circulation.

A morning walk in combination with a yoga series allows you to fully absorb the positive sun energy. Walking outside is better than walking indoors or on a treadmill, unless the weather is harsh, as it is holistic and allows you to both breathe fresh air and greet the first rays of the Sun. Moreover, one needs to walk before noon. As I have stated, during the afternoon hours the Sun's rays are no longer beneficial. Walk for as long as you like, consciously feeling all of the muscles of your body engage. When taken all together (walking, yoga and sunbathing), they form a comprehensive system that encourages optimum health. Remember, any part of the body that remains unused will deteriorate over time. The areas of the body that are not engaged in proper exercise are vulnerable to disease. This exercise system works every part of the body and involves the mind as well. Moreover, it improves your lung capacity, thereby increasing the level of oxygen supplied to your cells, particularly those of the brain. This, in turn, rejuvenates the cells, while helping to enhance proper functioning.

Becoming connected to the light of the Sun nourishes and cleanses both body and mind. Therefore, in addition to sunbaths and exercise, concentrate deeply and immerse yourself in the following meditation on the Sun, which involves training your brain to experience the sensation of sunlight pouring into your body. It will help you experience the radiance of your heart center and your boundlessness. You will feel yourself expand beyond time and space into a realm of total peace and joy.

Before we outline the meditation it is important to stress, once again, that the early morning hours, known as the ambrosial hours, are the best time to meditate. Sunrise is a time for rejuvenation and revitalization of the spirit with sunlight fluid. Our daily activities have yet to begin, and the Sun is distributing a great amount of prana to the Earth. Work to recharge your aura and fill your body with light before you face each day. Working with the Sun in this way is a spiritual cure that will bring balance to your energy flow, while restoring and recharging the divine protective shield around you. If this shield is strong, the negative energies that approach you can be transformed into positives in the way in which they affect your consciousness.

Whether sitting, lying down, or standing, your back needs to face the direction of the rising sun before sunrise. This is true even on cloudy days. The amount of healing and renewing energy you absorb during this time is equal to that which you can absorb by staying in the Sun all day. Focus your thoughts toward the rising sun with the knowledge that nothing, not even clouds, can counteract the vital, renewing energy of the Sun. Remember to stay with your back turned towards the Sun whether you find yourself in a good mood or bad or whether you are healthy or ill.

While the Sun is easy to recognize by its rays, it is also an invisible energy found in the air we breathe. In fact, this invisible energy surrounds and protects us at all times. With each breath, every organ in the body soaks up the Sun's energy much the way that a sponge soaks up water. Train your brain to experience the sensation of sunlight pouring into your body.

For a few minutes each day visualize the invisible sunlight force bringing you increased vitality, health, and spiritual and material richness with each inhale. Know that you are drawing the Sun's great strength into your system. Now visualize this force being distributed throughout your body. If you have a specific illness or diseased organ, concentrate on it and affirm that the Sun is centering its healing power on the area of disturbance, making itself particularly intense and active. Next, talk with the light of the Sun. If any part of the body is aching, expose it to the Sun's light; think of the light and its healing power, and your ache will disappear. Through concentration, faith, and the power of positive thoughts, the vital sun force can be administered to bolster any weakened organ or function.

We need to train ourselves to work with the Sun on a daily basis. The consistent practice of working with the Sun is a golden habit that makes for true happiness, healing, and bliss, as the Sun bestows the eternal fullness of joy, knowledge and love. Make every effort to work with the Sun. Pray that neither test nor temptation ever has the power to make you forget to connect with the Sun each day. In due time, its beautiful and healing brightness will shine throughout your body and radiate throughout every aspect of your life. By working with the Sun, your perception will become limitless and you will merge with the oceanic flow of the divine presence. Those who meditate and work with the Sun to connect with God on a daily basis are granted light and healing. Indeed, the two go hand in hand. The sun will brighten you so much that God will permanently reside in you. Regardless of what your mind may suggest, keep your sacred agreement to connect with the Sun each morning. Internalize the joyous presence of the Sun's light. In this way you will be laying the foundation stone of your happiness for the rest of the day.

*The physical appearance of disease
is only the result of some broken law of nature or karma
of some misspent emotion within the individual.
Law makes the universe absolutely dependable.
By studying and following the laws of nature,
one gains knowledge, power and wisdom.
As laws are the basis of the universe,
so do they govern every aspect of human life.
By working with these laws, we can improve
our health and bring order into our lives.*

CHAPTER NINE

THE LAW OF NATURE AND THE SEVEN CREATIVE PLANETS

THE PHYSICAL APPEARANCE of disease is only the result of some broken law of nature or karma of some misspent emotion within the individual. Laws make the universe absolutely dependable. For if our universe were not so dependable, sunrise would be as unpredictable as sunset. As a result, it would be almost impossible for anything to grow and even live. Laws are a sign of security, reliability and order. By studying and following the laws of nature, one gains knowledge, power and wisdom. For law always means a level of control and power. While human law may be restrictive, irrational and unpredictable, the universal laws are not; they are immutable.

As laws are the basis of the universe, so do they govern every aspect of human life. Knowledge of the laws of life can help ease our fears. By working with these laws we can improve our health and bring order into our lives. We must learn to work with the seven planets and renew our contact with heaven, so that the beneficial heavenly energies may circulate and flow through us and our lives, and we may regain our divine birthright. The study of the divine spiritual wisdom will engage the mind with healing and higher truth. Learning about the nature of the soul, and working with the seven planets, expands the mind and fights disease.

The seven creative planets are linked to the cosmic powers of the Archangels, and each of the seven planets is ruled by an archangel who in turn is subject to God. It is God Himself who rules over each of these planets. The person who knows how to work with the number seven can knowingly attract light and repel darkness.

God created the world with the 22 letters of the Hebrew alphabet, which relate to the 22 major arcana of the tarot, with the following pattern: three mother letters, seven double letters, and twelve single letters. The letters in this pattern not only correspond to the divine, astral and physical worlds, but they also reveal exactly where our consciousness dwells. For example, the 12 simple letters correspond in space to the 12 signs of astrology, and most of humankind dwells at that level of consciousness. That is why, one thing people often ask is what astrological sign you are. The fact that seven is the level above twelve, and God uses the pattern of 3-7-12 in the creation of the world should give us some food for thought.

It may also be interesting to describe here, in as few words as possible, the human spine and its connection to the divine number seven in relation to the pattern of creation. The spinal column is by some mysterious coincidence divided into 26 vertebrae, the exact number of the Kabbalah numerology of the sacred name of God—*Yod He Vav He*—which can only be pronounced with utmost reverence.

Still more extraordinary is the fact that the first section of the spinal column is divided into the seven cervical vertebrae, which corresponds to the seven double letters, the seven creative planets and the seven days of the week.

Further, the presence of the mystic number seven in the first group of vertebra is such a remarkable coincidence that one is forced to the conclusion that the disposition of the sections was purposely planned to come together for a definite reason. And that reason evidently being that the relation of such coincidence will inevitably strike a seeker of truth as an illustration of the power of the number seven as the key to penetrate the mysteries of life and nature.

In addition, the seven cervical vertebrae occupying as they do the remarkable position of being the first section, justifies the reason why humans need to work with the number seven, so as to understand and master the laws of nature. This disposition is the epitome of the great truth taught all through the arcanal wisdom.

The other fact is, next to the seven cervical vertebrae, we find the second section, and it is subdivided into 12 thoracic vertebrae, which correspond to the 12 single letters of the Hebrew alphabet, the twelve signs of the zodiac, and the twelve months of the year.

Not only is this a curious link to the order of creation, but it is doubly so because the seven planets rule the twelve signs of the zodiac. The five lumbar correspond to the the five fingers, the five elements of earth, water, fire, air and ether that make up time and space, and the five senses. This could only have been done by a supreme and infinite intelligence, in order to reveal to us that the mystic number seven, which is at the root of all the laws of nature, is also the key to our health and happiness.

THE SEVEN PERIODS

The year can be divided into seven periods of 52 days. Each period is ruled by one of the seven planets. The planet Earth goes through a yearly cycle. The planetary year does not start on January 1, even though this is what our current calendar system states. The new year actually begins on March 21, the first day of Spring. This is the first powerful day of the year, when the Sun releases vast amounts of energy into the Universe. Each individual has a personal yearly cycle as well, with the first day of the Sun period starting on your birthday. For example, if you were born on March 21, which is also the first day of the Earth's year, this is what the seven periods of 52 days would look like for you:

EXAMPLE: YEARLY CYCLE FOR A
PERSON BORN ON MARCH 21

Sun Period	March 21–May 11
Moon Period	May 12–July 2
Mars Period	July 3–August 23
Mercury Period	August 24–October 14
Jupiter Period	October 15–December 5
Venus Period	December 6–January 26
Saturn Period	January 27–March 20

The following is a description and detailed explanation of the jurisdiction of each if the Seven Creative Planets, their attributes, and how each pertains to your health.

SUN PERIOD

This potent Sun period begins the day of your birthday and, as with all periods, lasts for 52 days. Whenever you are planning to connect with heaven for assistance regarding your health, this is the time. Take advantage of this period by doing something worthwhile. Mentally create a picture of yourself vibrant with health. This is the time to achieve anything that you deem important in your life, realizing that the universe is cooperating with you during your Sun period. All your ideas, creative powers and plans will move forward with greater success if you start now. Remember to keep this in mind: Maintaining health through diet and exercise and attaining your health-related goals are entirely within reach during your Sun period.

This is a good time for you to remember your eyes, circulation, and heart. Most heart troubles come from cholesterol. The higher the cholesterol level, the greater the risk of heart disease. Cut back on foods such as french fries made with artery-clogging fats. Eat more fish and other foods such as soybeans, walnuts and flax seeds that contain healthy fats. Lower your cholesterol and risk of heart disease by eating foods with omega-3 fats like salmon and tuna, and avoid eating transfatty acids.

It has been found that hydrogenated fats tend to raise blood cholesterol levels. Therefore avoid foods like beef, pork and lamb. Stay away from fat in butter, milk, vegetable shortening, crackers, cookies, doughnuts and french fries. Get in the habit of drinking the juice of half a lemon in lukewarm water. Avoid palpitations, blood pressure, and keep your back healthy. Take herbs that improve digestion, promote circulation and functional activity.

In addition, you can add turnips to your diet; they have a splendid effect on the heart. You also can rebuild the body with cucumber juice, or a healthy drink made of ginger juice, cardamom powder, and grapefruit juice.

A person who is very sick can eat a cup of yogurt with saffron three times a day, or rice cooked with garlic and milk once a day.

Walk barefooted on cold grass in the morning. It will improve your eye sight and increase vitality. In the morning, after showering run cold water on the frontal lobe for 60 seconds or eat water chestnuts, in order to maintain healthy eyes, ears and throat. Also, carrots, spinach, and kale are excellent sources of beta carotene, which help the eyes function well.

Useful for this time is avocado and olive oil, they are good for the arteries, and they help lower cholesterol. Not only can you strengthen the nervous system with ginger, but also, it kicks out all the poisons of the body. This is a time to take advantage of its positive aspects of regeneration to renew yourself.

Since the heart is ruled by the Sun, here are some of the things you can do to heal and strengthen it. Grate a few carrots and add honey and lemon juice to make salad. Take this combination to cure all sorts of heart ailments resulting from ventricular or muscular disorders. For high blood pressure, drink goat milk twice a day.

Some studies have found that death from coronary heart disease is far less common in countries along the Mediterranean than in northern Europe.

A diet rich in fruits, vegetables, cereals, fish and beans can prevent heart disease or heart attack. Also, an intake of more dietary fiber, antioxidants and B vitamins found in fruit and vegetables can slow the arterial damage that precedes heart disease.

In addition, olive and flaxseed oil are not only rich in omega-3 unsaturated fatty acid, but also, these oils have several effects in the body that would be expected to prevent or reduce risk of blood clots, abnormal heart rhythms, inflammation and clogging of blood vessels by deposits of fat cholesterol and prevention of sudden cardiac death. Fish oil is also known to help prevent cardiac death.

People with a high level of omega-3 fatty acids in the blood have a lower risk of developing a recurrent heart attack or any cardiac problems.

To avoid heart attacks or the worsening of heart disease, eat foods that are high in omega-3 fatty acids. Eat foods like fish: salmon, mackerel, sardines, albacore and tuna, once or twice a week. They are good for the heart by making the blood less likely to clot. They prevent heart attacks and lower blood pressure.

Eating fish can prevent the potentially fatal disruption of heart rhythm. People who regularly eat fatty fish are less likely to suffer heart attacks. Fish oil reduces the thickness and stickiness of the blood, which, in turn, prevent blood and heart attack.

In a few rare cases, for seven days your Sun period may be overlapped by the cusp of the previous period, Saturn. In some cases, it may not come into full strength until about seven days after your birthday. Sometimes, for seven days before your Sun period ends, it gradually loses its strength on account of becoming overlapped by the cusp of the incoming Moon period.

MOON PERIOD

The next 52 days encompass your Moon period. The Moon period influences your sensitivity and personality improvement. Cultivate calm, tolerance, and acceptance of others. Be mindful of others and their needs. Try not to let disharmony and disagreeable situations take a toll on your nervous system. Avoid doing things in a hurry. Take care of your circulation and strengthen your digestive system, so that you may avoid skin problems, for example. Take good care of your kidneys, bladder and reproductive system. Avoid emotional upsets. Women may be challenged by PMS or pain in the breasts or reproductive system. To make the mind healthy or heal any type of psychosis, take brisk walks for 11 minutes per day or dance.

Herbs and foods such as cabbage, chicory, cucumber, lettuce, and melon can be good. Your Moon period is the time to cooperate with others and keep your temper on an even level.

For depression, drink a glass of cold water and splash the face with cold water five times.

To center your energy, combine in a blender and drink: *1 banana, 2 teaspoons of raisins, plain yogurt, water or apple juice.*

Add bananas and ginger to your diet. Aloe vera juice is also good for the stomach.

This period can affect your health and relationships with friends, loved ones and yourself. Meditation can give you the capacity for tolerance. Your spiritual discipline will develop in you the attitude of neutrality that sustains your projection in the midst of all the experiences that you attract. Instead of defending yourself from all the choices with fear and oversensitivity, you can respond with clarity, expansion and the joyful fulfillment of responsibilities.

MARS PERIOD

The next 52 days will take you through the Mars period. Check up on your health, for you are most susceptible to health problems and skin diseases at this time. It is here that one may contract contagious and lingering diseases. During this period, the Universe will put a lot of energy at your disposal, either to improve your health or to do anything of a physical nature. Mars is a planet of trials and tests. This challenging planet stands for guns, fire, accidents and sexuality. Exercise caution during this time. Mars can be a challenging planet that works on your strength, impulses and anger. Therefore, this is an excellent time for you to build your strength and energy. Beware of argumentative tendencies, control your temper and avoid family conflicts. Mars influences the immune system and the bone marrow, which manufactures white blood corpuscles to fight off viruses and bacteria. It has a direct relationship to the blood and is closely related to the muscular system. Add a lot of onion to your food to make your blood strong and healthy. Work out or do some yoga to stretch the body. Mars rules over courage which is directly related to blood sugar levels. Try not to drink alcohol, and moderate your coffee consumption and other caffeinated beverages. Keep your blood pure, and avoid throat troubles, bronchitis and laryngitis. Take good care of your adrenals. Try not to be impulsive in speech and action. Be calm and not quick-tempered.

Take care of digestive problems to stop possible skin problems. Build blood by eating large quantities of onion and turmeric separately or together. Zucchini, carrot and pumpkin have a splendid effect on the blood. Celery helps lower blood pressure, because of the blood pressure-lowering chemicals that it contains.

MERCURY PERIOD

The next 52 days welcome the Mercury period. Mercury is a neutral planet that influences your nervous strength and communication. During this time it will feel much easier to write or talk with everyone and make yourself understood. Steer clear of putting yourself under time limits and pressures.

Maintain a strong nervous system. Learning how to be calm will be vital here. Take good care of your kidneys and lungs. Take food, herbs and fruits that are good for the nerves, such as gotu kola, mint, fennel, and parsley. Avoid restlessness and insomnia. Induce restful sleep by drinking a juice made from lettuce. It is a powerful relaxant that will put you right to sleep. Reduce the salt content of the body; it will induce sleep quickly. Pay attention to your arms or hands.

Lemon is good in this period, because it contains magnesium, which will take care of your nervous and circulatory system. Asparagus is especially good for the central nervous system. Eggplant has a splendid effect on the adrenals. Corn has a good effect on the brain. Drinking cranberry juice is excellent for the kidneys.

JUPITER PERIOD

Jupiter has its say for the next 52 days. This is a time to seek help and engage in any form of money transaction. It is an excellent time to borrow money or work on your health. Jupiter rules the general medical realm and regulates financial matters and wealth. This is a time when you can recover from most illnesses. Do not be temperamental; avoid worrying. Keep yourself from overworking, which leads to stress and strain. This is a time when your mental outlook will be of major importance. Develop a positive mental attitude.

Since Jupiter is in charge of eating, make adjustments to your diet so that it works on all aspects of digestion, such as the assimilation and absorption of food. You need a diet that helps to promote digestion and disperse the accumulation of undigested food materials. Do not overeat. Take good care of your skin and liver. This is a good time to add to your diet olive oil, fish oils and most tonics if you haven't before. You can help prevent nervous disorders and congestive diseases by having a diet that helps dispel mucus, which clogs and stagnates the stomach and intestines. Avoid digestive weakness that is born from anxiety, depression and worry.

This is a good time to go out and absorb as much sunlight as possible. It is especially recommended that you lie on the grass or on the sand on the beach in the sunlight in such a manner as to permit the rays to strengthen your health. Also, lying in the sun so that it will shine on the solar plexus, or central part of the abdomen, is an excellent practice, especially in the early morning hours when the Sun is not too strong. Unless disease attacks the inner part of the body, the organs lying immediately around the solar plexus are the last to break down and wear out.

This period is good for anyone to project or send treatments, to do good spiritual work, or to do anything that calls upon the creative strength and vitality of the spiritual centers.

VENUS PERIOD

The next 52 days belong to Venus. Loosen up. The Venus period is time to rest, play, and have fun. This is a good time to take it easy. It is also an excellent time to tap into the healing aspect of good music and uplifting art. You should now take good care of yourself and treat yourself right. Avoid promiscuity, and be moderate with your love of pleasure. Although this is a period for you to play and have fun, you will need to practice moderation to prevent impulsive behavior that may lead you into bitter experiences that come from extremes. Do not be caught in loyalty to a dream as an ideal picture of perfect love. Through your spiritual practice, you must develop an awareness that will guide you into safe situations. Make it your duty to strengthen your electromagnetic field on a daily basis, so that you may channel your emotions constructively and avoid the devastating pain that comes from a broken heart. Do not be overly emotional. Stay away from lust. Take care of your reproductive system, urogenital area, hair, and kidneys. Avoid constipation and throat problems. Take foods and herbs that work on the heart, kidneys and reproductive system. Venus is mainly in charge of cooling herbs such as aloe vera and saffron.

Drinking cranberry juice is an excellent support for the bladder and the kidneys, and also helps block infectious bacteria. Drink as much water as you can in order to flush out your system.

SATURN PERIOD

The next 52 days will require precise attention to detail and emotional balance. Check up on your health, for you are most susceptible to health and skin diseases at this time. It is here that one may contract contagious and lingering diseases. You may feel confined or restricted. Saturn is often a challenging period that works on your fear. Steer clear of being fearful, withdrawn and melancholy. Keep a positive attitude. Spend a lot of time reading spiritual books.

Saturn, which is the balancer of karma, is also referred to as the planet of darkness. It brings disturbance to the mind, body and spirit, making you lonely and frustrated. It is confining and limiting.

Pay attention to your bones, joints, and liver. Strengthen your spleen, and take care of your digestive system so as to avoid colds. Keep your kidneys in good shape, and eat plenty of fresh fruit, herbs and vegetables. Take care of your eating habits in order to avoid problems such as hemorrhoids. Take care of your ears and teeth. Add celery and spinach to your diet. Take care of arising problems before they get worse.

You can prevent arthritis by eating fatty fish, such as sardines, salmon, tuna, etc. Golden milk is also excellent. Take turmeric to keep the bones and joints flexible.

You can prevent bone fractures and even osteoporosis by eating pineapple. Pineapple contains manganese.

This is a time to study yourself, your friends and your environment with a detachment that is cool and clear. Your spiritual practice will give you the ability to choose the right direction. It will help you develop intuition in this karmic period.

THE MOON

The moon follows a 28-day cycle, during which it travels once around the earth at an average distance of 250,000 miles. During those 28 days, the moon experiences the same influences the sun experiences during its 365-day rotation. Therefore, as you can imagine, the moon cycle is one of intensity.

The moon's 28-day rotation is divided into phases which directly impact all living beings on Earth, including man. In other words, the moon not only influences the tides and plant growth, it also influences our health. As human beings, we are affected both psychologically and emotionally by the moon's phases. When we know how to work with the moon's energy, we are able to tap into universal healing forces in order to restore and maintain health.

Logic dictates that because our bodies are composed of 75% to 80% liquid, the moon, which influences the waters of the Earth, would exert great influence on our systems. When faced with health challenges, one should immediately begin working with the moon. On a physical level, the moon is represented by water and therefore, one must drink sufficient amounts, and on the spiritual level, one can breathe solely through the left nostril to access the lunar energy, which renews the blood, sharpens intuition and enhances overall health. The expression "calling upon the hands of God" refers to the water element. Water is the best natural medicine for the liver and kidneys. It is used by the liver to detoxify impurities, and the kidneys use water to flush these toxic substances and waste materials out of the body. Therefore, drink a lot of clean water to heal the body and maintain health. Plenty of water is a necessity to keep the body chemistry (pH) in balance.

The four most powerful days in the 28-day moon cycle are the new moon, full moon, and the tenth and eleventh days of the moon. During these days, the moon generates a certain pressure on the endocrine system, so that it is able to properly secrete and cleanse itself. Fasting on these days, in particular the eleventh day, is highly recommended. Fasting is a therapeutic application that can be implemented in order to restore and maintain the body's equilibrium. When we give our bodies a break from the stresses of digestion and elimination, our immune systems are strengthened.

There are two main phases of the moon cycle. They are termed waxing and waning. The waxing moon begins with the new moon, when just a small slice is visible, and lasts for about two weeks. These two weeks are called the waxing moon phase because during this time the moon becomes increasingly larger and more luminous until the day before the full moon. While the moon's light is increasing, vital forces tend to be more potent.

This moon phase is particularly favorable for spiritual and material expansion. Indeed, from the time of the new moon to the time of the full moon the body's spiritual centers are active and efficient. Those who use this time wisely will gain assistance from the universe and experience positive results. Harness your creative energy in the service of healing or spiritual work. Take advantage of the constructive energy of the waxing moon to start a new project or business, and improve or maintain your health. In general, the phase of the waxing moon is beneficial for making additions to your life, environment and body. This is a time where you are bringing something into your life. Most complex health work, plastic surgery, dental implant, or all surgical procedures that involve adding something to the body should be conducted during the waxing moon.

The phase of the waning moon, conversely, is beneficial for removal. This phase begins with the full moon and also lasts for approximately two weeks. During these two weeks, we experience the moon as a decreasing light, and the effects produced are entirely different from those of the waxing moon. As previously stated, this is the most beneficial time to rid your life of unwanted or unnecessary habits and conditions. Moreover, all surgical procedures that involve removing unwanted tissue should be conducted during the waning moon.

THE SUN

The sun is a tremendous source of healing and strength. Its light is the carrier of life. Therefore, it is important to absorb as much sunlight as possible. Working with the sun will revitalize and energize your entire system.

The healing energies of the sun can be accessed in a variety of ways. Perhaps the easiest is to allow the sunlight force to enter the body through the pores of the skin. This method is particularly helpful to those who are experiencing health challenges. Lie on a patch of grass, sandy beach or the floor of a sun-drenched room in such a way that the sun's rays are able to penetrate the entire skin surface. Be sure that the sunlight shines on your solar plexus. Fifteen minutes of daily exposure will greatly benefit the spiritual centers of the body, boosting their healing properties so that the body is strengthened and health improves.

The healing, life force of the sun is ever present. While the sun is easy to recognize by its rays, it is also an invisible energy found in the air we breathe. In fact, this invisible energy surrounds and protects us at all times. With each breath, every organ in the body soaks up the sun's energy similar to the way a sponge soaks up water. Train your brain to experience the sensation of sunlight pouring into your body. For a few minutes each day, visualize the invisible sunlight force bringing you increased vitality, health, and spiritual and material richness with each inhale. Know that you are drawing the sun's great strength into your system. Now visualize this force being distributed throughout your body. If you have a specific illness or diseased organ, concentrate on it and affirm that the sun is centering its healing power on the area of disturbance, making itself particularly intense and active. Through both concentration and faith, the vital sun force will be administered to bolster the weakened organ or function.

The invisible sunlight force contained in the air we breathe is the living spirit, the universal life that emanates from all things. It is the omnipresent, projected God; the infinite, omnipotent principle. When you consciously relate to the sun through meditation, the universe relates to you.

The early morning hours are referred to as the ambrosial hours. Our daily activities have yet to begin, and the sun is distributing great amount of prana to the earth. This is one of the best times to meditate, as sunrise is a time for rejuvenation and revitalization of the spirit with sunlight fluid. It is recommended that you work to recharge your aura before you face each day. Again, as a therapeutic method, the sun is most potent during the fresh hours of each morning. If you are experiencing illness, choose this time to expose yourself to its healing rays. Sunset, on the other hand, is a beneficial time for balance and protection.

Take advantage of the changing tides of sunrise and sunset to bolster your life force, and strengthen your aura, or magnetic field. At sunrise you will attract all manner of health and well being, while at sunset you will create a shield that protects you until the following morning. For more details on the power of the Sun, you may wish to read *The Healing Fire of Heaven (previously title The Splendor of the Sun)*.

Connecting with the Sun for Energy

- Sit erect and relaxed with hands in your lap.
- Visualize the sun or fountain of light and energy.
- Mentally lift your consciousness from your body and go "in spirit" to the sun itself.
- Have the sun send a tremendous energy flow through your entire being, invigorating and strengthening every particle.
- After a few minutes, return your awareness to your body, rise and go on with your daily tasks.

As you practice this simple exercise, you will find yourself becoming less tired and more energized.

CHAPTER TEN

PLANETARY INFLUENCE

THERE IS A MYSTICAL system of inestimable value for anyone looking to improve their health. It is based upon the planets of our solar system and the influence those planets have upon the systems of individual members of humanity. Planets are the framework of the universe and he who knows how to work with them becomes all-powerful. Planets are magnetic forces. Every human being has a specific primary and secondary planet and if he knows them, he also knows exactly where he fits in the universe. Each person who comes to earth is determined by the fundamental planets allotted to him by divine intelligence, and based upon what he/she has earned for himself/herself through the way he/she lived in previous incarnations. Each person has a primary and secondary planet, which hold sway over events, tendencies and patterns in our lives. Whether you know about them or not, these planets have a hidden influence on all aspects of your life, and often foreshadow the future. Learning what planets guide and govern you and your loved ones can aid in diagnosing, curing and preventing illnesses, as well as creating and maintaining health. But knowing your influencing planets is not enough; it is also important to have a firm understanding of the characteristics each planet represents. Each planet contains both positive and negative aspects, and knowledge of the aspects of one's ruling planet is not only useful, but essential to a healthy and successful life.

The planet that rules the day of the week on which you were born is known as the "primary planet." Your day of birth is full of information, as the vibration of that day is recorded deeply in your energy system. When your primary planet is learned, and its aspects understood and applied, it becomes a master key to revealing your personal strengths and weaknesses.

What is called the "secondary planet" is also based upon the time of the year you were born, and can be learned by consulting the next chart. Together, the primary and secondary planets shape your own particular vibration, and this fundamental vibration, determines your destiny and your path in life, your health, the shape of your physical body and even the cast of your features. You will find that one of these planets is often more active in your life than the other.

Again, it is important to keep in mind that there are both positive and negative aspects to each of the planetary energies. The negative influences can sometimes manifest as health problems. You will also find that certain illnesses are particular to specific planets. Most health disturbances will come to you through the diseases that are particular to your ruling planets, but there are foods and herbs designed to heal or prevent illnesses and bring the positive influences of these planets into your life. For example, if you are ruled by Mercury, most of your health disturbances will manifest as the diseases listed under Mercury. It is important to learn the challenging aspects of your planet so that you may prevent it's particular tendencies to specific illnesses through lifestyle adjustment. Therefore, eating the herbs and foods under your ruling planet can reduce the possibility of having the health challenges of the planet manifest in your life and let you maintain optimal health. In other words, there are many benefits to be derived from the intelligent use of planetary herbs. Just remember that your destructive patterns will often manifest through the negative aspects of the planet that rules your day of birth. And, by living consciously, you will be most likely to manifest your planets positive aspects. As you can see, those who learn more about their planets will certainly be thrice-armed in battling unhealthy patterns, and consequently moving their life to a healthy and harmonious one.

FINDING YOUR PRIMARY AND SECONDARY PLANETS

PRIMARY PLANET
THE DAYS OF THE WEEK AND THE RULING PLANETS

Sunday	Sun
Monday	Moon
Tuesday	Mars
Wednesday	Mercury
Thursday	Jupiter
Friday	Venus
Saturday	Saturn

Note: If you do not know the day of the week you were born, you can consult an ephemeris, Lifting the Veil *or* Alchemy of Love Relationships.

SECONDARY PLANET
DATES OF REFERENCE

Mars	March 20–29
Sun	March 30–April 8
Venus	April 9–18
Mercury	April 19–28
Moon	April 29–May 8
Saturn	May 9–18
Jupiter	May 19–28
Mars	May 29–June 7
Sun	June 8–17
Venus	June 18–27
Mercury	June 28–July 7

Planetary Influence 103

Moon	July 8–July 17
Saturn	July 18–27
Jupiter	July 28–August 6
Mars	August 7–16
Sun	August 17–26
Venus	August 27–September 5
Mercury	September 6–15
Moon	September 16–25
Saturn	September 26–October 5
Jupiter	October 6–15
Mars	October 16–25
Sun	October 26–November 4
Venus	November 5–14
Mercury	November 15–24
Moon	November 25–December 4
Saturn	December 5–14
Jupiter	December 15–24
Mars	December 25–January 3
Mars/Sun	January 4–5
Sun	January 4–13
Venus	January 14–23
Mercury	January 24–February 2
Moon	February 3–12
Saturn	February 13–22
Jupiter	February 23–March 4
Mars	March 5–9
Mars/Jupiter	March 10–14
Jupiter	March 15–19
Mars	March 20–29

HELPFUL PLANETARY INFLUENCE

Certain herbs, gemstones and behavior patterns have been found by the ancient students of nature to be in harmony with the ruling planet. Taking the beneficial herbs, vibrating the proper sound, wearing the proper gem, or behaving in the positive aspect of your planet, can attract its positive influence in your life and improve your health.

Procedure For Vibrating the Sound Relating To Each Planet

- Sit in a meditative position, eyes closed, hands resting on lap.
- Inhale and hold the breath for a few seconds. Chant the planetary sound aloud in full voice on the exhale, extending the sound until you run out of breath.
- Repeat 7 times.
- Then sit quietly and breathe deeply for a few minutes.

Note: You can also use the sounds whenever you need the desired effect.

SUN

PERSONAL INFLUENCE:
Positive: Generous, warm-hearted and loving. Enthusiastic, helpful within boundaries. Purposeful, inventive, kind, original, nobleminded, socially inspiring. Live consciously; resist stress (build a strong nervous system); be clear, joyful; laugh a lot. Be creative and create new ways of self-support.

Negative: Domineering, impractical and irresponsible. Ruthless or selfish. Sensitive about one's importance, prestige, honor, character, pride or ambition. Lazy, unbending, obstinate, reckless, too critical. Demanding attention all the time and needing of approval or validation. Egotistic, worried about what others think.

HEALTH SUSCEPTIBILITIES: Sun people tend to suffer from heart troubles, displayed by their nails going blue. They tend to have problems with their circulation, heart, or eyes. Palpitations, blood pressure, stamina, spine, and skin. Also, they are prone to accidents and susceptible to sunstroke or acute attacks of fever.

GEMSTONES: Yellow diamond, topaz, carnelian

BENEFICIAL HERBS, FRUIT OR FOOD: The Sun, in general, is in charge of hot, spicy and pungent herbs, such as cayenne, black pepper, ginger, cloves, cardamom, bayberry, and long pepper. They are largely stimulants and increase digestion, improve perception, and promote circulation and functional activity. Other suggested herbs/foods: chamomile, cloves, dates, gentian root, honey, lavender, lemons, myrrh, nutmeg, oranges, raisins, saffron, St. John's Wort, sorrel, thyme.

SOUND: **EHM**
This sound is pronounced like the word *aim*. It affects the thymus gland and is very helpful in case of heart disorders. The musical note is B above middle C.

SUGGESTED AFFIRMATION: *I radiate love in thought, words and deeds. I am a source of blessings. God and me, me and God, are one.*

MOON

PERSONAL INFLUENCE:
Positive: Calm, warm, and centered. Imaginative, creative and having determination. Intuitive, compassionate and cooperative. Sharing, creating partnership, changeful.

Negative: Indecisive, fluctuating, oversensitive, timid, deceitful, lying, indifferent. Doing things in a hurry. Secretive, self-centered or procrastinating. Undiplomatic, reactive or possessive.

HEALTH SUSCEPTIBILITIES: Moon people tend to suffer from poor circulation and a weak digestive system, which leads to skin problems. They are also susceptible to troubles with the kidneys, bladder or reproductive system. Also, breasts, lymph, ovaries, stomach, gastric troubles, inflammation of bowels, internal growths, emotional problems, rheumatism.

GEMSTONES: Moonstone, pearl, black onyx, quartz crystal

BENEFICIAL HERBS, FRUIT OR FOOD: The Moon predominates over cool, sweet or salty herbs and spices, such as comfrey root, chickweed, Irish moss, sandalwood and slippery elm. They are demulcent and emollient herbs. Some of them are lung tonics. Other suggested herbs/foods: cabbage, chicory, cucumber, lettuce, melon, water plantain.

SOUND: **RA**
This sound pronounced RRRAAAA is chanted on the note **A** above middle C. It produces great physical energy.

SUGGESTED AFFIRMATION: *The universe loves and supports me. I release the past and reclaim my good now. God and me, me and God, are one.*

MARS

PERSONAL INFLUENCE:
Positive: Energetic, loyal, magnetic. Physically active. Using exercise, dance, yoga; developing determination; building vitality or strength; being peaceful, courteous, generous, or conservative.

Negative: Aggressive, quarrelsome or vindictive. Anger; passivity; lack of initiative; outspoken, argumentative, negative talk, arrogance, obstinate or overbearing, ill-tempered, warlike, impulsive in speech and action, quick-tempered. Must avoid impulsive behavior. Reckless or accident-prone.

HEALTH SUSCEPTIBILITIES: One should avoid drinking alcohol or coffee. Watch for fevers, blood disorders, throat troubles, bronchitis and laryngitis. Anemia, colds, red corpuscles, muscular system, sinuses, adrenals, skin problems, hearing and sight.

GEMSTONES: Bloodstone, diamond, garnet, ruby

BENEFICIAL HERBS, FRUIT OR FOOD: Mars predominates over garlic, mustard, damiana. Mars herbs/foods are largely stimulants; most are aphrodisiacs. Other suggested herbs/foods: ginger, horseradish, leeks, onion, pepper, spear wort.

SOUND: **MA**
Chanted on the note **A** above middle C like MMMAAAAAA. MA produces a feeling of comfort and being cared for.

SUGGESTED AFFIRMATION: *I feel invincible and connected to the light. I am divine and I am positive. God and me, me and God, are one.*

MERCURY

PERSONAL INFLUENCE:
Positive: Adaptable, eloquent, intelligent. Communicative; straightforward; flexible, adaptable, or changeable.

Negative: Dishonest or superficial. Restless; inability to plan; not straightforward. Manipulative, deceitful, hurrying, aloof, or trivial.

HEALTH SUSCEPTIBILITIES: All afflictions to the brain, twitching face, nervousness, eye problems, insomnia, vocal cords, thyroid, respiration, solar plexus, mental problems, memory. Afflictions to the arms or hands. Those ruled by Mercury must watch their nervous system and keep it strong. Learning how to be quiet is very important, as well as sleeping restfully. They are also susceptible to kidney, lung and urinary disorders.

GEMSTONES: Emerald, jade, opal, agate

BENEFICIAL HERBS, FRUIT OR FOOD: Mercury herbs are mild, harmonizing and good for the nerves, such as gotu kola, mint and ginkgo. Other suggested herbs/foods: bread, fennel, carrots, mushrooms, hazelnuts, oatmeal, parsley, thyme, walnuts.

SOUND: **THO**
Chanted on the musical note **F-sharp** above middle C, like ZZOOO. Stimulates the throat center and is excellent for any trouble with the thyroid gland. It develops the power of adaptability.

SUGGESTED AFFIRMATION: *Every day and in every way I am getting better and better. God and me, me and God, are one.*

JUPITER

PERSONAL INFLUENCE:
Positive: Straightforward, sociable, optimistic. Confident; expandable; disciplined. Having a positive mental attitude. Enthusiastic, joyful, hopeful, or charitable.

Negative: Intolerant, bossy or temperamental. Lack of confidence; doubting; worrisome, conceited. Saying yes to everything, overeating, or overly critical. Overworking leading to stress and strain. Selfish. Controlling or excessive.

HEALTH SUSCEPTIBILITIES: Skin problems, liver, hips, thighs, intestines, cells, nutrition, formation of hemoglobin. Many of Jupiter people's health problems come from food. They often have liver and/or stomach troubles. They often have affliction to the lungs, such as asthma.

GEMSTONES: Amethyst, lapis lazuli, sapphire

BENEFICIAL HERBS, FRUIT OR FOOD: Jupiter rules sweet and tonic herbs and substances, such as licorice, ashwagandha, ginseng, sesame oil, olive oil, other oils and most tonics. Other suggested herbs/foods: almonds, apples, asparagus, bayberries, beets, cherries, cloves, dandelion, figs, gooseberries, grapes, hazelnuts, mint, mulberries, nutmeg, olives, peaches, pineapples, pomegranates, saffron, sage, St. John's Wort, strawberries, wheat.

SOUND: **KHEI**
Chanted on the musical note **F** above middle C. It strengthens the adrenals and helps all kinds of illnesses.

SUGGESTED AFFIRMATION: *I am a source of miracles. I am open and receptive to blessings. God and me, me and God, are one.*

VENUS

PERSONAL INFLUENCE:
Positive: Gentle, graceful and sociable. Cheerful, well-disposed and responsible. Hospitable, good-humored, sociable and courteous. Graceful; enjoys having fun and being playful; creating beauty in one's environment.

Negative: Promiscuous, vain and vacillating, extreme love of pleasure, envious, timid, seductive, careless, unconsciously amorous. Overly emotional; ruled by lust.

HEALTH SUSCEPTIBILITIES: Reproductive system, urogenital area, hair, kidneys, digestion, constipation, varicose veins, breast problems, throat, nose, upper part of lungs, venereal diseases, thymus, complexion.

GEMSTONES: Emerald, jade, malachite, turquoise, rose quartz, diamond

BENEFICIAL HERBS, FRUIT OR FOOD: Venus is mainly in charge of cooling herbs and often fragrant flowers: Aloe vera, gardenia, hibiscus, lotus, red raspberry, rose, and saffron. Foods and herbs under Venus work on the heart, kidneys and reproductive system. Other suggested herbs/foods: almonds, apricots, apples, beans, legumes, figs, melons, mint, musk violets, peaches, pomegranates, rose leaves, vervain, walnuts, wild thyme.

SOUND: **RAMA**
Chanted on the musical note **A** above middle C, like RAAAMM-MAAA. It raises the awareness and is of strengthening and protective nature.

SUGGESTED AFFIRMATION: *I am fearless and optimistic. God and me, me and God, are one.*

SATURN

PERSONAL INFLUENCE:
Positive: Good morality, trustworthy and stable. Wise; patient, developing the ability to listen; having good values; disciplined; organized; practical, persistent, serving a greater cause, grateful, wide circle of friends. Structured, philanthropic.

Negative: Fearful, withdrawn and melancholy. Anxious, isolated, hypocritical, scheming.

HEALTH SUSCEPTIBILITIES: Bones, joints, rheumatism, liver, intestines, headaches, skin problems, spleen, tendons, colds, congestion, consumption, kidney, blood and urinary trouble. Those born under Saturn should eat plenty of fresh fruit, herbs and vegetables. They have a tendency to suffer from bile poison in the blood, leading to paralysis of the lower limbs, varicose veins and hemorrhoids. They may also have eye, ear or teeth troubles.

GEMSTONES: Amethyst, black onyx, sapphire

BENEFICIAL HERBS, FRUIT OR FOOD: Saturn herbs are cold, bitter, astringent and detoxifying, such as bayberry, dandelion, gentian, golden seal, selfheal, and uva ursi. They are natural antibiotics, anti-tumor and anti-fever herbs. Other suggested herbs/foods: angelica, celery, gravel root, plantain, sage, solomon's seal, spinach, vervain, wild carrot, wintergreen.

SOUND: **ONG**
Chanted on **D** above middle C, like ONNNNNG. It has a great effect on the third eye.

SUGGESTED AFFIRMATION: *God and me, me and God, are one. My ways are the ways of the light. I am intuitive and successful.*

CHAPTER ELEVEN

VITAL FOODS FOR HEALTH

HUMANS CAN TONIFY, rejuvenate, cleanse and rebuild the body by eating the proper food. In fact, a good diet can ward off most health problems. But eating the wrong food not only lowers your life force (prana), it also is the physical source of most diseases. The stressful impact of modern life and the toxins in our food and environment are causing the human immune system to become less efficient. The modern lifestyle, in general, disrupts our connection with the life force and our spirit, making us prone to low energy. Unfortunately in addition, the traditional methods of treating diseases, such as antibiotics and other pharmaceuticals, further reduce vitality. Access to healthcare has become a luxury today due to the soaring costs of medical care. With the continuous increase of virulent pathogen strains that are drug-resistant, along with autoimmune diseases and the various chronic illnesses that seemingly have no cure, it is now more than ever, necessary to redefine diet. The goal of a healthy diet should not be just about avoiding weight gain. It is one of the most powerful modalities for healing. Creating a "medicinal diet" requires some education that goes beyond just counting calories and avoiding fat.

The fact is, synthetic medicine does not have the capacity to bring the healing vibrations of prana into the atomic structure of each of our 100 trillion cells. Therefore, we must try to eat the purest, life-force–filled foods available, while avoiding heavily processed and prepared foods—since most of the vitalizing prana in the foods has been removed, as well as the essential vitamins and minerals. Many chemical food additives destroy the liver and kidneys. Use utmost moderation or stay away from chocolate, tobacco, coffee, black tea, salt, and caffeinated soda, especially colas. They will not only overstimulate your nervous system and drain your adrenal glands, but they will also disturb the electrolyte balance and generate vascular and cardiac pressure. When we choose our food, we must consider it not only in terms of vitamin, mineral, calories and fat content, but also in terms of the amount of life force that it contains. Ask yourself: *Will this sustain, nourish and vitalize my body, or will it do nothing but drain my vitality?*

Ingredients such as refined sugar, white flour and alcohol have no life force; they are completely dead. Dead food neither enlivens nor sustains you; and it will eventually kill you. Refined sugars contain no vitamins, enzymes, and minerals. Refined sugar is nothing but concentrated, simple carbohydrates, which are extremely difficult for the body to digest and metabolize. The reason sugar is so popularly used is because it has a long shelf life. It will skyrocket your pancreatic insulin levels and throw your blood sugar levels out of balance, thereby leading to either hypoglycemia or hyperglycemia. Refined sugars create the precondition for arteriosclerosis by increasing the level of free-floating acids in the blood. In addition, sugar is bad for the complexion and the empty calories cause obesity. As a person gains weight, they ironically lose precious vitamin and mineral stores during the body's effort to metabolize these nutrient-poor foods. Therefore, regardless of the addictive quality of these foods, you must use your willpower to protect your body from them.

Mother Nature, in her limitless and generous wisdom, has provided us with inexpensive and easily obtainable foods to help improve, strengthen, and heal all of the major body systems. Eating the right food has been shown to augment the body's natural ability to resist disease by strengthening and potentiating our immune system. In this regard, "fresh vegetables have long been praised for their healthful benefits. Vegetables and fruits should be viewed as an extension of herbal medicine because their healing properties are very similar. Experts are now beginning to hone in on the scientific reasons why. They think that the class of compounds known as phytonutrients found in plants holds great promise for warding off breast and prostate cancers and for reducing the risk of heart disease and an age-related eye disorder called macular degeneration. Vegetables that are dark green, deep yellow and orange—and fruits such as tomatoes and blueberries—revive the body's natural defense system."

Dr. John Glaspy, a researcher at UCLA's Jonsson Comprehensive Cancer Center noted that Japanese women tend to have a lower incidence of breast cancer than Americans. He is testing their traditional diet—heavy in the omega-3 fats found in fish, and soy products—on a group of American breast cancer patients who have been treated and are currently cancer-free. Foods that range from blueberries to chocolate and from alcohol to garlic already have shown evidence of lowering cholesterol, neutralizing cancer-causing substances, reducing blood pressure, soothing the symptoms of menopause, and preventing the growth of new blood vessels that feed tumors. Some may even boost the immune system. Women who are menopausal are advised to "drink soy milk, which is thought to ease hot flashes and other symptoms. Fish that is high in omega-3 oils, like salmon, herring and mackerel, are recommended for patients at risk of cardiovascular disease or breast cancer. Men who fear prostate cancer are advised to consume more tomato-based products, such as spaghetti sauce, because tomatoes are high in lycopene, thought to reduce the risk of this disease." In fact, the rate of prostate cancer among the Italian male population is low, due to the extensive use of tomato sauce and spaghetti.

It is also wise to consume organic foods, free of pesticides and chemical fertilizers, especially if you are using these foods for healing purposes. These chemicals contain xenoestrogens, which fill the estrogen receptor sites, disturb the hormonal system and promote cancer.

Many people who suffer from gas and bloating after eating, feel tired after eating or have low enzyme production cannot eat raw or lightly steamed vegetables. The result of doing so causes diarrhea, bloating and stomach pain. Because some plants have a relatively hard cellular structure, the body's digestive system is required to produce more acid and digestive enzymes to break that structure down. Many people, because of weakness, are incapable of producing it, so they are unable to make the best use of the nutrients presented to them. In general, steaming vegetables until soft aids the digestive process. Although cooking reduces the amount of vitamins and live enzymes, it becomes much more assimilable for people who have weak digestion. Very feeble people—those who have deadly diseases, those who are convalescing or young children—may require vegetables to be cooked in a soup. Consuming the broth of a soup or the water produced from steaming allows the person to benefit from more of the healthy nutrients of the vegetables and fruits. These broths may also be used to cook rice or pasta or as the base of a soup.

Another helpful way of promoting efficient digestion is to add a small amount of spice, such as cardamom, mint, basil, fennel, ginger, garlic, rosemary, nutmeg or black pepper. Please note that consuming highly spiced foods may not be appropriate for everyone, especially children, the elderly and those with hot conditions such as cancer, as they may be too warming to the body. Please use moderation. After the age of 35, lower your intake of salt by avoiding foods that have a high sodium content.

The following foods and herbs have been studied because they are believed to have health benefits for specific diseases. These foods can be incorporated into your diet according to your needs as a regular part of preventive maintenance. In essence, avoid refined sugar, high sodium foods, fried foods, saturated fats, white flour, and caffeinated beverages.

BANANAS contain serotonin and norepinephrine, which cures depression, so eat a couple of bananas and keep depression away. Those who eat this fruit will experience less pain. Bananas are high in potassium and help women maintain their youth. Avoid them in cases of copious mucus and phlegm production. If you feel that you want to eat bananas, but are fighting obesity or sinus congestion, eat them with cardamom and ginger sprinkled on top. Ginger is good for the nervous system and cardamom is good for the colon, which helps counteract the difficulty one may have with digesting bananas. *(See page 119 for more on ginger.)*

BEETS can beat anything! Beets are recommended when the red blood cell count is low. Everyone, however, can benefit from a 40-day dietary regime of beets, combined with black pepper, ginger and oregano. This mixture will shine you up.

BLUEBERRIES are excellent for the kidneys and revive the body's natural defense system.

BROCCOLI SPROUTS contain sulforaphane and can regulate the insulin levels in the blood, because they are rich in chromium. They also prevent cancer. People with weak digestion can steam them until they are very soft, and also drink the steamed water.

CABBAGE reduces the risk of breast cancer by controlling the estrogen levels in the body. It also prevents colon cancer. Cabbage has been found to contain an anti-ulcer compound as well; for this purpose juicing cabbage is highly beneficial. For cases of weak digestion, cook until soft.

CARROTS contain betacarotene, which is an antidote to lung cancer. Eating carrots regularly can help prevent this condition.

CAT'S CLAW cleanses the intestinal tract and enhances the action of white blood cells. It also acts as an antioxidant and anti-inflammatory. Good for intestinal problems and viral infections. May be helpful for people with arthritis, cancer, tumors, or ulcers.

CHICKWEED reduces mucus build-up in the lungs. It is useful for bronchitis, circulatory problems, colds, coughs, skin diseases, and warts. A good source of vitamin C and other nutrients.

CRANBERRY JUICE takes care of the kidneys and bladder. It blocks infectious bacteria from becoming lodged in the bladder walls. It is especially good for women. For best results during an infection, drink unsweetened juice. Another great way of getting the benefits of cranberry is to purchase frozen raw unsweetened cranberries and include 5 or 6 of them in a blended fruit smoothie.

GARLIC: The ancients knew that garlic had tremendous medicinal properties and that it could be used as both an antiseptic and a natural antibiotic. It wasn't until 1858 that Louis Pasteur discovered that garlic does indeed kill bacteria. Garlic contains a complex compound that bolsters the immune system. It has also been used to prevent heart disease and cancer. Dried and uncooked garlic has a very warming and drying property. Cooked garlic, which is less potent and more neutral, is better tolerated by those who feel warm all the time. Dried and uncooked garlic is best used for people who have copious body fluids. If you want to use garlic long-term for prevention or to promote healing in a chronic condition, use the form of garlic that is most appropriate. For those who have dry skin or any dry condition, who feel hot all the time or who sweat easily, cooked garlic incorporated into your food is best. If you feel you need the most potent form, then you may want to use it in pill form in small doses and choose another food that has a cooling nature to counteract the heat production. Over a long period of time, it will dry body fluids and increase the heat in your body.

Garlic is also a potent antifungal. For vaginal yeast infections, use one large peeled clove. Make three very light, one-centimeter incisions on the soft skin of the garlic. Thread a needle and pull a string through the center of the garlic. Use it as a vaginal suppository, allowing the string to remain outside of the body. Repeat the process with a new clove until it clears up. This is an extremely effective remedy!

Garlic can be used to aid digestion when incorporated in recipes. It also prevents food poisoning as it is antiparasitic. It is good for ear infections and acne, tonifies yang for low energy and combats male infertility.

GINGER will enhance your circulation and rejuvenate your entire system. Oriental medicine has successfully used ginger to treat rheumatism, inflammation of the testicles, and malaria. Moreover, ginger has been known both to lower cholesterol levels and especially, to kill vaginal trichomonas when taken orally. It is often used to treat cramps in the intestines and abdominal area. The juice can be used to energize muscles. Mixed with oil, it can be used in massage to relieve stiffness. This root of the sun will provide you with nourishing heat to keep the body strong through old age, as ginger is a very warming herb. When dried in spice form or in a tea bag it is most warming; when fresh it is less warming. To mitigate some of its heat, you can add soymilk or peppermint to your tea. When juiced, you can add celery or carrot to reduce its warming property. Conversely, because many foods that are very cooling in nature are difficult to digest, ginger's warming quality may be added to aid or "warm" the digestive process.

Because ginger is antiparasitic, it is used in high quantities in some cooking to prevent food poisoning. If you think that you may have had food that was not fresh, you can drink a few strong cups of hot ginger tea. Cut three, one-eighth inch slices and boil for 20 minutes in 3 cups of water.

Ginger is excellent for menstrual cramps. When experiencing menstrual cramps, make the tea described above. You can also soak a washcloth in ginger tea and place it on the abdomen. Cover wash cloth with another hot towel to keep it warm.

GRAPEFRUIT JUICE lowers cholesterol levels and prevents colon cancer. The citrus pectin may also inhibit tumor cell growth. It has been found to interfere with the way cancer cells form in animal tests. Its bitterness helps to cut through phlegm or mucus conditions when the juice is consumed fresh or as sliced fruit.

GREEN TEA is known to contain epigallocatechin-3-gallate, and can prevent stroke and cancer.

KALE contains lutein, and is known to prevent age-related blindness.

LEMON cleans dirt from the body. It helps you fight germs and infection. The combination of minerals it contains make it healing in many ways. It is rich in calcium to makes your bones strong. It contains large quantities of potassium to tone the liver and digestive system. The high level of magnesium heals internal and external wounds. Magnesium will take care of your nervous and circulatory system. Because of its acidity, it is best to drink lemon water or tea with a straw. Although lemon is very acidic in flavor, it ironically helps the body to become more alkaline once it has been digested because of its high mineral content. Avoid in cases of acid indigestion. Never eat lemon seeds. The best lemon is bright yellow. Lemon, lime, grapefruit and orange peel, when added to boiling hot water and steeped, helps cut through phlegm and mucus and aids digestion. It helps you fight germs and infection.

Regarding the white or pith of citrus peel:
This part of citrus is very high in bioflavonoids. They are anti-inflammatory and excellent for strengthening and cleansing arterial walls. They can be used for hemorrhoids, as they strengthen the intestines. These bioflavonoids have a special property of breaking down hydrogenated and partially hydrogenated oils that come from margarine, shortening, and other processed foods such as candy bars, crackers, cereals, preserved sauces and many other foods. The FDA recently released a report saying that no level of hydrogenated oils is safe for consumption because the body is largely unable to break them down. These oils have been implicated as the major cause of arteriosclerosis as they build up in the arteries and eventually lead to the blockage of blood flow. The peel can be eaten daily or consumed in pill form as "Citrus Bioflavonoids."

OATS harmonize the digestive system and help the body to use insulin more effectively, because of their high protein content.

Oats/grits regulate wasting disorder and are high in fiber. Oats generally have a calming effect. The fiber of oats binds with cholesterol, helping the body to excrete it in the stools. For best results, do not use instant oatmeal, but rather the "Old Fashioned" style, steel-cut rolled or whole oats.

ONION is not only a tonic, but it also makes the blood very strong. It is often recommended to eat lots of onion before traveling to bacterially infected locations. Those who have asthma should regularly eat an abundance of onions in their diet, because onions contain at least three anti-inflammatory elements. Those who have tumors or cancer should eat 1 raw or lightly cooked brown onion daily.

PINEAPPLE: You can easily take care of your joints whether they are stiff, swollen, or in pain by eating pineapple. Pineapple contains bromeliad, and is rich in B1 and B6. It fights arthritis by dissolving joint debris and calcium deposits that clog the cells, cause pain and discomfort, and inhibit mobility.

TOMATOES contain lycopene, which is a potential agent against cervical and prostate cancer. Also, pancreatic cancer can be prevented by eating tomatoes. Men who fear prostate cancer are advised to consume more tomato-based products. Tomatoes revive the body's natural defense system.

SWEET POTATOES contain betacarotene and can prevent lung cancer.

APPLES, ONIONS, RED WINE, and TEA contain flavonoids and can prevent heart disease.

FISH OILS: Fish that is high in omega-3 oils, like salmon, herring and mackerel, are recommended for patients at risk of cardiovascular disease or breast cancer.

SOY, TOFU, or SOY MILK can prevent cancer and heart disease.

These foods can be incorporated into your diet, according to your needs, as a regular part of preventive maintenance.

PARSLEY AND TURMERIC: Parsley, which is an antidote to the bad smell that garlic gives, is also used to expel gas from the body. Turmeric, which is known to feed the blood, has the additional function of calming the stomach and healing wounds. When parsley and turmeric are taken together, they neutralize indigestion and take care of bleeding ulcers. This combination has been successfully used for spleen, thymus, lymph, kidney, bladder and liver problems. In addition, this combination is beneficial for the skin, joints, lungs and bronchials. It is good for cardiovascular and cellular detoxification.

TRINITY ROOT is a very divine combination of three roots: onion, garlic and ginger. It renews completely the spinal serum, thereby restoring the life force to its optimal level. Yogic records report that it is good for all brain functions, brain tissue, pH balance, colon toxicity, viruses, bacteria, fungus, allergies, the digestive system, the endocrine system, testes, joints, weak muscles, the cardiovascular system, liver, spleen, thymus, lymph, connective tissue, cellular detoxification, back pain, and for sexual function. It is also good for the musculoskeletal system and body maintenance.

Onion stimulates the production of blood—the river of life that takes nourishment to the different parts of the body and carries waste material away from them. During periods of illness especially, an adequate supply of blood is essential to make certain that the toxins in the body are carried away from the diseased area. Onions are best raw and can be used generously in cooking.

Garlic has medicinal properties and will act to increase the production of semen in the body, which is essential for healthy nerves. Garlic acts to purify the blood as well by drawing poison to it. And it is a natural antibiotic that can be used during almost any illness. It is best taken raw, for it loses its potency when cooked. Garlic powder can also help in the absence of fresh garlic. Garlic can be eaten by taking a few cloves and biting into them one at a time and swallowing with water without touching the tongue more than necessary. Eating parsley can help reduce garlic odor.

Ginger nourishes the nerves of the body and allows them to carry more energy. It may be helpful in correcting spinal difficulties and the health of the life nerve. Ginger tea is a great energy booster, especially for women during the menstrual period. All three can be used in abundance in the daily diet, and specifically at a time of disease.

Use trinity root as a means of cleaning our bodily system of chemical wastes. The fact is, most of us spend the major portion of our lives eating foods that contain a variety of chemical pollutants, many of which remain in our body. As a result, the body has made minor and major adjustments in its manner of operating and in the nature of its organs. Our nerves, sinuses, kidneys, intestines, practically every part of our body has had to alter its normal mode of action, in order to accommodate this chemical warfare. The combination of garlic, ginger and onion can purify the body of these unwanted additions. They can stimulate unused and misused parts of our body so as to drive out impurities and reestablish a normal functioning.

Trinity Root Healing Drink
Good for infections and energizing the body.
1 medium onion chopped
1-3 inches ginger root, peeled and sliced thinly
1/2 bulb of peeled and sliced garlic
1 quart of goat milk (OK if powdered with water)
1 teaspoon turmeric
Cook on medium fire for 20 minutes and drink.

Energizing Morning Drink
2 ounces ginger juice
2 ounces lemon juice
1 teaspoon of olive oil or flax seed oil
Adding water is optional

Drink first thing in the morning and wait 20 minutes before eating anything. Olive oil is better for the liver and brain, and flax seed is better for the heart.

Morning/Evening Light Tune-up
This makes a very healthy, light and easy-to-digest breakfast or night meal.
1/4 cup old-fashioned style oats
1 handful blueberries
1 handful blackberries
1 banana, sliced into pieces
1 apple, chopped
1/2 cup boiling hot water

Put into a blender and blend until completely smooth.

Food for Purity
Soak 10-15 raw almonds overnight. Then, peel and blend them in a blender with one jalapeño and a serving of rice and milk. (Cow's milk may be used, but soy, rice, almond, or goat milk is preferable.) Drink and enjoy. Your entire body will benefit and change.

REGARDING WATER

Three-quarters of the body is made up of water, yet many people drink anything but water. You can improve your health by drinking lukewarm water first thing in the morning and right before retiring at night. Do not give your body the chance to feel thirsty, so drink 6 to 8 glasses of water throughout the day.

REGARDING MILK

Within the health industry, milk is a highly controversial topic. Dairy products such as milk, yogurt, pudding, cheese, butter and ice cream can be difficult for the body to assimilate. Allergic reactions that manifest as gas, bloating and diarrhea are common. Moreover, a dairy allergy can manifest in some as chronic illness including, but not limited to, arthritis, sinusitis, headaches, irritable bowel syndrome and eczema. Genetic predisposition, along with unhealthy farming practices (hormones injected into cows and/or pesticide and antibiotic consumption), contribute to dairy intolerance and allergic reactions in humans. In addition, the proteins contained in cow's milk are difficult for the human body to break down and digest. Those with adverse reactions to cow's milk may want to try goat's milk. Goat's milk is much more akin to human breast milk and, therefore, easier for the human body to deal with. It is my recommendation, however, that whether you consume cow or goat milk, you limit your dairy consumption to the occasional yogurt or piece of cheese. In recipes that call for milk, goat's milk, soymilk and almond milk can be used as substitutions, and rice milk is indicated for those prone to high mucus production.

While it is a commonly held belief that we must consume milk in order to provide our bodies with an adequate amount of calcium, it is easy to get the calcium we need by eating dark green vegetables. These vegetables include: kale, chard, broccoli, cabbage, collard greens, dandelion greens and kelp. Calcium is also present in foods like oats, prunes, blackstrap molasses, figs, soybeans, sardines and soups cooked with bones in the broth. Moreover, some herbs contain calcium. They include: alfalfa, chamomile, burdock root, chickweed, chicory, fenugreek, fennel seed, nettle, parsley, raspberry leaves, red clover and rose hips. Do your research, and then choose the herb that is best for you. A variety of calcium rich foods and herbs should be consumed on a daily basis to ensure that your body is receiving what it needs.

It is more beneficial to receive your daily intake of calcium via food than via supplements. If you do take calcium supplements, however, be sure to use a liquid version. The most absorbable forms of calcium, when taken as a supplement, are calcium gluconate, lactate and citrate.

Whether you receive calcium from food, herbs or supplements, be aware that the caffeine found in coffee, tea and cola drinks both inhibits your body's ability to absorb calcium and depletes existing calcium reserves.

CHAPTER TWELVE

HEALING CANCER

A RECENT GOVERNMENT STUDY on mortality found that between 1973 and 1999, the percentage of deaths due to heart disease had decreased by 21 percent, while the percentage of deaths due to cancer had increased by 30 percent. Each year, 1.3 million Americans are diagnosed with cancer. (In particular, incidences of breast, testicular, thyroid and lymphatic cancers have risen sharply.) Of this number, more than half a million will die. With more than 40 percent of men and one-third of women developing some form of the disease, cancer has become an illness of "mass destruction."

It seems that the money we spend on cancer research has failed to produce a significant reduction in deaths. How can this be? Every year, billions of dollars are spent on finding a cure. Very little, however, is allocated for prevention. Common sense dictates that the best way to combat any illness is to focus an equal amount of resources on both prevention and cure. By addressing disease before and after it has occurred, we give ourselves the best opportunity for survival. In the case of cancer, one must ask why the medical establishment's attention remains primarily fixed on damage-control measures, diagnosis, treatment and related research. Who benefits from such a one-sided approach?

Drug development and marketing is a highly profitable industry. Pharmaceutical companies earn tremendous profits from the treatments they devise. What would happen to these companies if their drugs were no longer needed in such vast quantities? The National Cancer Act calls for an expanded and intensified research program for the prevention of cancer caused by occupational or environmental exposure to carcinogens. To date, the medical establishment has failed to embrace this mission. Moreover, it has suppressed evidence that demonstrates the link between exposure to carcinogens and rates of cancer.

The cost of treating cancer is a burden for the afflicted individual and our national health care system. The war on cancer is certainly winnable, but we must shift our focus from cure to prevention. We must begin to place a greater value on saving lives than accumulating wealth. Indeed, by choosing prevention we will ultimately save both lives and dollars. This chapter is designed to reveal to you various methods of prevention and healing.

Cancer is an astral disease that comes from various emotional infections, such as insecurity, anger, resentment, fears, dislikes, worries, envy, jealousy and irritation, which consume our life force far faster than any human equipment can replace it. This leads to the depletion of prana in every organ system in the body. This is the main cause of all the wasting diseases such as ulcers, skin disturbances, nerve disorders and cancer. It is the toxic thought patterns and negative emotions that consume the spirit that ultimately deplete the physical body of its vital life force. All of these illnesses in their later stages end up as wasting diseases with malnutrition-like symptoms. In order to better understand the mechanism whereby disease takes hold in the physical body, we should first review the anatomy of the spiritual body. The body is divided into three major sections: head, chest and abdomen. The head, which corresponds to the divine or mental plane, relates to the world of ideas or thoughts. The chest, which corresponds to the astral or spiritual plane, relates to the world of feelings and emotions. The abdomen, which corresponds to the physical world relates to actions and visible manifestations.

In the head of man is to be found his intelligence, whose job it is to control and direct all his lower faculties according to their particular laws. In other words, you are what you think. Think straight and life becomes straight. Think twisted and life becomes twisted. The head represents the intelligent nature, the command center of the body, and the stomach represents the material corporeal nature. These two parts are united and joined by the chest, which is the world of feelings and emotions. For it is in the chest that we feel the acts of our intelligence working, whereas the only purpose of the lower part of the body is purely for material acts. The heart, located in the chest area, is the seat of the emotions and sentiments of humanity and further, it pumps the lifeblood throughout the body.

The head, which is the storehouse of life force, gives birth to the thoughts that it manifests. Likewise, the chest generates feelings and emotions and also is the seat of prana. Above all, it gives birth to life, which it preserves within it.

As you can deduce, the chest, or astral body, governs our emotions and feelings. Cancer is an astral disease that originates from unhealthy emotions. For example, chronic anger can poison the blood, disturb the digestive system, affect the health of our cells, and eventually lead to cancer. Likewise, feelings of joy, peace and contentment can charge the blood with healing prana and restore harmony. Emotions are a key component in the development and cure of cancer.

It is important to know that our body is equipped with three lines of defense. They all need to be functional in order to implement a cure. These three lines of defense consist of the immune system, electromagnetic field and digestive system. As stated previously, they correspond to the head, chest and abdomen. Love strengthens the immune system, faith enhances the electromagnetic field and hope balances and tonifies the digestive system. A person must be equipped with the spiritual shield of love, faith and hope in order to overcome cancer. You need love to experience the reality of forgiveness, compassion, tolerance and gratitude so that you may neutralize anger, guilt and jealousy. Love provides the protective shield from the divine world. All fear, hatred, jealousy, envy, and greed disappear when love is in your life. Where there is love there is no place for those negative emotions and destructive forces. The key is love; it is the most important lesson to learn. You have to learn to love what you're doing, to love the people around you, to love the very air you're breathing, and the very ground you walk upon. Love everything you set your eyes upon. Faith grants the protective shield from the astral or angelic world. Where there is faith you cannot find doubt. And remember that when you are negative you draw negativity to yourself. Hope gives the gift of protection from the physical world. If you have hope and you are constantly positive, seeing the good in everything and everyone, there is going to be a blue sky and sunshine all around you and within you. So fill your life with love, faith and hope. Learn to love life and if you do, your life will be a constant prayer of grace. For prayer is the food of the spirit and the nourisher of the soul.

In essence, love, faith and hope are the three blankets of light that you need to raise your vibration and liberate yourself from the grip of any challenging illness or situation. Unconditional love, faith in the helping forces of the unseen world, and hope for the best possible outcome can bring harmony into any condition. Heaven is the source of all things. Love, faith and hope will bring you heavenly help.

Although there are many varieties of cancer, and each of the various types of cancer behave differently, the end result is malnutrition. The ultimate cause of death from cancer is usually an organ failure. The symptoms of the end stages of cancer are similar to malnutrition syndromes in third-world countries: weakness, fever and water retention causing the liver to swell, or creating lymphatic congestion. In countries where food is abundant, malnutrition is ultimately caused by the body's inability to assimilate nutrients.

The fact is, when the digestive system becomes weak, due to a poor diet or negative thought patterns poisoning the blood stream, food residue accumulates in the digestive tract, creating mucus or phlegm. This sticky substance is the body's way of isolating toxins or unneeded substances, so that it may be removed from the body. People who are constantly exposed to toxins, either through an inappropriate diet, drugs, alcohol or other poisons in their environment, will have an abundance of phlegm. That phlegm becomes difficult to get rid of, either because of weakness, lack of body fluids to flush them out or poor circulation. When this phlegm retention becomes chronic, toxic heat and blood accumulation combine with it to create cancerous growths.

The following are the general causes of the development of cancer. All are related to poor circulation of one or a few different substances.

Retention of phlegm and mucus due to deficiency of body fluids

Body fluids are required to cleanse the body. As we age, body fluids may become scarce. This dryness is also often associated with hormonal imbalances. Dryness in the body may also be from consuming drying constituents such as spicy food, smoking, certain drugs, caffeine and stress. Dryness may also be a result of sexual overindulgence, which may weaken the hormones and drain those body fluids that are hard to replace.

Chronic inadequate circulation of blood and prana

Inadequate circulation of blood and prana will hamper the body's ability to flush out toxins. This phenomenon occurs with stress and chronic emotional imbalances. Leukemia or solid masses are often the end result of this pattern, because blood, which is pumped by the heart in the chest, is closely related to the emotions, and as aforementioned, excessive anger poisons the blood, leading to the development of this disease.

Exposure to toxins

These may include several sources.

a. *Xenoestrogens* are commonly found in our food and water through the use of pesticides and herbicides, certain fuels, and the by-products of incineration of plastics and hazardous wastes. They behave in the body similarly to natural estrogen, and in so doing, throw the hormones out of balance. A preponderance of natural estrogen should also be avoided; this may occur when chronic stress depletes the progesterone levels. Estrogen dominance may result in breast cancer, fibroids, endometriosis in women and may be related to testicular cancer, urinary tract disorders and low sperm count. Dioxins are one kind of xenoestrogen.

b. *Nitrates* — Wheat absorbs nitrates from the soil at a very high rate and should be avoided for cancer. Many meats and cheeses are preserved with sodium nitrite.

c. *Sugar* feeds cancer and promotes phlegm production. In cases of cancer and for cancer prevention, it is important to avoid simple processed carbohydrates such as bread, crackers, processed sweetened cereals and pasta, which all have a similar effect on the body. The glycemic index gets very high, which is not good for cancer. Sugar, along with alcohol, yeast- containing products and antibiotics promote fungal infections in the intestinal tract. Fungal infections have a huge impact on the health of the digestive and immune system. Because one of the side effects of chemotherapy is fungal infection, it is advisable to avoid sugar at all costs. Complex carbohydrates, such as whole grains, are okay.

d. *Other Factors* — There are many other contributing factors such as: chronic electromagnetic field exposure, ionizing radiation, nuclear radiation, mercury toxicity, parasites, viruses and many more. These toxic exposures are all combined with the first or second disease patterns to create the predisposition for cancer to take hold. Not everyone exposed to cancer-causing agents gets cancer. The physical and spiritual body must be out of balance in a particular way for cancer to develop.

INTERNAL HEAT

Tissue damage is a characteristic that involves every type of cancer as a result of cellular mutation and death. Heat, caused by dietary toxins, emotions and infections will eventually dry body fluids, reducing the integrity of the surrounding body tissue. These may affect any area of the body: lungs, digestive tract, cervix, skin or liver. Regardless of the location of this toxic heat, when it is present for a long enough time, the heat damages the digestive system, impairing the body's ability to assimilate fluids and nutrients. At that point, the body has the toxic heat to contend with and cannot regenerate itself; this leads to increased rate of cell death and general weakness or even organ failure.

Consuming extreme foods on a regular basis will eventually damage the digestive system. Extreme foods include spicy, fried, high sodium, high sugar, high fat or raw food diets. Well-balanced, slightly bland and lightly cooked foods on a consistent basis are easier to digest and assimilate and less likely to create phlegm, mucus, water retention or heat.

Poor Elimination

The body must eliminate toxins and waste. This must occur via sweating, urination, bowel movements, breathing and, in women, menstruation. If any one of those is blocked, the body has to store waste, which leads to waste build-up and eventually, toxic heat that is fodder for disease development. Sweating should occur from all natural areas, including the armpits, which empty the lymph nodes of the upper body. For those concerned with lung or breast cancer, blocking the upper lymph nodes with antiperspirants is not a good idea. Rather, crystals and natural deodorants that do not contain aluminum will allow the body to sweat properly.

A person should have a bowel movement at least once a day, if not two to three times per day. Fecal matter retained in the intestines is a huge toxin resource that promotes poor circulation in the lower part of the body, especially the reproductive system and lower back.

From an energetic perspective, metastasis, or spreading of the cancer, occurs when the body can no longer eliminate a sufficient amount of toxin via the normal routes. Instead, it is forced to spread the heat toxin accumulation to other areas of the body.

Hidden Heat Toxins

Some people accumulate heat toxins but, because they cannot eliminate them, the body stores them to come out at a later date. Sometimes this will happen as a result of a person being on "survival mode," like a single mother who must expend all her energy on raising her children. Once they are grown and some of the burden has been lifted, the body begins the painful process of releasing many years of stored toxins. This may or may not be in the form of cancer, yet it is a common explanation for why some seemingly high-energy people suddenly get very sick after years of extremely hard work. When the body's ability to store this toxin has been used up, the toxin must come out in some way. This may be in the form of cancer. In this case, people often say that "it just came out of the blue, one day I was completely fine and the next I had a life-threatening disease." On the outside, their health might have appeared strong, because the body was hiding it well. But once those stores were full, it became apparent that this health was only superficial. These toxin stores may be in fatty locations of the body or in fatty tumors, organs, hidden tumors, tooth abscesses, sensory organs and all elimination organs.

Coffee enemas can be an excellent method for helping the body eliminate toxins via the intestines.

Lack of Vitamin D

Scientists are now linking low levels of vitamin D to cancer, hypertension, diabetes and osteoporosis. More and more evidence is mounting that the vitamin plays an absolutely pivotal role in all aspects of human health.

Vitamin D can be found in cold-water fish like salmon and mackerel as well as fortified milk.

Most of the vitamin D is supplied by the sun. A D-related hormone in the skin soaks up the ultraviolet rays in sunlight and travels to the liver and the kidneys, where it picks up extra molecules of oxygen and hydrogen. This process transforms the pre-vitamin D into a potent hormone called calcitriol.

Part of the evolving understanding is that scientists think many tissues in the body—not just the liver and kidneys—can convert the pre-vitamin D and make their own disease-fighting calcitriol.

Let the sun warm your unprotected arms and face for a few minutes (the early morning hours are the best and gentlest), and you will make all the vitamin D you need. Sunscreen reduces vitamin D absorption to nothing.

Without sunlight, the body runs through its vitamin D reserves in just a few weeks. People who consume the most vitamin D in their blood have a lower risk of colon cancer. The chances of dying from cancer are reduced for people living in the sunniest areas.

Prostate cells produce the hormone calcitriol, which can act as a break on cell growth. When the cells cannot get enough vitamin D's precursor to make calcitriol, they start to multiply uncontrollably and create a platform for prostate cancer. Therefore sunlight is not only providing us with many important vitamins such as D, but it also can help heal us and strengthen our health.

Remember that everything that takes place in your life happens because of your level of consciousness. Raise your consciousness and you'll raise your whole being, improve your health and your whole outlook on life, and you will start to live a life full of grace.

Keep in mind that you have within you all power, all wisdom, all strength, all intelligence and all understanding. Connecting with your spirit—the God-force working through you—will cause you to accomplish the seemingly impossible. The more love, faith and hope you have, the quicker your health or challenging condition will change for the better, but it all starts in you, with your spirit. The sooner you realize this, the sooner changes will take place all around you. So be positive and always expect the best in your health situation. Love, faith and hope lead to power. Pessimism and doubt lead to weakness and defeat. Work with love, faith and hope and let your spirit shine in and through you, creating health and harmony in your life. When your outlook on life is optimistic, you improve your health and increase your lifespan. There is always hope in life, even if it is a tiny flickering spark to begin with. When it is surrounded with faith, hope and love and the right atmosphere, that tiny spark will be fanned into a flame and it will grow and grow until you are on fire with the healing fuel of the spirit, which is unquenchable and inextinguishable. Once it has been ignited, nothing will be able to stop the spread of its healing power within and around you.

EXERCISES TO OVERCOME HEALTH CHALLENGES

The following exercises can be applied to face cancer, AIDS and other health challenges, as well as to build general strength and balance in the body.

Working with the Healing Space: Tree of Life Hand Symbol

There is a symbol which is referred to as the *Tree of Life Hand Symbol*. Actually, I believe it is a potent healing symbol, which has already been empowered in the collective psyche. It is a particular formula which helps resolve one's problems in life. This symbol brings your consciousness into the moment. It changes your attitude by moving you outside of the duality of this planet into a state of oneness. It is the highest level of facing any moment. It will completely revibrate your life. We are not time and space; we flow through time and space. This flow is called the life-flow. Any mental, emotional and physical blocks in this life-flow manifest as disturbances, and if not attended to, eventually manifest as disease. Disturbance, or disharmony, is only possible when the masculine and feminine principles are out of balance.

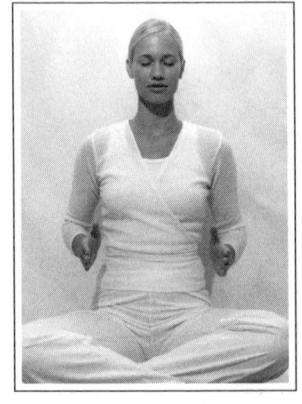

The Tree of Life Hand Symbol corrects the flow of energy and dissolves any blocks. It will bring balance to all areas of your life. It can be used whenever you have a question or problem that needs resolution. The answer will soon come to you. It is also an effective tool to use in combination with visualization. You can chant any mantra in this position or do breath-work.

Position:
Sit in a chair with your feet flat on the floor or sit cross-legged in a comfortable meditative pose. Bring both hands before your heart center, palms facing each other about 6 inches apart, elbows bent and relaxed. Eyes are closed and focused between the mid-brow point.

Mantra:
RA-MA-DA-SA
SA-SAY-SO-HUNG

Chant the RA MA DA SA mantra in this posture along with the CD for 11 to 31 minutes.

For those who can hold the breath longer: Inhale for one cycle of the mantra, hold for another cycle, and exhale as you chant the mantra. Repeat breath cycle for 11 minutes.

This breath will bring the entire nervous and glandular system into balance. The beauty of life is based on the breath. It is the link between God and you.

Comments:
In this position, you are creating the three pillars of the Tree of Life. Your right hand is the Pillar of Mercy, the masculine principle; your left hand is the Pillar of Severity, the feminine principle; and you are in the middle, the Pillar of Equilibrium. This posture will take you beyond time and space into a healing space. It will connect you to the fountain of light, the source of all.

Inner Sun: Immune System Booster

This meditation works on cleansing and rejuvenating your whole system. The immune system will have new vigor and will not be blocked by inner conflict.

Position:
Sit in Easy Pose with a straight spine. Close your eyes and concentrate at the brow point. Left hand: bend your elbow and raise your hand to shoulder level, as if taking an oath. Touch the tip of the ring, or Sun finger to the tip of the thumb, called Surya Mudra. Right hand: Make a fist, then extend the index finger and use it to close off the right nostril.

Breath:
Begin a steady and powerful Breath of Fire—a rapid equal inhale and exhale from the diaphragm—through the left nostril.

Time:
Start with 3 minutes, then gradually work up to 31. To end, inhale deeply and hold the breath. As you hold, interlace the fingers of the hands 4 inches away from the face, palms facing towards you. Try to pull the fingers apart, using resistance and creating a great tension. When you must, exhale. Repeat 3 more times. Relax.

Comments:
This breath meditation strengthens the immune system by allowing us to access the healing and nurturing energy from the Moon, mother of life, in order to renew the blood, help the nervous system, and take care of the glandular system. Our fears, insecurities, shame, anger, frustration, and guilt are destructive and unhealthy emotions that lead to depression. They prevent the immune system from working properly. This lunar breath heals the emotional body by helping to clear out these unhealthy energies. The left nostril not only benefits meditation, but it also helps remove sorrow, pain and depression and assists in restoring

consciousness. It is also good for music, dancing, and enjoying poetry. The best time to accumulate spiritual energy is when the left or moon nostril is operating properly. The moon energy is needed during the day to compensate for the predominance of solar energy; and the right or sun nostril to compensate for moon predominance at night. During this meditation, you may go through emotional shifts while your body is regaining balance. Then you will begin to experience the calm, peacefulness and harmony that comes with its healing impact.

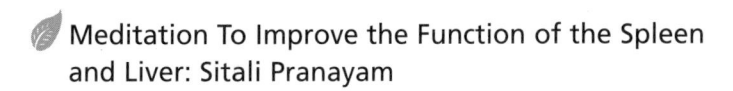

Meditation To Improve the Function of the Spleen and Liver: Sitali Pranayam

Position:
Sit in a comfortable position with the spine straight. Hands are either relaxed on the lap, or you can spread the fingers and touch the fingertips of both hands together at the level of the solar plexus (between heart and navel). This hand position seals in the energy, so it can be contained and used for healing. Close the eyes and focus at the brow point.

Breath:
Inhale through a curled tongue, as if you are sipping through a straw. Hold the breath for as long as possible. Exhale slowly through the nose. Continue the breath cycle.

Time:
Start with at least 11 minutes. There is no time limit.

Exercise To Cleanse the Blood

Position:

- Sit with a straight spine, palms pressed together, touching at the chest, arms hugging the ribs. Gently focus the eyes on the tip of your nose. Mouth is open.
- Inhale in four equal strokes through the mouth, mentally concentrating on one syllable of the mantra WA-HE (pronounced "hay") GU-RU with each stroke, and on the breath as it crosses the tongue tip.
- Exhale in four equal strokes through the mouth, concentrating on each syllable of the mantra WA-HE GU-RU and on the breath as it crosses the tongue tip.

Time:
Continue for five minutes. Then rest for a minute. Repeat all of the above twice.

Comments:
Anyone who can practice this kriya an hour a day is greatly strengthened against diseases of the blood. Doing the breath described in this kriya 108 times purifies and oxygenates the blood. Doing it as described above for 18 minutes a day for 40 days will rejuvenate an old body.

Meditation To Get Disease Out

Position:
- Sit in easy pose, with the spine straight.
- Raise the right hand to the side as if taking an oath, palm facing forward.
- Raise the left arm parallel to the ground and bend the elbow, so that the hand is in front of the chest. Palm faces down. The eyes are closed.

Breath:
Form an "O" with your mouth and breathe powerfully through it. Inhale with four segmented breaths, and exhale with one big breath out.

Time:
Continue for 22 minutes. To end, inhale as deeply as you can, relaxing your diaphragm and opening up the cavity of the breath of life. Hold the breath and stretch both hands straight up as high as you can possibly reach, with the fingers spread and tight. Cannon-fire the breath out. Repeat two more times. Relax.

Comments:
This is a powerful breath to increase your prana and raise your energy to a level that leaves no room for disease.

Exercise to Open all the Channels for Health: Sodarchan Chakra Kriya

Here is a meditation that makes use of prana to cleanse mental garbage, open the channels in the body for health, and purify the mind. It is also an excellent meditation to do in your Sun period and during the season of Spring.

Of all the 20 types of yoga, including Kundalini yoga, this is the highest kriya. It will give you a new start. It is a simple kriya, but at the same time hard. It cuts through all darkness and all barriers of a neurotic or psychotic nature. When a person is in a very bad state, techniques imposed from the outside will not work. The pressure has to be stimulated from within.

The tragedy of life occurs when the subconscious releases garbage into the conscious mind. This kriya invokes the Kundalini to give you the necessary vitality and intuition to combat the negative effects of the subconscious mind.

Position:
Sit with spine straight (either on the floor with legs crossed, or sit in a chair with feet flat on the floor). The eyes are focused at the tip of the nose, or closed if you prefer.

Mudra and Breath:
1. Block off the right nostril with the right thumb. Inhale slowly and deeply through the left nostril and hold the breath. Mentally chant WAHE GURU 16 times, while pumping the navel point 3 times with each repetition (pump once on WAA, once on HAY and once on GURU), for a total of 48 pumps. WA is infinity; HE is the presence of the finite in infinity; GU is darkness; and RU is light. Together WAHE GURU means *Indescribable Wisdom*.

2. Unblock the right nostril and use the right index or pinkie finger to block the left nostril. Exhale slowly and deeply through the right nostril. Continue, inhaling left nostril, exhaling right.

To end the meditation, inhale and hold 5–10 seconds. Exhale. Then stretch and shake the body for about 1 minute to circulate the energy.

Time:
Suggested length for this kriya is 31 or 62 minutes a day. The ideal is to start at 31 minutes, but you can begin with 11 minutes, then build up to 31, then 40, and eventually 62.

Comments:
There is no time, no place, no space, and no condition attached to this meditation. Each garbage pit has its own time to clear. If you are going to clean your own garbage, you must estimate and clean it as fast as you can, or as slowly as you want. You have to decide how much time you have to clean up your garbage pit. If you can do this meditation for 62 minutes to start with, then build up to the point where you can do it 2 1/2 hours a day (1/10th of the day), it will give you Nao nidhi, athara sidhi, which are the 9 precious virtues and 18 occult powers. In these 27 total virtues of the world lies the entire Universe.

Practiced 2 1/2 hours every day, this meditation will make you a perfect superhuman. It will purify the subconscious and take care of your life. It will make you extremely intuitive. It brings together all 27 facets of life and makes people saintly, successful and qualified. This meditation also gives you pranic power. This kriya never fails. It can give you inner happiness and bring you to a state of ecstasy in life.

Exercise For Balance and Purification of the Blood

Position:
- Sit in easy pose with the legs crossed or in any comfortable meditative sitting posture with a straight spine.
- Press the palms together in prayer pose at the heart center.
- Close the eyes and focus the eyes at the brow point.

Mantra:
Inhale deeply and chant on a single breath:

RAA-RAA-RAA-RAA
MAA-MAA-MAA-MAA
RAAMAA-RAAMAA-RAAMAA-RAAMAA
SAA-TAA-NAA-MAA

(*Ra* is the Sun energy, *Ma* is the Moon energy)

Time:
Continue for 11 to 31 minutes. Then inhale, hold the breath and press palms together strongly. Exhale. Repeat three times and relax.

Comments:
This healing meditation mixes and balances the solar and lunar forces of the body. It purifies the blood and increases creativity while charging and strengthening the electromagnetic field.

Exercise for Mental Harmony and To Balance the Tattvas: Kirtan Kriya

Our five fingers correspond to the five tattvas (elements) of which everything in this universe is made. Prana is the expression of the five elements in harmonious action. This simple exercise balances the five elements, thereby bringing the mind, body, emotions, and spirit into harmony.

Position:
Sit in easy pose, spine straight, elbows straight, wrists resting on your knees. You will be pressing your thumb to alternating fingers with each sound. Keep your eyes closed.

Mantra:
Chant in an even rhythm for 11 minutes: **Sa–Ta–Na–Ma**

a. *Sa*: Press the thumb to the index finger. (Jupiter/Water element/*Existence*)

b. *Ta*: Press the thumb to the middle finger. (Saturn/Fire element/*Life*)

c. *Na*: Press the thumb to the ring finger. (Sun/Air element/*Death*)

d. *Ma*: Press the thumb to the baby finger. (Mercury/Ether element/*Rebirth*)

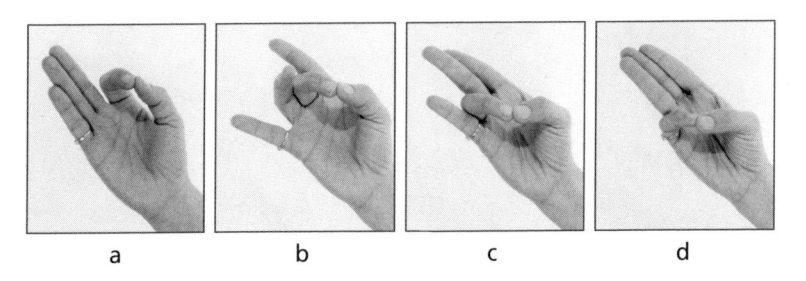

a   b   c   d

End:
Inhale deeply, then shake the hands vigorously above the head. Finally, exhale, relax the arms onto your lap and sit calmly to absorb the benefits of this meditation.

Exercise to Strengthen the Lifeforce & Rebuild the Body

Position:

- Sit in easy pose with the legs crossed or in any comfortable meditative sitting posture with a straight spine. Close the eyes and focus the eyes at the brow point.
- Place the hands on the knees palms facing up. Press the tip of the thumb, ring and pinkie fingers together. Extend the index and middle fingers.

Mantra:

Inhale deeply and chant: RA-MA-DA-SA-SA-SAY-SO-HUNG

Time:

Continue for 11 minutes a day for 40 to 120 days.

Comments:

The silver triangle mudra strengthens your energy body and builds your overall power of recuperation. This hand position causes sickness to leave and all bad omens to fall from the being. All physical body ailments will be spiritually healed. Do not think that it is you who are doing the healing; it is the grace of the infinite conscious energy. This hand position energizes the body and improves vitality and eyesight. It is good for those who feel nervous, tired and weak. With practice, your life will be longer and well-balanced. Working with the silver triangle bestows revitalizing energy, nervous strength, and good health. The prolonged practice of this posture normalizes the natural equilibrium of the body. It increases the glow, or luster, of the body, imparting goodness and transcendental spiritual qualities. The ring finger symbolizes the Sun or Uranus. The Sun represents energy, health, and sexuality. Uranus represents nervous strength, intuition, and change. This position increases general immunity to disease. It builds the nerve strength and rebalances the magnetic field of the body.

CHAPTER THIRTEEN

HEALING HEART DISEASE

MOST HEART TROUBLES come from cholesterol. The higher the cholesterol level, the greater the risk of heart disease. Cut back on foods such as french fries made with artery-clogging fats. Eat more fish and other foods such as soybeans, walnuts and flax seeds that contain healthy fats. Lower your cholesterol and risk of heart disease by eating foods with omega-3 fats, and avoid eating trans-fatty acids.

It has been found that hydrogenated fats tend to raise blood cholesterol levels. Therefore, avoid foods like beef, pork and lamb. Stay away from fat in butter and milk, vegetable shortening, crackers, cookies, doughnuts and french fries. Get in the habit of drinking the juice of half a lemon in lukewarm water. It will also heal high and low blood pressure. For high blood pressure, drink goat milk twice a day.

Grate a few carrots and add honey and lemon juice to make salad. Take this combination to cure all sorts of heart ailments resulting from ventricular or muscular disorders.

Some studies have found that death from coronary heart disease is far less common in countries along the Mediterranean than in northern Europe.

A diet rich in fruits, vegetables, cereals, fish and beans can prevent heart disease or attack. Also, an intake of more dietary fiber, antioxidants and the B vitamins found in fruit and vegetables can slow the arterial damage that precedes heart disease.

Olive and flaxseed oil are rich in omega-3 unsaturated fatty acids, and additionally have several effects in the body that help prevent or reduce risk of blood clots, abnormal heart rhythms, inflammation and clogging of blood vessels by deposits of fat cholesterol as well as preventing sudden cardiac death. Actually, fish oil is known to prevent cardiac death.

People with a high level of omega-3 fatty acids in the blood have a lower risk of developing a recurrent heart attack or any cardiac problems.

To avoid heart attacks or the exacerbation of heart disease, eat foods that are high in omega-3 fatty acids. Eat fish, including salmon, mackerel, sardines, albacore and tuna, once or twice a week. The omega fatty acids are good for the heart by making the blood less likely to clot. They prevent heart attack and lower blood pressure. Eating fish can prevent the potentially fatal disruption of heart rhythm. People who regularly eat fatty fish are less likely to suffer heart attacks. Fish oil reduces the thickness and stickiness of the blood, which in turn prevents blood clots and heart attacks.

THE HEART CENTER

It is important to mention here the heart chakra—the center of unconditional love. At this level the feelings of universal brotherhood and tolerance begin to develop and all beings are accepted and loved for what they are.

The heart center is governed by the element of air, known as *Vayubhuta* or *vayu*. The *gunas* or forces of sattva and *rajas* manifest in the Vayubhuta, the element of air. This vayu is the vital force or prana in the body. It produces the cells and precious seeds. It is vayu that keeps all the bodily organs active and healthy and circulates the blood and other fluids throughout the body. Vayu is not as subtle as ether, also known as *Akasha*. The element air is tactile. Air is the protective element in the body. It is the vital force. The fourth chakra rules the chest region, known as *vayu-granthi*, which includes the lungs, heart, thymus, cell producers and all their subsidiaries. When you are in possession of strong vayu-granthi, self-control, balanced temperament, purity of thought and unselfishness are yours.

The heart center is the most important of our spiritual centers. It is one of the two centers which is in direct contact with the higher self and through which soul energy and the other higher energies enter our being. The second entrance is the head center, which is located in almost the exact center of the head in the vicinity of the pineal gland.

In addition, *ojas*—the essential energy of the body—is located in the heart from where it pervades the entire body, giving stability and support. Ojas, which means *vigor*, is the ultimate essence of the reproductive system and the heat of the tissues. It is the subtle essence of the reproductive system and all the vital secretions. It is not a physical substance. Ojas is the sap of our life energy and exists on the subtle level in the heart chakra. It is the essential energy of the immune system. When it is sufficient there is health; when it is deficient there is disease. Disease strikes at the location where it is weakest. When it is destroyed, one dies; when it is sustained, one lives. From a Chinese medical point of view, the heart is affected by anxiety and excess joy and passion. These intense emotions, when not rooted in pure balance, are detrimental to the ojas, as they burn yin. The leader of one of the four great medical schools of thought in the Chinese system, Dr. Zhu Dan Xi, held that the root of all disease comes from "Heart Fire." This is a term that means that the burning pursuit of desires creates excess heat in the heart, which ultimately consumes yin. Yin is the water-like substance that composes our flesh. Any intense emotion such as anger, stress, excessive sexual indulgence, greed and any drive that causes us to make poor decisions and lifestyle choices will cause premature depletion of the precious yin. When the yin becomes deficient, symptoms such as hormone deficiency, reproductive problems, fatigue, dry skin, thin bones and immune weakness arise. According to Chinese thought, the yin cannot be replaced through food or medication. The only source of yin replenishment lies in the Universal Energy itself and is obtained within the body through meditation.

Ojas is decreased by factors such as anger, hunger, worry, sorrow, and overwork, which disturbs the senses. Decreased ojas results in: a general lack of color to the skin tone, a lack of strength, the mind becomes weakened, and there is a physical wasting. Qualities such as patience and faith disappear and are replaced with fear.

On the physical level, the heart center is associated with the heart, lungs, circulatory and respiratory systems. When the heart center does not work properly, one can get heart and lung diseases, including asthma, which reflects deep-seated issues of identity, emotions and self-consciousness. Heart diseases include heart attacks, strokes, angina, arteriosclerosis and hypertension. Heart attacks are often preceded by palpitation, insomnia, numbness, or severe pain in the chest or middle back that radiates down the arms. Causes of heart diseases include an unhealthy diet, physical or emotional trauma, congenital or hereditary factors, suppressed emotions, or excess strain or anxiety.

The first thing to do in order to heal the heart involves an extended period of rest or reduced activity, both physical and mental. Strain and worry should be set aside. Heavy exercise and travel should be avoided. Sufferers of conditions such as anemia, hypertension, palpitations, tuberculosis, asthma and bronchitis may concentrate on their heart center while performing asanas and other yogic techniques.

The heart center is the point of balance in the human body where spirituality takes one higher and deeper. Most people die of broken hearts or spiritual starvation. A connection to the God of one's heart is crucial. People must get in touch with their real hearts and discover what they really want to do in life, and do it!

Exercise To Prevent Heart Attacks

Position:
With a straight spine, sit with the left heel at the perineum. The right knee is at the chest, right foot flat on the floor. Forearms are parallel to the floor, right palm resting on top of the left hand. Both hands are flat; tips of the thumbs are touching. Eyes are only 1/5 open. Focus downward as far as possible.

Breath:
Completely inhale in 4 equal sniffs. Exhale completely in 4 equal sniffs. (this is called segmented breath.) You may use any mantra you wish with the breath. A good one is ONG ONG ONG ONG repeated mentally on the inhale and SO-HUNG SO-HUNG SO-HUNG SO-HUNG repeated mentally on the exhale.

Time:
Continue for 7 minutes. Adding 5 minutes for each week of practice, you may work up to 31 minutes.

Comments:
The 4-fold breath stimulates the center where the ida, pingala and the shushmana meet. It assists in the absorption of oxygen into the lungs and purifies the blood. As the exhale is 25-30% greater than usual, old toxins are forced into the blood stream.

The pressure of the right knee on the liver helps balance the liver and the spleen. This mudra stimulates and regulates the interaction of the pancreas, adrenals, and kidneys. Stimulation of the perineum balances the sexual glands. Regular practice of this kriya helps prevent heart attacks. It is a very powerful aid to a longer life.

Exercise for Heart Problems

Position:
Sit in easy pose with a straight spine. Place the palms gently together with the fingers extended and joined and the thumbs crossed. With the elbows straight, extend the arms 60° up and as far to the left as possible. The fingertips of the right hand cover the mounds at the base of the fingers of the left hand. Be sure to keep the elbows stretched out and up and locked throughout the meditation.

Breath:
Inhale powerfully and deeply through the nose. Exhale powerfully through the mouth, pushing the navel deeply in toward the spine. Concentrate on the breath.

Time:
Continue for 11 minutes. (You can build up to 31 minutes with practice.) At the end of the meditation, inhale deeply, exhale very powerfully and completely, hold the air out for 10-15 seconds, then relax.

Comments:
This meditation is good for people who have any kind of heart problem, tension, or poor circulation. It is also good for the glandular system and depression. Various meridians in the shoulders and elbows will hurt as the body corrects itself, but keep the elbows locked regardless! If you've been eating junk food you may find it hurts more; you will feel very weak no matter how strong you may be!

Exercise for the Physical and Emotional Heart

Position:
Sit in easy pose with a straight spine.

Place the hands on the knees, palms facing up. Fold in the index finger to touch the fleshy mount at the base of the thumb. Touch the thumb tip to the tips of the middle and ring fingers. Extend the pinkie finger.

The eyes are closed focused on the point between the brow.

Mantra:
Inhale deeply, and on the exhale chant:

RA-MA-DA-SA-SA-SAY-SO-HUNG

Time:
Continue for 11 minutes daily for 40 to 120 days.

Comments:
The benefit of this hand position, called heart mudra, is to divert the flow of prana from the hands to the heart area, thereby improving the vitality of the physical heart. The middle and pinkie fingers relate directly to nadis, or channels, connected with the heart, while the thumb closes the pranic circuit and acts as an energizer, diverting the flow of prana from the hands to these nadis. This hand position is beneficial for heart ailments, especially ischemic heart in acute situations.

The heart is the center of emotion. Heart mudra helps release pent up emotion and unburden the heart. It may also be practiced during emotional conflict and crisis.

*The heart center is the most important
of our spiritual centers.
It is one of the two centers which are
in direct contact with the higher self
and through which soul energy and
other higher energies enter our being.*

CHAPTER FOURTEEN

SPIRITUALITY AND DEPRESSION

AT THE VERY HEART of the healing of depression lies the quiet song of the soul. It is this eternal part of us that often gets buried amidst the chatter, hurriedness, clamor, and pain of our life's journey. While depression is a serious condition and requires immediate attention, it is important to understand its energetic underpinnings. While depression can be brought on by a number of factors, including genetics, chemical imbalance, inappropriate medication and stress, all forms of depression are linked by the common denominator of unresolved issues that manifest as a depressive energy pattern. This energy pattern then further depletes the weakened electromagnetic field, or aura.

The soul, which is the eternal part of us that is the accumulation of our many lifetimes of experiences, and the electromagnetic field are intimately interconnected. The electromagnetic field is the energy that surrounds our physical bodies. Its size and strength are determined by the extent to which we have rid our lives of negative patterns, the integrity of our belief system, the purity of our heart and our physical health. When the electromagnetic field is large and strong, we are able to deflect negativity and draw positivity into our lives. Our immune system is bolstered, and we are not subject to fluctuating emotions. Our normal feeling of happiness, connection and well-being depend on the balance of our individual psycho-electromagnetic field.

When your energy field is strong, it causes your muscles to obey the message nerves. As a result the message nerves give a good perception to the brain. Your nerves must be strong and balanced. Also, the circumvent magnetic force of your aura must be so strong that negativity cannot enter your field. Proper maintenance of the nerves depends on the basic elements and hormones in the constitution of the blood. Blood is the life supply line to the cells. The protective aspect of the electromagnetic field can be compared to the protective light the sun provides to the Earth and universe.

We are generally able to sympathize, to a certain extent, with depressed friends and family members, because most of us have experienced some form of depression. In certain instances, however, depression overwhelms its victim, causing extreme feelings of hopelessness, worthlessness, helplessness and despair. The afflicted individual is rendered incapable of performing even the most basic of tasks. Their depression has reached such a high level of intensity that those around them become uncomfortable and are no longer able to relate. Sympathy surrenders to the self-protective disdain that expects the depressed individual to snap out of it and regain control of their lives. Unable to simply snap out of it, the depressed person withdraws and their depression is reinforced.

If you are depressed, or know someone who is, the following questions can be useful in determining the extent to which the depression has taken hold:

Has the person been depressed for a long time?
Is depression a side effect of prescribed medications?
Does the person have a glandular disorder?
Has the person's work life changed?
Has something affected the person's home life
or social relationships?

Pharmaceutical anti-depressants are often prescribed for depressed individuals. These medications succeed in alleviating the symptoms of depression, because they increase the levels of serotonin, a chemical responsible for one's sense of well-being, in the brain. While pharmaceutical remedies may help the depressed person feel better, they do not heal the negative patterns that are at the root of the illness. In other words, pharmaceutical remedies cannot strengthen our electromagnetic field.

Our electromagnetic field is strengthened by the practice of self-healing, which is achieved through meditation and chanting. This is the key to alleviating depression. It is the only permanent cure. Our unhealthy patterns create mental and emotional conflicts that disrupt our lives and inhibit self-healing. While some will spend a lot of money and years in therapy, the truth is that no one can heal you but yourself. Only you have the power to clean your mind. The only thing another person can do is offer you the tools. The rest is up to you.

The electromagnetic field is strengthened when we chant. *(See The Healing Fire of Heaven for more information on Sacred Sound.)* As we chant, eighty-four acupressure points on the roof of the mouth are stimulated through the vibration of the tongue. In turn, this vibration has a powerful impact on our brain and heart.

Chanting works on the glandular system. Our glands are the guardian of our physical health, including our stability to infinite consciousness. Their secretion determines the chemistry of the blood, and the blood in turn, determines the composition of our personality. For example, if you lack proper iodine from the thyroid gland, you will lack patience and seldom succeed in staying calm and cool. Through chanting the mantras revealed in these books you will gain mastery of unlimited consciousness in yourself by mastering your physical consciousness. This spiritual practice takes care of your glandular balance now, so that age, depression, stress, disease and fatigue may not interfere with the enjoyment of the God consciousness you can build for your happiness. Chanting enhances the function of the pineal, pituitary and thyroid glands, while helping to facilitate the building of strong character and morality. The stimulation of the thyroid gland causes it to secrete and open circulation to the brain. This clears our thinking and adds energy to the will.

The parathyroid glands are exceptional, because they ease pain and equalize the distribution of the psychic and physical vibrations of the human body so as to establish a harmonic condition between them. Each of us generates energy from our mind/psyche and our body. These must be integrated for our total being to function well. The parathyroid glands are responsible for this. It is here where one can easily and automatically synchronize one's circumvent force with the universal magnetic field, for through the functioning of the parathyroids the aura of the physical body is adjusted in its rate of vibration to be harmonious with the Cosmic vibrations.

The thyroid gland is significant in that it controls the rapidity and intensity of exchange between subjective and objective consciousness. In other words, the thyroid helps us integrate what we feel with what we know.

A healthy thyroid indicates that a person will have a quick, delving mind. Indeed, the mind aided by normal thyroid functioning will be keen and possess the ability for rapid adjustment. Conversely, a weak or malfunctioning thyroid slows mental reactions, producing dullness, a general lack of interest and an inability to deal with the problems of life. These qualities can then lead to irresponsibility and a tendency to adopt the line of least resistance. Human beings have both a larger thyroid than other animals and a greater level of mental, emotional and physical activity. Thyroxin has a tremendous effect on the nerve cells in the adrenals glands and the ganglion cells throughout the sympathetic nervous system. We know that the nervous system controls the body, and one needs a strong nervous system to neutralize the negative effect of depression. Since the thyroid exerts such influence over the nervous system and also regulates the short wave emanations given off by the body's cells, it follows that the thyroid is one of the chief governors of the body.

Thyroid abnormalities cause severe health problems. One of the common symptoms that accompany hypothyroidism is a bad temper and moodiness that gets expressed in an angry way. The thyroid gland then greatly effects one's mental actions and reactions. In turn, the functioning of one's physical muscles and organs is also affected. Physical fatigue results from an underactive thyroid. Moreover, the thyroid gland is important psychically, as it acts as a sort of speed control for the interchange of objective and subjective impressions. It is not the place where these impressions actually change from the objective to subjective, or vice versa. Rather, it is the mechanism that controls how rapidly the change will occur. In addition to the crucial role the thyroid plays with iodide, and its cooperative function with the pituitary gland, the thyroid works closely with the adrenals as well. Working with the adrenals, the thyroid is referred to as the body's shock absorber. In this way, it helps the physical body adjust to its emotional environment.

There are several mantras, offered on the CDs *Blissful Spirit* and *Soul Trance*, that are helpful for combating depression. They include the following:

Wahe Guru Wahe Jio: This is a mantra for dancing with the soul and translates as *God, God, God, Oh my soul.* Chanting this mantra initiates a subtle rub against the center of the palate, and stimulates the 32nd meridian, known in the West as the Christ Meridian and in the East as the *Sattvica Buddha Bindu.* Chant the mantra 8 times per breath to increase your stamina, while making your thinking clear, your perceptions more honest and your actions more in line with your higher self.

Ganputi Kriya: Ganputi Kriya is called the impossible-possible kriya, whereby all negativity from the past and present will be redeemed. Ganputi is sometimes called *Mangalam*, the God of happiness. This mantra is linked to samskaras, karma and dharma. It will remove the negative karmas you carry from past lives and are paying for now. (All current suffering, unhappiness and misfortune are the result of past debts.) Ganputi Kriya also clears the karma you create in your daily life and makes way for dharma. The good you do today will be rewarded tomorrow.

Soul Trance: *Soul Trance* awakens the soul so you are able to manifest your highest destiny. It gives you the ability to construct healthy boundaries and make clear decisions, creating internal stability and harmony. It purifies the mind, helping you live life with a higher degree of consciousness, light and effectiveness.

Meditation allows us to bring out the negative karmic experiences that inhabit the deep recesses of our consciousness. Through mantra, coupled with the power of the breath, these karmic experiences are neutralized and then constructively assimilated into the consciousness. Therefore, they are no longer able to transform into the chaotic energies that dwell in the unconscious and disrupt our lives. They are effectively transmuted from negative to positive, and are reintegrated into our personalities as beneficial parts of our psyche.

Meditation on the Sun can be particularly helpful, as the Sun is the mathematical center of the universe and is analogous to the human heart. When we meditate on the Sun, we attune ourselves with its energy and our aura becomes brighter. We have the light, under whose gaze the darkness of depression cannot survive.

During the process of meditation, you will occasionally revisit early, often painful, experiences in order to evaluate how you react emotionally. As you analyze your feelings at these times, you will uncover the source of your unconscious reactions to various situations in your current life. The emotional reactions during meditation, then, serve as the foundation for modification of conscious actions. When you are able to objectively observe the nature of your negative karmic influences, you are better able to detach yourself from them. Consistent meditation allows you to gradually free yourself from the grip of negativity.

Meditation and chanting are arts of surrender; surrender to the inner power that can help you restore mental stability. They renew your energy and allow you to face the challenges of time and space with divine grace. You begin to live in the here and now, and life becomes a creative enterprise. No matter how humble your lot, or how limited your environment, you begin to make life a sanctuary of joy. Employ meditation and breath in the service of merging with the harmonious flow of divine grace that stills the sense organs and the mind, so that you can face your true self and experience ultra-consciousness.

CHAPTER FIFTEEN

SPIRITUALITY AND STRESS

THE DEMANDS OF LIFE produce stresses that we are constantly called upon to relieve. A modern day reality, stress has been described as mental, emotional or physical tension and strain. Physical, egotistic and social forces motivate the responsibilities of life, and represent the source of human nature. Indeed, modern life is characterized by a plethora of economic necessities that must be met, social standards that must be upheld, educational requirements that must be achieved, and political influences that must be addressed. Each area of life is capable of producing stressful conditions. Moreover, each area of life is intimately linked to the next. Therefore, human beings are always faced with environmental stressors. We must adjust ourselves to these stressors, finding both a mode of self-expression and a manner in which to contribute to an ever-changing social order. This is no small task. How one adjusts to life's recurring demands, however, determines both his level of stress, and the impact it has on both his personality and physical health. Stress cannot be ignored if health and a balanced personality are to be achieved.

For most of us, stress is associated with work. The three main sources of job stress are: The relationships we have with our co-workers, our work environment, and our expectations around our jobs. Stress, however, can come from anywhere, and at anytime while working, socializing or at home. While those with a weakened nervous system are more susceptible to stress, we all need to learn how to manage the stress in our lives.

Each of us is capable of handling stress in a healthy or unhealthy way. When handled constructively, stress can become a motivator. You develop a new life philosophy that transforms intolerable problems into tolerable troubles that can be dealt with. When handled poorly, stress becomes frustrating at best and destructive at worst. You are waylaid by physical and mental exhaustion. How you manage the satisfactions or frustrations that are related to the source of your stress, then, will determine how agitated you feel.

Situations and conditions will arise that seem unchangeable and inevitably, require us to alter our perspective. In our efforts to both satisfy our needs and reach the goals we have set for ourselves, we experience many tensions. To help reduce your level of strain and tension, you must first identify the cause of your stress. Once you become aware of the primary stressor, you have conquered one-third of your battle. After you've identified the issue or area causing you to feel stress, strategize. What can you do to alleviate the problem? Can you ignore or eliminate the source of your stress? Can you do something that will change the stressful situation? If you can't alter the source of the stress, can you change your reaction to it? Often, people tend to look for the easy way out of obligations. This tendency is a personality-destroying sin of "babying the self." Instead of trying to change another person or social order, we must recognize and acknowledge our own weaknesses and understand that perhaps, not all of our troubles originate in the nature of the requirements to which we must adjust. Often, by changing our reactions to the stressful conditions in our lives, we create the space for alternatives to exist. Finally, adopt a constructive habit that allows you to re-channel your stressful energy and eliminate it from your system. Take up a hobby or spend time with friends. Physical exercise and mental relaxation can greatly help to increase your overall ability to deal with stress. The aforementioned tactics can aid you in significant ways by reducing the tension created by the suppression of our fundamental wants.

It is strongly recommended that you choose to handle your stress in a positive, constructive manner. If you are feeling stressed out, be sure to talk to friends and loved ones. When we internalize our stress, our physical health suffers and we have a greater tendency to rely on negative coping mechanisms. Using alcohol or drugs to manage stress may initially seem beneficial, however, these chemicals only serve to mask our stress. The stressor itself, remains unchanged. Moreover, the use of chemicals to alleviate stress creates additional problems such as dependency and poor health.

TWO TYPES OF STRESS

There are two types of identifiable stress: acute and chronic. Acute stress is a sort of conscious peak experience that forces us to be aware of our external circumstances. In other words, acute stress forces us to pay attention to the details of everyday living. Very often it shocks us out of the daydream we have retreated into in order to escape the rigors of life. (This is especially true of those who are introverted.) When we experience acute stress, our hearts race, our senses are heightened, and our minds are alert. We need a certain amount of acute stress. Otherwise, we would sleep-walk through our lives.

Unlike acute stress, chronic stress is generally quite unconscious. Our first experience with chronic stress is at birth. Indeed, this first imprint of stress on the consciousness renders us susceptible to particular triggers and may actually be the basis of chronic stress as we move into adulthood. From a Jungian perspective, chronic stress is often related to what is known as the inferior function. Far from being an inferior function when properly understood, chronic stress has the potential to reveal who we are and what makes us tick.

All stress, whether acute or chronic, is linked to the inbred, biological mechanism commonly called fight or flight. The fight or flight mechanism is a reaction to the law of self-preservation. In nature, this law manifests as the preservation urge that resists change. It is an instinctual part of memory, deeply imbedded in the psychic body of every living being. When a biological system (i.e. a human being or animal) perceives danger or threatening conditions, the fight or flight mechanism swings into full gear in order to eliminate the threat (fight) or remove the being from the situation (flight.) In either instance, it is the urge for self-preservation that becomes paramount.

When in a given situation, we conclude that we are free to either fight or flee, we have some measure of control. This is a situation involving acute stress. But what happens when we reach the conclusion that we are neither free to fight or flee? What if we cannot cope? When we determine that we are stuck, that we have lost capacity to alter a situation, we are experiencing chronic stress. When we are unable to work effectively to combat chronic stress, the harmonious flow of energy in the psychic body is disrupted, leading to physical health problems. In this way, chronic stress becomes a killer. Therefore, it is imperative that we examine our lives, determine where we feel stuck, and remedy all chronically stressful situations.

In order to understand why chronic stress is so detrimental to our mental, emotional and physical health, let's briefly examine the physiological changes that occur in response to stress of any kind. When one perceives impending danger, the hypothalamus, as part of the emotional center of the brain, releases a hormone that instructs the pituitary gland to release additional hormones known as Adreno-Cortiso-Tropic Hormone (ACTH) and Thyroid Stimulating Hormone (TSH.) ACTH acts on the cortex, or outer portions, of the adrenal glands. At the same time, neuronal messages act on the medulla, or inner portion. Steroid hormones are released into the blood via the adrenal cortex, while adrenaline and nor adrenaline are released via the medulla. The combined effect of this simultaneous release is a further release and breakdown, via the liver, of sugars and fats. This results in a surge of energy for physical activity. In addition, TSH acts on the thyroid gland to release the hormones T3 and T4. T3 and T4 contribute on a cellular level to the energy production initiated by ACTH. Interestingly, adrenaline is the hormone associated with fear, while nor adrenaline is the hormone associated with anger. Stress reactions, then, can be regarded as expressions of either fear or anger, or both. Fear induces flight, while anger induces fight.

While our hormones are preparing us for fight or flight, our vagus nerve is assisting in the process. The vagus nerve is the tenth of the twelve cranial nerves, esoterically known as the psychic antenna. It transmits messages directly to the heart and lungs, thereby regulating our rate of breathing and circulation. Without the function of the vagus nerve, we would neither have the appropriate supply of oxygen necessary for the energy production so crucial to an effective fight or flight response, nor would we experience proper metabolism or adequate waste removal.

The preceding paragraphs outline the wisdom of our life force. If one is to engage in the physical response of fight or flight, energy must be made available to our muscles. The life force also prepares our blood for the preservation response. During times of stress, our blood momentarily moves away from non-essential activities, such as digestion, toward the brain and voluntary muscles. This allows for quick decision-making and action. The thymus is stimulated to release immune boosting cells into the blood, so that the chance of physical injury is reduced. When injury does occur, the presence of immune boosters allows the organism to effectively combat invading microbes. Moreover, the blood begins to clot at an increased rate of speed. Therefore, the possibility of bleeding is greatly reduced.

While we need and appreciate the body's protective adjustments during times of stress, imagine the effects of prolonged conditions of stress on the human system. Imagine the cumulative effects of faulty breathing and digestion. Imagine the detrimental effects of sustained release of certain hormones. Under such conditions we begin to suffer from glandular exhaustion and the concomitant breakdown of certain tissues, as well as the weakening of our immune defenses. Moreover, under conditions of chronic stress our mental ability for accurate analysis is depleted and our psychic energies are restricted to psychological defense.

The human system is wonderfully constructed. The power to determine what is a threat and what is not a threat carries grave responsibilities. While a healthy level of caution is indispensable for survival, prudence dictates that we strike a balance between caution and curiosity. Remember, caution is the law of self-preservation, curiosity the law of evolution. Living with the perception that one is susceptible to dangers and threats on all sides is accompanied by severe consequences. These consequences are experienced as physical disease. We are each responsible for the ills that befall us.

Understand that our experiences are in line with the Law of Attraction and carry great possibilities for personal growth and evolution. Just as the food we eat nourishes our physical bodies, the experiences of daily life nourish our psychic and spiritual bodies. The subtle bodies of our being can extract nutrients from our experiences when they are properly digested. Think of it this way, when the digestive enzymes work to break complex foods down into their simpler elements, these simpler elements are absorbed into the blood in order to facilitate cellular function. Adequate oxygen supplied to these cells further allows the body to benefit from the food we ingest. If, during the first step of this process, the digestive enzymes malfunction, we experience discomfort. Similarly, if the first step of assimilating the value of our experiences is inadequately performed, we experience the discomfort of psychic indigestion; the unconscious condition which manifests as chronic stress.

A Ritual from the Oriental System to Aid in Stress Reduction

At the back of the neck, there is an area known as the crucifixion center. It is said that the negative and positive currents of the body cross paths at this center. The following ritual uses this assumption to rid us of physical and psychological habits, as well as likes and dislikes.

Imagine a current of positive energy entering your solar plexus and filling the right half of your body. Next, imagine a current of negative energy entering your solar plexus and filling the left half of your body. Hold your breath and tense your body. With the breath held and the body tensed, send both currents to the crucifixion center with a positive suggestion to subconscious mind that will assist in the destruction of physical and psychological habits, as well as likes and dislikes.

CHAPTER SIXTEEN

※

HARMONYUM

DID YOU KNOW that in your bones is buried the most potent healing energy ever known to humankind? First, imagine yourself without bones. You would be a formless mass of flesh and blood. It is strange to think about, isn't it? Bones are crucial to our structure and support as a human being. Human bones are actually composed of the highly concentrated light of the Sun. The quality of life force that radiates in our bones is superior to anything else in the body, because of the enduring strength of the skeletal structure. We can see proof of this because what remains after we pass from this life are our bones, which survive long after the flesh and viscera have decomposed. In fact, bones endure for such a long time that there are still bones in existence from early humans, *Australopithecus*, which have survived over a million years.

The healing and invisible spiritual force of the Sun which penetrates, surrounds, and binds everything in the seen and unseen worlds lives and breathes in our very bones. That omnipresent, omnipowerful force permeates every man and woman and directs the flow of life from our skeletal foundation. This potent vibratory energy buried in our bones gives us what is known as the *body of light*, and it has been found to have genuine therapeutic values. Advanced spiritual mystics also refer to this body of light as the body of resurrection mentioned in the New Testament. When the spiritual force contained within our bones is properly used, there is no affliction or disease that cannot be cured.

In the mystery schools of Lemuria, Atlantis, and ancient Egypt, people with pristine power had complete knowledge of the body of light. This precious information showed the profound connections between the body of light and the Akashic records; all karmic influences are recorded within it. By accessing that body of light one is able to dissolve any blocks to the free flow of life force throughout the whole body. By using Harmonyum, a transcendental healing system that originates from Universal Kabbalah, disease, destructive habits, or bad luck simply disappear as if they never existed.

Harmonyum raises the vibratory frequency of the whole spiritual body so as to neutralize negative karmic influences or energy blocks from the past while releasing the life force in the body, thereby activating the body's innate healing mechanism. It gracefully directs the spiritual force to feed and nurture every single nerve and cell and clear away debris in the astral body that creates disease and adversity, thus initiating healing on all levels. Harmonyum can heal chronic illness and neutralize traumatic experiences which may have occurred during childhood, the birth process, or even in past lifetimes. Those who receive Harmonyum understand it to be a simple, subtle and gentle process that instigates profound and permanent healing.

In human beings, the destructive energy patterns or negative karmic influences imprinted on one's aura create a blueprint for recurring illness in the physical body or adversity in one's life. These patterns act like a photographic negative; you can destroy the photograph, but this doesn't eliminate the negative. When modern medicine uses curative methods to eliminate the symptoms of disease, this process destroys only the photograph. Therefore, the energy pattern imprinted in the negative can reproduce the illness at any time in the future. This explains why some illnesses reappear during times of stress, and others are called incurable. Harmonyum creates permanent healing within the body through the elimination of these energy patterns.

Some believe that an arduous healing process must occur before the body is truly healed. Harmonyum is diametrically opposed to this viewpoint; the application of this system that originates from the Kabbalah of the Sun is gentle, yet completely effective. In fact, the world's most powerful healers practice their art without any pain whatsoever experienced by their patient. As we live in an increasingly complicated world, we often think that the most complicated method is the best; we look for deep contact to relieve our aches and pains, yet healing energy is actually much more powerful when we barely touch the body. Harmonyum works with the auric body to clear away all accumulated karmic debris. Deep contact treatment, such as massage, is only related to the grosser healing energy of matter; light touch or even no touch accesses the subtle and high vibrational healing forces from the spirit.

HARMONYUM AND THE NERVOUS SYSTEM

As previously mentioned, we are governed by two main nervous systems: the cerebrospinal nervous system, or central nervous system, which is associated with the cortex and cerebration; and the autonomous nervous system, connected with the viscera and inner centers of the brain. Harmonyum regulates the autonomous nervous system, which controls and activates our biological functions, specifically those that regulate and affect temperature, metabolism, endocrine gland secretion, digestion and sleep. When our nervous system is working properly, we have perfect health in our bodies and minds. All organs and their functions are in perfect harmony within the body.

The two divisions of the central system—the sympathetic and parasympathetic—condition the equilibrium of our body; it is the balance and regulation of these that govern health. Harmonyum balances the fluctuations between the sympathetic and parasympathetic systems, so that circulation, breathing, digestion, sexual energy, and sleep may return to normal. Many people erroneously believe that diet or medication can regulate health, when in fact, this is simply more manipulation of the photograph rather than looking at the photographic negative.

The autonomous nervous system is affected by the cerebrospinal nervous system, and it acts independently of our consciousness.

After a Harmonyum treatment, the outer brain grows quiet, and the internal structure can exert a balanced control over the autonomic nervous system. The resulting hormone secretion interacts with the autonomous nervous system and calms the cortex, thus enabling a healing rhythm to be restored.

The sad truth is that in some of our scientific explorations, we have forgotten about the simplicity and beauty of the natural self-regulation of the body, its automatic wisdom. We subject these regulating centers to all kinds of violence that disrupt their natural rhythm. This is the chief cause of all the diseases, from mental neuroses to cancers, that we see today. Harmonyum increases the pranic supply to all body cells while nurturing all the internal organs. It calms the nerves and connects you with your own limitless happiness and contentment.

Harmonyum is the divine doctor for this age and beyond. It balances the three nervous systems and positively charges the spinal fluid to assist in the healing process, allowing us to tap into the ever-flowing energy of the universe. Not only does it help repair the energy drained through long-term stress, but it also has a soothing effect on the personality. Harmonyum encourages the body to establish a rhythmic breath that purifies the blood, strengthens the heart and elevates the power of the mind. It promotes general longevity and strengthens the entire body for maximum benefit.

THE HARMONYUM AND UNIVERSAL KABBALAH CONNECTION

Let's define Kabbalah both in relation to healing and the process of manifestation of a thought pattern in the physical plane. Kabbalah is like an astral tree whose seed is in the mental body with its fruit in the physical body. Therefore, to completely heal, you must understand that the mental seed of a negative thought pattern grows into a tree in the astral body, and eventually reaps destructive fruit. This may be illness that manifests in the physical body or adversity that we attract. Since habitual mental tapes are very difficult, but not impossible to change, it is easier to work with the astral body, because it is mid-way between the mental and the physical levels. By purifying the astral body, you can create positive changes in the mind and heal the physical body.

Technically, if you experience pain or disease, it means that your astral body is transmitting through the sympathetic nervous system unhealthy vibrations to your physical body. Indeed, when we allow reoccurring thoughts of anxiety, doubt, hatred, anger and fear to invade our mind, our mental body directly impacts our astral body. The astral body in turn transmits via our sympathetic nervous system unhealthy or disturbing nerve impulses to our physical body, thereby creating disease with clear pathological intentions.

Harmonyum cleanses the astral body so as to balance the mind, body and spirit and transmit through the sympathetic nervous system positive nerve impulses to our physical body. As a result, all our cells vibrate with pranic light and new life. Those who receive Harmonyum find that their energy blocks within themselves are removed, freeing their paths for creative purposes, with an expanded awareness and acceptance for themselves and others.

There is a fascinating key to the mystery of how to heal the human body contained within the very structure of the body itself. Imagine a person standing with legs apart and arms outstretched inside a vertical circle, as in Leonardo DiVinci's famous drawing of the Vitruvian Man. The contact points are the feet, hands and head, with the spine at the center of the circle. The striking coincidence is that located at each of these contact points are 26 bones exactly. We have 26 bones in our head, 26 bones in each hand, and 26 bones in each foot. Furthermore, the spine, which is located at the center of both the circle and the five contact points, has 26 vertebrae as well.

Why the number 26? Is this by chance? Let's investigate this mystery further. In Kabbalah, the addition of 2 and 6 results in 8, which is the number of infinity and healing. Eight is also the number of Saturn, Lord of Karma. By using the Kabbalah numerology of the Hebrew name of God, master of the universe, the creator of all—*Yod He Vau He* (Yod=10, He=5, Vau=6, He=5)—this also adds up to the number 26. This is a compelling indication that God's name is not only written in the five points of contact of the star figure in the circle, but also, in the spine of the sixth point. By working on one or all of these areas, it is thus possible to completely heal the human body, curing it of all illnesses and neutralizing negative karmic influences.

Another interesting aspect of the mysterious divine healing power released by Harmonyum is the fact that it is connected to a mighty and misunderstood Kabbalah symbol: the five-pointed star, or pentagram. This star has been often used to represent the smiling Sun. In actuality, it is an active symbol of condensed sunlight fluid—a symbol whose light is so blinding that it dispels all darkness. When a person stands like the Vitruvian man, he symbolically represents the pentagram. The use and understanding of this symbol is one of the greatest guarded secrets of the Kabbalists. As we talk to God through mantras and prayer, so we communicate with the invisible world through symbols. The pentagram is the symbol of Human-God, the perfect human. In addition, it is believed to be one of the most powerful, beneficial and highly protective ancient symbols. Not only does it bring the awesome creative power and divine cleansing light of the cosmos to those who know how to use it, but it is also written that all sorrow and hardship is totally banished from its protective light. When you receive a Harmonyum treatment, your rhythms are aligned to the perfect balance of the pentagram; you become like the Vitruvian Man, in ideal health and harmony.

It has long been understood by most healers that there are spiritual centers responsible for our health and well-being located inside the head and along the spine. By working with the spine, Harmonyum gradually awakens these centers from latency. They, in turn, pour forth a stream of highly concentrated life force and power into the body and mind. Many illnesses are caused by a deviation of the spinal column, a pinched nerve, or an injured disc. Since the organs are dependent on the nerves, you cannot cure a diseased organ if you ignore the nerves that support it. All the nerves in the body eventually run through the spinal column. As the spinal column is not only the Sun or mathematical center of the skeletal system, it also serves as a bridge between the brain, the organs and the rest of the body. If the bridge is in poor condition, it will lead to abnormalities in the organs. Harmonyum restores the normal functioning of the organs by healing the nerves that run throughout the spinal column.

The rest of the treatment focuses on the head, which sits on top of the spine. On the Tree of Life, the head corresponds to the sphere called Kether, which is ruled by Metatron—the chief of all the Archangels of God. The two divine glands, the pituitary, known as the master of the glandular system and the seat of the third eye, and the pineal, the center of awareness and cosmic consciousness, are located in the head area. Working on your head stimulates the divine glands and enhances your spiritual vitality while nurturing your brain. It protects the brain cells and nerves from degeneration due to aging and damage due to poor circulation.

The spinal column corresponds to the middle pillar, known as the pillar of the Sun on the Tree of Life. A perfectly working middle pillar brings health, grace and balance. Proper work along the spine frees the balancing and healing energy of cosmic love which then floods each cell with pranic light. This explains why within the first few minutes of this Universal Kabbalah treatment, the recipient always experiences peace and nurturing divine Love while the light is being released.

RESULTS FROM A HARMONYUM TREATMENT

After the treatment, one experiences a deep sense of calm, relaxation, and vitality. Every part of the body is charged with a gentle pulsing of the pranic current. As a result of the Harmonyum treatment, the eyes become bright and the complexion noticeably radiant. Furthermore, it makes the aura beautiful and magnetic. Some people have reported the disappearance of chronic conditions after only a few treatments; more serious conditions may need regular sessions in order to completely rejuvenate the body.

Harmonyum gently and effectively sends you to the divine or astral world to restore your body's natural healing mechanism. When you touch a person's heart you touch his whole being. When you heal a person's heart you heal his whole being. Harmonyum heals the heart and brings healing into the whole human being and touches the heart of the skeletal system. By giving Harmonyum you are opening and healing the heart of a person and connecting him/her to the heart of the universe by means of soft and harmonious touch.

A Harmonyum treatment gently eliminates destructive energies such as anger, fear, stress and anxiety and replaces them with feelings of peace and serenity. It induces a psychological shift, which allows you to become aware of the causes induced by your thoughts and actions. In other words, Harmonyum creates self-healing by also expanding your awareness to recognize the laws of nature, primarily how cause-and-effect impacts your life. By changing behaviors and attitudes, you may undo and control the damages caused by living in disharmony. In addition, your daily practice in awareness starts to free your power of choice in how to think and act. This in turn replaces the habits that keep you in the cycle of negative patterns. Then you begin to understand and know your body and how it reacts to your attitudes. In other words, your growing awareness enables you to make conscious choices to behave in ways that support your positive growth, thus replacing the cycle of negativity with living in new positive possibilities.

Harmonyum is one of the rare healing systems known to nurture and give unconditional Love that can be automatically experienced by the recipient. Since the whole universe is kept together by the energy of Love, when that energy properly flows in our body, we are happy and healthy. It is becoming common knowledge that hurt feelings, emotional entanglements, resentment, fear and frustration can cause the ever-flowing energy of Love to become blocked, thereby manifesting disharmony and disease. Harmonyum reconnects us with the natural flow of Love in the body, wiping out every weakness in our destiny. When you receive Harmonyum, you will feel the love flowing through you as all resentments, fears and doubts drain away. At this point, you move gently and completely into the healing space.

Harmonyum is a cosmic dance in which harmony is established between heavenly and earthly energies. It turns your whole body into an energetic lighthouse, while promoting health and longevity and developing your own profound intuition. It is the supreme healing system for this age and beyond.

*The magnet is a perfect expression of the
basic principle of governing life:
electricity and magnetism.
These two principles rule everything.
The human body has an electromagnetic field,
which is composed of an electric
and magnetic principle.
Physical pain, discomfort and disease
come from an imbalance of these two principles.*

CHAPTER SEVENTEEN

THE HEALING POWER OF MAGNETS

I HAD ALWAYS HEARD about the healing power of magnets, but I never really took it seriously until I went to Hawaii. It was there that I met a doctor and his wife whose life experience with magnets made me cosmically curious.

A few years before, his mother, who is a heavy smoker, was diagnosed with small-cell carcinoma—a most virulent and deadly form of cancer. The survival rate is one to two months, but she decided not to do chemotherapy. She chose instead another healing route—the use of a powerful magnet. She was asked to sit on the north pole of a 4,500 gauge magnet for no more than three hours per day, one hour at a time, for six days a week. This was done while she was eating, watching TV, reading, etc... Besides the three separate hours of sitting, she was to apply the north pole of the magnet for one hour on the spleen, because not only does the spleen purify the blood, it is also responsible through its etheric counterpart for the transmission of the life force coming from the sun. In this way, the body can absorb this energy and be healthy.

After 24 months of use, to the amazement of her doctors, she was still alive with no discomfort whatsoever. She lost only ten pounds, and continued smoking and living a regular life. I thought that if it works for her, there is no reason why it should not work for others. Therefore, I decided to look into the universal principles at work in a magnet.

The magnet is a perfect expression of the basic principle governing life: electricity and magnetism. In other words, life—which is a vibration of up and down—is the result of the magnetic and electric forces. These two principles rule everything. You will even find them in the atom as the proton, or electricity, and as the electron, or magnetism. Giving and taking also displays respectively electric and magnetic forces.

The human body, which is a living magnet, has an electromagnetic field called the aura, which is composed of an electric and magnetic principle. Physical pain, discomfort and disease come from an imbalance of these two principles.

By virtue of the law of sympathy, if you hang out with healers, you directly or indirectly become a healer. If you hang out with polished people, you become polished. If you hang out with positive people, you become positive. If you hang out with criminals, you become a criminal.

The same law can be applied with a magnet. Since a magnet is the perfect expression of the balance of magnetic and electric principles, if our human magnet is unbalanced, all we have to do is hang out with a perfect magnet and we will become like it. In other words, if a sick person sits on the north pole of a magnet for some time, by virtue of the same law of sympathy, the perfect healing blueprint will be transmitted to the 100 trillion human cells and health will progressively be restored.

A magnet has a north pole, or magnetic force, and a south pole, or electric force. The north and south poles correspond respectively to the lunar and solar energy. The lunar force is the mother energy; it is the nurturing and rebuilding force. The north pole gives inner strength. It is the north or magnetic pole that awakens the life force and heals by redirecting all the constructive forces of the body, so that health may be restored. This pole stops malignant growth of any kind in the body. This pole is also the moon or water energy. As you may know, 75% of the body is composed of water. Therefore, it is logical to assume that the moon pole will at least empower that 75%, thereby creating harmony in the remaining 25%. Water washes impurities from the body. It will draw the bacteria to it in order to give the white cells a chance to wipe them out.

The south pole, on the contrary, will accelerate a condition already in place. Therefore, since you do not know how healthy you are or if something is growing in your body, leave the south pole alone. Do not leave room for mistakes. Focus on the north pole.

Here are some ideas obtained by research with the north pole:
- Cancer was arrested to the point where the living system took over and cured it.
- Put a glass of water on a magnet for 20 minutes and drink the magnetized water a few times a week to enhance your health.
- Apply the same water topically for bites, cuts or skin problems.
- Use the magnet to slow down the aging process, revitalize the body and increase life span.

ABOUT EASY POSE

The term *easy pose* refers to any posture in which one sits comfortably, with the spine straight and shoulders relaxed. The most common easy pose posture is sitting in a chair, with the feet flat on the floor. The ideal easy pose posture, however, is assumed by sitting on a mat with a pillow or folded blanket placed under the buttocks. This facilitates a release in the hips and a straightening of the lower back. Although it is advisable to avoid using a wall for support, those who sit against a wall must still sit on a folded blanket or pillow so that the hips and buttocks are positioned slightly higher than the feet. In cases of debility, it may be necessary for a person to lie down. When lying down, do not use a folded blanket or pillow.

People in the United States are less accustomed to sitting on the floor than people in other cultures. As a result, many Americans have inflexible hips, knees and lower backs. Indeed, many Americans have difficulties just getting out of a chair due to a loss of strength and flexibility. I recommend, therefore, that one make a habit out of the simple practice of sitting on the floor in easy pose. This will help you maintain strength, flexibility and circulation in the hips, knees and lower back. While sitting on the floor, massage your feet and pay attention to your breath (you should breathe deeply). The time you devote to this exercise now will greatly benefit your health and quality of life when you reach old age.

CHAPTER EIGHTEEN

HEALING REMEDIES AND YOGIC PRACTICE FOR SPECIFIC CONDITIONS

Exercise for Addiction

This "Medical Meditation for Habituation" is effective in overcoming such physical addictions as smoking, overeating, alcohol and drugs. It also works on subconscious addictions that lead us to insecure and neurotic behavior patterns, and on phobic conditions.

Position:
- Sit in easy pose with a straight spine, making sure that the lowest six vertebrae are pushed forward.
- Make fists of the hands. Extend the thumbs straight and place them on the temples in the niche where they fit.
- Lock the back molars and keep the lips closed. Vibrate the jaw muscles by alternating the pressure on the molars. A muscle will move in rhythm under the thumbs. Feel it massage the thumbs as you apply a firm pressure with the thumbs.
- Keep the eyes closed. Look to the third-eye point.

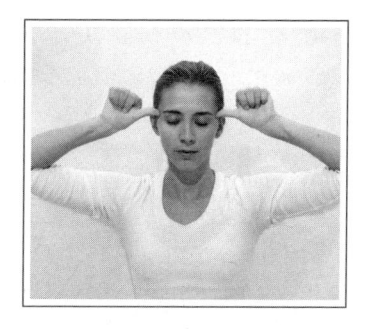

Mentally vibrate the mantra: SA-TA-NA-MA (*ah* as in "father") at the third-eye point.

Time: Continue 5-7 minutes. The time may be expanded to 20-31 minutes with practice.

🍃 Exercise for Adrenal Gland Imbalance

This meditation is a direct healer for the kidneys and adrenal glands. Consequently, it helps repair the energy drained by long-term stress. It alleviates problems of the lower spine, and helps the heart. Be sure to allow yourself at least as much time afterwards to relax as it took you to do the exercise.

Position:

- Sit in easy pose. Make sure the spine is pulled up and stretched straight.
- Extend the right arm straight up, hugging the ear. Extend the left arm to 60° from horizontal, with the palm facing down. On both hands, put the thumb onto the mound just below the little finger. Keep the eyes slightly open. Look down toward the upper lip. Press the elbows straight. Stretch the arms up from the shoulders.

The breath will automatically become longer and deeper as you continue. It is important to hold the arms perfectly still at the angles given, with a stretching feeling in the shoulders to receive the full benefit. Continue for 11 minutes.

ARTERIES

Avocado and olive oil have been known to be good for the arteries. Also, they help lower cholesterol.

ARTHRITIS

All physical conditions have a spiritual foundation. Arthritis is an often painful and debilitating condition ruled by Saturn. In order to gain insight into the spiritual aspects that underlie this condition, sufferers and health practitioners should learn as much as possible about Saturn's influence. *(See page 68)**

**The Healing Fire of Heaven (Splendor of the Sun)*, *Alchemy of Love Relationships*, and *Lifting the Veil*, by Joseph Michael Levry, also provide an in-depth description and analysis of the seven creative planets, including Saturn, and their attendant energies and influences.

Exercise for Arthritis

Sit down with legs spread as wide apart as possible. Catch your heels. Touch your forehead to the floor. Make sure the legs stay straight. Breath is normal. Continue for 1-3 minutes.

Comments: This exercise is also good for constipation and eyesight.

The following suggestions help to alleviate the physical aspects of arthritis:
- Maintain bowel health. *(See section on Constipation.)*
- Treat yeast overgrowth in the intestines. *(See section on Yeast.)*
- Avoid foods that you are allergic to, as they will contribute to inflammation. In order to determine if you have any food allergies, have your physician administer a food allergy blood test.
- Avoid nightshade vegetables such as eggplant and potatoes.
- Remove coffee, soda, alcohol, spicy foods, sugar and white flour from your diet.
- Walk every day, taking care to dress warmly in order to avoid exposing the joints to cold and wind. Sweating, via daily exercise, cleanses the body.
- Never walk around with wet hair or damp clothing, and avoid damp environments.
- Fast on vegetable soup to help cleanse the body.
- Apply this poultice to painful joints: combine 2 tablespoons of mullein and slippery elm powder, 1 tablespoon of lobelia, and 1/2 teaspoon of turmeric powder. Boil for five minutes in 1 1/2 cups of water, then steep for 5 minutes. Remove herbs to cool slightly. When the mixture is sufficiently cool, place on joints in a 1/4 inch layer and wrap. Allow it to remain for one hour.
- Apply a castor oil poultice to painful joints.
- Liquid multi-minerals with copper, zinc, manganese and sulfur.
- Liquid multi-vitamins with vitamin A, C and E.

- The following herbs are also helpful; research and choose the best ones for you: burdock root, turmeric root, yucca, black cohosh, chapparel and guggul.
- Cold showers are excellent for arthritis, but do not precede or end your cold shower with warm water.
- You can prevent arthritis by eating fatty fish, such as sardines, salmon, tuna, etc. Golden milk is also excellent.

ASTHMA

It has been found that smog and other forms of air pollution can have a long-term effect on children's lungs and could be the contributing cause of asthma. A study conducted in southern California found that pollution affects the breathing of girls more than it does of boys. Boys are more likely to get respiratory diseases like asthma and bronchitis at an early age.

- Eat an onion regularly, because it contains at least 3 to 4 anti-inflammatory elements.
- Add the juice of half a lemon to lukewarm water and drink.
- Combine and drink: 1 part lemon juice to 1 part ginger juice to 2 parts water.
- Trinity root, *page 122*.
- Add turmeric and parsley to your diet.

Exercise for Asthma (1–3 minutes)

Stand up, heels together. Hands are overhead with palms together. Lean back as far as possible and do Breath of Fire for 1-3 minutes. To prevent falling, stand over a gymnast's horse or a soft sofa back or get someone to stand behind you to catch you if you lose your balance. You must bend back as far as possible.

Comments: This exercise is said to make asthma fly away like a crow at the clap of your hands!

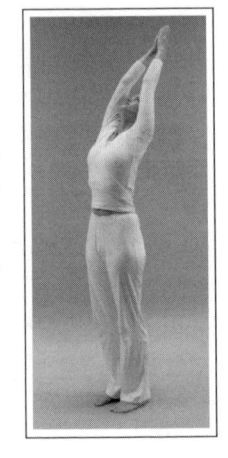

ACIDITY

Burning sensations in the chest are the result of an accumulation of acidic content in the body. Combine: *lemon juice, ginger juice, and lukewarm water*. Drink this to clear up discomfort very fast.

ALLERGIES

Eat cooked eggplant with garlic and onion.

Exercise for Allergies or Chronic Diseases

Sit in a comfortable meditative position. Make a fist with your left hand with the thumb on top. Wrap the right fingers around the left fist, and cross the right thumb over the left.

Mantra:

Inhale deeply, and on the exhale repeat the mantra 7 times per breath. Continue for 11 minutes minimum, working up to 31 minutes maximum.

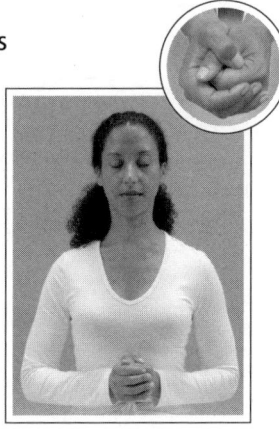

> Sat nam, Sat nam, Sat nam, Sat nam,
> Sat nam, Sat nam, Wa-he Guru

BACKACHE

- Massage the spine with ginger juice mixed with massage oil to nurture the spine.
- It is important to strengthen the abdominal muscles to help support the spine and protect the back from injuries.
- To gently stretch, massage and relax the back, do Cat-Cow *(page 217)* and end with Baby Pose *(page 189)*.

BAD BREATH (HALITOSIS)

Bad breath comes from poor dental hygiene, improper diet, indigestion and liver malfunction. Put golden seal in warm water and keep in mouth for 3 minutes, or steep a quarter of a teaspoon of golden seal in warm water and rinse mouth with solution. Swish solution of golden seal with warm water in your mouth for 20 to 30 seconds. Repeat a couple of times a week. Also, you can put a little of the golden seal tea on a toothbrush and thoroughly brush your teeth and gums. The result will be most satisfactory. Parsley is excellent because it is rich in chlorophyll. Green drinks are very helpful. Drink a glass of water with lemon juice in the morning and before sleep. You can repeat this process a couple of times during the day.

BLADDER

Cranberry juice is extremely good for the bladder and the kidneys, because it blocks infectious bacteria.

BLOOD

- Clean your blood by drinking a lukewarm glass of water with lemon juice, morning and night for at least a week.
- Build blood by eating large quantities of onion and turmeric separately or together.
- Red wine (in small amounts) has the capacity to ward off blood clots, because it is full of blood thinners contained in grape skins.

BLEEDING

- To stop internal and external bleeding, add the juice of two lemons to a glass of water and drink. Repeat if needed.
- Honey is a renowned blood coagulant. Apply it on a cut; it will stop the bleeding. Not only will it act as an antiseptic, but it will also heal the wound speedily.
- Put some turmeric powder on the cut; it will stop the bleeding.

Exercise To Balance Red and White Blood Cells
(11 minutes/day for 40 days)

Position:
- Sit in easy pose with a straight spine.
- With the right elbow bent and relaxed near the body, raise the right hand up to the side as if taking an oath. Middle and index fingers of the right hand are pointed up, the other two fingers are curled down under the thumb.
- Hold the left hand in the same mudra, with the two outstretched fingers touching the heart center, midway between the breasts. Make the outstretched fingers as straight as possible.
- Eyes are either closed or focused on the tip of the nose.

Breath:
Breathe slowly, meditatively, and with control, taking the breath mentally from the third-eye point and then down to the heart where the fingers are.

Time:
Continue for 11 minutes. Then inhale and exhale deeply three times, and relax.

Comments:
This meditation helps balance the distribution of the white and red blood cells. This balance is intimately involved in the proper functioning of the body's immune system. Do the meditation once a day for 40 days in order to perfect it.

Exercise for Blood Disease
(18 minutes, 1 hour, or 108 breaths)

Position:
Sit with a straight spine, palms touching at the chest, arms hugging the ribs. Focus on the tip of your nose.

Breath:
Mouth is open. Inhale in 4 equal strokes, mentally concentrating on one syllable of the mantra WA-HE GU-RU with each stroke, and on the breath as it crosses the tongue tip. Exhale in 4 equal strokes, concentrating on each syllable of the mantra WA-HE GU-RU, and on the breath as it crosses the tongue tip.

Time:
Continue for 5 minutes. Then rest for a minute. Repeat all of the above twice.

Comments:
Anyone who can practice this kriya an hour a day is greatly strengthened against diseases of the blood. Doing the breath described in this kriya 108 times purifies and oxygenates the blood. Doing it as described above for 18 minutes a day for 40 days will rejuvenate an old body.

BLOOD PRESSURE

Celery lowers blood pressure, as it contains pressure-lowering chemicals.

Exercise for High Blood Pressure (1–3 minutes or 31 minutes)

Position:
Sit in easy pose. Use the thumb of the right hand to block the right nostril. Fingers of the right hand are together, pointed straight up.

Breath:
Do Breath of Fire through the left nostril while pumping the navel point in and out. (Breath of Fire is a very rapid breath from the diaphragm, with equal inhale and exhale.) The more completely you can pull your abdomen in and push it out, the more effective will be the kriya. Continue for 1-3 minutes.

Time:
For longstanding problems of high blood pressure, do 31 minutes daily of normal left nostril breathing (without Breath of Fire or stomach pumping).

Comments:
Breathing through the left nostril stimulates the cooling, relaxing functions in the body. Your breath, which switches from mainly right nostril to mainly left nostril every 2 1/2 hours throughout the day, can be automatically channeled to the left nostril by holding the left hand under the right armpit, with the right arm pressing in on it slightly in its normal relaxed position. Try it!

Exercise for Low Blood Pressure (1–3 minutes or 31 minutes)

Position:
Sit in easy pose. Use the thumb of the left hand to block the left nostril. Fingers of the left hand are together, pointed straight up.

Breath:
Do Breath of Fire through the right nostril while pumping the navel point forcefully in and out. Continue for 1-3 minutes.

Time:
For longstanding problems of low blood pressure, do 31 minutes daily of normal right nostril breathing (without Breath of Fire or stomach pumping).

Comments:
Breathing through the right nostril stimulates the "sun" functions of the body—when you have a lot of sun energy you do not get cold, you are energetic, extroverted, and enthusiastic. It is the energy of purification. This breath holds the weight down and aids digestion. It makes the mind clear, analytical, and action-oriented. Your breath, which switches from mainly right nostril to mainly left nostril at intervals during the day, can be automatically channeled to the right nostril by holding the right hand under the left armpit, with the left arm pressing in on it slightly in its normal relaxed position.

BLOOD SUGAR

To regulate the insulin and blood sugar levels, eat broccoli or lentils. Broccoli is especially rich in chromium, which regulates insulin and blood sugar.

Exercise for Hypoglycemia (1 1/2 minutes)

Lie down on your stomach. Grab the ankles and arch up into bow pose. Bend the neck to touch the left ear to the left shoulder. Hold this position for 45 seconds. Then change so that the right ear touches the right shoulder. Hold for another 45 seconds. *(See contraindications for Bow Pose on page 202.)*

Comments:
Use of the diaphragm lock is also helpful in cases of hypoglycemia.

Exercise for Leukemia

Part 1:
Sit in easy pose with your hands in gyan mudra. Eyes are closed and pressed up toward the third-eye point.

Inhale completely in either 3, 4, or 5 parts (broken breath) through the nose.

As you exhale, chant out aloud

> WA-HE(Y) GURU, WA-HE GURU
> WA-HE, WA-HE, WA-HE GURU

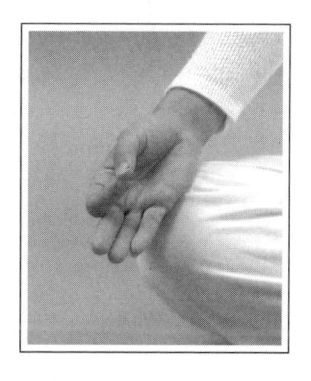

Start with 11 minutes and build up to 2 1/2 hours.

Part 2:
Now sit in easy pose with your left hand behind and at the middle of your back, palm outward at the level of your heart. The right palm is on your chest, in the middle, at heart level.

Chant:

> ECK ONG KAR(a)
> SAT NAM(a)
> SIRI WA(a)-HE(Y) GURU

The navel point is pulled in sharply on ECK. On each high-pitched "a" sound (pronounced like u in "but") the diaphragm is pulled up so that the rib cage lifts. On HE (pronounced "hay") the diaphragm and stomach relax. Low-pitched a's are pronounced as in "father." As you chant, visualize the energy spinning from the base of the spine upward through the top of the head to infinity. Continue for 3 or 11 minutes.

Comments:
This meditation is helpful in cases of leukemia, arthritis and to cleanse the blood.

BONES
- Take turmeric to keep the bones and joints flexible.
- Recipe for Golden Milk:
    1/8 tsp. turmeric
    3 cardamom pods (opt.)
    1/4 cup of water (approx.)
    Simmer 5-7 minutes, then add:
    1 cup milk
    2 Tbs. cold-pressed almond oil
    Bring up to boiling point, but do not boil!
    Sweeten to taste with *honey* or *maple syrup* (opt.)
- You can prevent bone fractures and even osteoporosis by eating pineapple. Pineapple contains manganese.

BRAIN

KELP is a type of seaweed that can be eaten raw, but it is usually dried or ground into powder. Kelp is a rich source of vitamins, especially the B vitamins, as well as many valuable minerals and trace elements. It is reported to be very beneficial to brain tissue, the membranes surrounding the brain, the sensory nerves, and the spinal cord, as well as the nails and blood vessels. It has been used in the treatment of thyroid problems because of its iodine content, and is useful for other conditions as varied as hair loss, obesity and ulcers. It protects against the effects of radiation and softens stools. Kelp is recommended as a daily dietary supplement, especially for people with mineral deficiencies.

GINKGO: As we age, there is less flow of blood to the brain. Ginkgo improves brain functioning by increasing cerebral and peripheral blood flow, circulation, and oxygenation. It is good for depression, headaches, memory loss, and ringing in the ears. Ginkgo helps relieve leg cramps by improving circulation. It is also beneficial for asthma, eczema, heart and kidney disorders. It is helpful in preventing altitude sickness.

GOTU KOLA: The gotu kola plant *(centella asiatica)*, referred to as *Brahmi* in Indian Ayurvedic medicine, has been used to heal the body, mind and spirit for over 2,000 years. Renowned in China and India as a brain and nervous system tonic, it is said to have remarkable rejuvenating properties. Indeed, this medicinal plant carries with it a wealth of positive attributes. Not only does it promote intelligence and stimulate the central nervous system, gotu kola helps with the elimination of excess fluids, decreases fatigue and depression, increases one's sex drive, energy and ability to concentrate, and shrinks unwanted tissue. In addition, this valuable herb may neutralize blood acids and lower body temperature while aiding in productive heart, liver and metabolic functioning. As if that weren't enough, gotu kola can stem the progression of cardiovascular, circulatory, connective tissue, appetite and sleep disorders. Gotu kola can also be used externally. When applied as a juice or poultice of fresh leaves, the herb aids in the healing of bruises, inflammations, eczema and ulceration. It has also been said to stimulate hair growth and stop hair loss when taken regularly.

Gotu kola is the main revitalizing herb for the nerves and brain cells. It increases intelligence, longevity, memory; it decreases senility and aging. It fortifies the immune system, both cleansing and feeding it, and strengthens the adrenals. Gotu kola has been used by yogis in the Himalayas as food for meditation and to awaken the crown chakra. Gotu kola helps to heal and balance the interaction of the left and right brain hemispheres.

NOTE: *This information should in no way be considered a substitute for proper medical care. As with all foods and medicines, please be aware that consuming very large quantities of gotu kola at one time may be harmful. Seek care from your medical professional whenever necessary.*

Exercise To Rejuvenate the Brain

This exercise changes and replaces the grey matter in the brain.

Position:
Sit in easy pose with your hands on your knees. The chest is out and the shoulders are back. Begin vibrating the front of your face using very rapid, short up-and-down vibrating motions. Try to move just the forehead. The brain will adjust itself.

Continue for 8-9 minutes.

BREAST CANCER

Take the following for 6 days. Take a break for one to two days, then repeat. *(See also Women's Health)*
- Astragalus for the immune system.
- Red clover for circulation and brain.
- Burdock to cleanse the blood.

Frog Pose

Frog pose is excellent for the prevention of breast and prostate cancer. It is also good for circulation and raising the energy from the lower to the higher centers.

Position:

Squat low with the hands on the floor between the knees, which are spread wide. The heels are touching. Keep the spine erect and the face forward (figure a). If possible, tip the chin in and down, placing it firmly into the cavity at the very top of the breastbone.

figure a

Inhale deeply as you straighten the legs and lift the hips high (figure b). Drop the head. Keep the hands on the ground, and if possible, stay up on the balls of the feet. Exhale completely as you return to the original position (a).

Repeat 26 times. End in position b on the inhale. Hold the breath, then relax on your back.

figure b

CHOLESTEROL

- One-half cup of cooked beans daily reduces cholesterol by 10%. Also, monounsaturated oils help lower your HDL level. *(See also Chapter 13: Healing Heart Disease)*
- Eating oatmeal is also excellent for regulating cholesterol. Try oatmeal cooked with sliced apple and flax oil.

CLEANSING THE BODY

- Drink lime and honey with mineral water for one week.
- Drink or eat melon and watermelon.
- Maintain a light diet throughout 15 days and go on this regimen:
    Day 1-3: *eat melon*
    Day 4-6: *eat watermelon*
    Day 7-9: *eat papaya*

Day 10-12: *drink honey, lemon and water*
Day 13-15: *drink lemon and water*
- Eat mung beans and rice for a week.

COLDS & FLU

- During the flu season, first thing in the morning drink:
   2 oz. ginger juice
   1 oz. lemon juice
   1 oz. oil of choice (sesame or flaxseed oil for the heart or olive oil for the brain)
- Ginger strengthens the nervous system; it kicks out all the poison from the body.
- To avoid colds, coughs and flu:
   Cut ginger into a few pieces and add olive oil; cook well.
   Add 1 cup of plain yogurt and eat first thing in the morning.
   Optional: add 5 nuts of any kind (cashews, walnuts, pistachios, or almonds with skin on).
- For colds and cough combine:
   2 parts ginger
   1 part black pepper
   5 parts basil leaves
   1/2 clove garlic
   Boil in milk and sweeten.
   Drink it before you retire for the day.
- Whooping cough: add garlic juice to a glass of warm milk, sweeten and drink.
- Garlic is an excellent cold medication, because it helps with decongestion. It also strengthens the immune system.

Most colds and flu come from an energy imbalance that starts in the digestive tract. (*See Digestion*)

🍃 Exercise: When You First Feel the Signs of a Cold

This exercise will help you get rid of colds in their early stages before they set in.

Position:
Sit erect and relaxed with feet squarely on the floor but touching each other. Your hands must also be touching at the fingers. Hold them in front of the body at the chest level, thumb touching thumb and each finger touching the tip of its corresponding finger on the other hand.

Breath:
Now close your eyes and take a deep breath. Exhale slowly and when the air is all out of your lungs, hold it out for the count of five. Then breathe easily and slowly for about five or six breaths until you are once again relaxed. Then repeat, holding the breath out for the count of five. Repeat the entire procedure seven times, then stop, breathe normally and put the entire procedure out of your mind.

COLON/BOWELS

- Wheat bran cereal and cabbage are a good prevention for colon cancer.
- Rice bran is a great natural laxative. It is even better than wheat bran. Aloe vera juice is also good.

COLITIS

Colitis is associated with stress and emotions, especially fear and anxiety. The physical causes may be certain antibiotics, *E. Coli*, or food allergies. Other contributing factors include prolonged constipation, a diet high in sugar and white flour, and drinking too much liquid while eating food, which overly dilutes the digestive enzymes. An overgrowth of yeast in the intestines can cause irritation of the intestinal lining as well. Chronic and recurrent cases may be the cause or a contributing factor in several diseases such as arthritis, all autoimmune disorders, chronic fatigue syndrome and endometriosis as the toxic contents of the intestines are allowed to exit into the blood stream.

If you suffer from colitis it is important to be under the care of a physician. However, becoming educated about the illness, understanding the contributions of natural medicine and diet, as well as meditation and yoga will make a significant difference in one's ability to overcome difficult cases.

- A wholistic approach to colitis involves keeping the diet extremely bland and free of roughage and avoiding raw and cooked vegetables. Rather, one may receive the important nutrients that vegetables provide by juicing carrot, beet and spinach or by making a broth and only drinking the liquid.
- You can eat white rice, but stay away from fried foods.
- For many people, it is important to totally avoid dairy products.
- A diet high in protein and essential fatty acids will aid the reconstruction of the damaged tissues in the intestines.
- Fluid and electrolyte replacement is of the utmost importance when there has been frequent diarrhea. Drink water, juice or broth in minute sips, taking care to mix the liquid with the digestive juices in your saliva.
- Avoid taking pills as they are difficult for the fragile digestive system to break down. Liquid forms are easier on the system.
- When in an acute flair up, specific herbal treatment is highly individual, as each person is able to tolerate something different. It is important to work with a knowledgeable herbalist, Chinese Medical practitioner, Homeopath or Naturopath.
- Taking a food allergy blood test may be very helpful in determining the precise foods that you are sensitive to.

During this time as well as before and after the flare up, meditation, breathing and spiritual work are extremely important, as it reaches the core causes, increases your intuition for medical care and has no chance of side effects. Other important healing factors are Harmonyum (see *Chapter 16*) and Sun Healing (see *The Healing Fire of Heaven*). Remember that the intestines are ruled by the Moon energy. Learn all there is to know about the physical and spiritual characteristics of the Moon to help you to pinpoint areas for self-growth, as well as beneficial stones, colors and mantras for healing. *(For further information on the Moon, read the planetary sections in Joseph Michael Levry's other books.)*

CONGESTION

Hot red pepper, like cayenne, has been known to help clear congestion because it contains capsalcin, which is similar to what one finds in cough syrups.

CONSTIPATION

In a healthy individual, a bowel movement once, if not twice, per day is preferable. Constipation leads to a build up of toxins in the system. These toxins contribute to a whole host of ailments including acne, eczema, allergies, headaches, gas, poor digestion, joint pain, gynecological problems and even intestinal cancers. Constipation can also aggravate menstrual cramps. There are several causes of constipation. If you suffer from constipation, consider the following factors and address those that apply. In extreme cases, the sufferer may need to consult with a medical doctor and an herbalist.

Before we continue, it is important to note that the autonomic nervous system plays a key role in the movement of the intestines. This means that bowel movements are closely related to one's feelings, sense of well-being and stress level. Meditation and chanting is very helpful as it helps you connect old patterns to your current health habits, thus allowing you to resolve them quickly. The following are the various causes and treatments for constipation.

1. A LACK OF DIETARY FIBER

Fiber helps to move the bowels. If you suffer from constipation, your diet may be lacking in a sufficient amount of fiber. The following foods are rich in fiber and can, therefore, help to alleviate the problem of constipation. Wheat bran, rice bran, and oat bran, along with cabbage, work as natural laxatives. Wheat bran and cabbage also help prevent colon cancer. However if you are sensitive to wheat, you should choose another option. Dried prunes and prune juice are very also very helpful.

FLAX SEED/MEAL   Flax seed or meal is an excellent source of fiber. Begin by ingesting 1 tablespoon. A maximum of 4 tablespoons can be used to induce bowel movement. Flax seed/meal can be taken on its own, or added to oatmeal, juice, water, yogurt, smoothies or applesauce. It has the additional benefit of providing essential fatty acids. It is best stored in the refrigerator.

2. INTESTINAL BUILD-UP
A build up of rich foods in the intestines creates a sticky environment that is not conducive to easy bowel movements.
- Avoid sticky, rich foods such as peanut butter, ice cream, cakes, over indulgence of meat, fried food and breads.
- Use digestive herbs and teas such as ginger, unsweetened chai and peppermint, as they help to facilitate proper digestion and elimination.
- Chew on some fennel seeds after a meal.
- Take chewable digestive enzymes.

3. INTESTINAL WEAKNESS AND TENSION
Weakness in the intestines can cause difficulty in pushing out the fecal matter. Tension in the abdomen and intestines can also prevent the stool from passing.
- On a daily basis, massage the intestines in a clockwise circle for 3 minutes to promote peristalsis.
- Practice the *Daily Exercises* and the *Five Tibetans* described in the next chapter.
- Apply a hot water bottle to the abdomen and lower back.
- In cases of tension, herbs such as aloe vera in pill form are very helpful. However, aloe vera should not be consumed by people with weakness, convalescence and debility.

5. INTESTINAL DRYNESS
- Aloe vera gel or juice nourishes and moistens the membranes of the intestines. Dilute with water to drink or take in pill form.
- Castor oil packs applied externally on the abdomen for 30 minutes with a hot water bottle on top is very helpful.
- Increase intake of good oils such as fish oil and flax oil.
- Eat homemade tapioca pudding, made with extra tapioca. This is particularly helpful after childbirth
- Drink a glass of warm prune juice. This will provide your intestines with both moisture and fiber.
- Increase your water intake.
- Eat a handful of unroasted nuts. Always store nuts in the refrigerator to maintain freshness.

DIABETES
- Drink milk with turmeric and honey for 40 days, or take turmeric with parsley.
- Take lemon juice with lukewarm water.

Exercise for Diabetes

Position:
Sit in easy pose. Inhale completely. Exhale completely, and hold the air out as you pump the navel in and up, then out, again and again. Continue on the held exhale for 15-60 seconds. When you need to take a breath, inhale, exhale and begin pumping again on the held exhale. Continue this technique for 1-3 minutes.

Comments:
This technique takes sugar out of the bloodstream. It is not recommended for hypoglycemics. Other techniques that help this condition are Beak Breath (the mouth is pursed in a tight "o" like a beak and the breath inhaled either in one long stroke or in short sips) for 31 minutes and foot massage at the pancreas point.

Bow Pose

Contraindications: People who suffer from a weak heart, high blood pressure, hernia, colitis, and peptic or duodenal ulcers should not attempt Bow Pose. This posture should not be practiced before sleep at night as it stimulates the adrenal glands and the sympathetic nervous system. Also, wait at least three hours <u>after</u> a meal before doing this pose.

This posture works on the navel, heart and throat centers. The entire alimentary canal is reconditioned by this posture. The liver, abdominal organs and muscles are massaged. The pancreas and adrenal glands are toned, balancing their secretions. The kidneys are massaged and excess weight is reduced around the abdominal area. This leads to improved functioning of the reproductive organs. It helps remove gastrointestinal disorders, dyspepsia, chronic constipation and sluggishness of the liver. This posture is recommended in yoga therapy for the management of diabetes, incontinence, colitis, menstrual disorders, and under special guidance, cervical spondylitis. It enhances blood circulation generally. The spinal column is realigned and the ligaments, muscles and nerves are given a good stretch, removing stiffness. It helps correct hunching of the thoracic area of the spine. This posture is also useful for relieving various chest ailments, including asthma, and for freeing nervous energy, generally improving respiration. (This posture can be added to the Kundalini yoga set in the next chapter before Triangle pose, page 241, to stimulate the sexual, navel and heart centers.)

Position:

Lie flat on the stomach with the legs and feet together, and the arms and hands beside the body. Bend the knees and bring the heels close to the buttocks, clasp the hands around the ankles. Place the chin on the floor. This is the starting position. Tense the leg muscles and push the feet away from the body. Arch the back, lifting the thighs, chest and head together. Keep the arms straight.

Final position: The head is tilted back, and the abdomen supports the entire body on the floor. The only muscular contraction is in the legs; the arms and back remain relaxed. Hold the final position as long as is comfortable and then, slowly relaxing the leg muscles, lower the legs, chest and head to the starting position.

Breath:
Inhale deeply in the starting position. Option 1: Hold the breath while raising the body. Retain the breath inside in the final position, then exhale as you slowly return to the starting position. Repeat 1 to 3 times. Option 2: Practice slow, deep breathing so that the body rocks gently in unison with the breath for 1 to 3 minutes. At the end inhale, exhale as you slowly return to the starting position.

Bow pose is ideally practiced after cobra pose and should be followed by a forward bending posture, such as baby pose for 1 to 3 minutes.

DIGESTION & NAUSEA

Regarding the digestive system:
The importance of enzymes in the proper functioning of the digestive system is vital. Enzymes may be the best-kept secret in maintaining health and fighting disease. Our body contains more than 3,000 kinds of enzymes performing different jobs. Without them, there is no breathing, digestion, growth, blood coagulation and reproduction.

Our digestive enzymes help break down the food we eat into its smallest components, so that the body can more easily absorb the nutrients. The majority of this work is completed in the stomach and subsequently in the small intestine, including amino acids, mono- and disaccharides, and esters.
- Pineapple and especially papaya, because of the enzyme papain, have been used for numerous years to aid digestion.
- Always take lemon juice and lukewarm water on an empty stomach.

- For colic pain, combine and drink:
  juice of 1/2 lemon
  glass of lukewarm water
- For nausea chew a clove of garlic and swallow the paste. This is helpful for all types of nausea, including pregnancy.
- Eat rice cooked with lots of turmeric.
- Eat homemade yogurt mixed with black pepper.
- Drink mint tea.

Moistening grains
Barley liquid is good for childhood digestive weakness. Non-pearled barley moistens the intestines, which helps childhood lactose intolerance. Boil and mix with soup to help digestion. It also helps to stop lactation. Chinese pearl barley, which is a larger grain than western varieties, has many medicinal properties. It is a diuretic for edema and water retention. It helps to resolve pus, vaginal discharge, acne, and swelling from arthritic pain. Pearl barley increases natural killer-cell levels and is useful against HIV, hepatitis and many other viruses. Oats harmonize the digestive system and because of their high-protein content, helps the body use insulin more effectively. Oat and grits regulate wasting disorders and are high in fiber. Oats generally have a calming effect. The fiber of oats binds with cholesterol, helping the body to excrete it in the stool. For best results, do not use instant oatmeal but rather "old fashioned" style, steel-cut rolled or whole oats.

Meditation for the Digestive System: Vatsar Dhouti Kriya

This kriya should only be done on an empty stomach. Don't do it more than twice a day. It should also be the last of your daily morning or evening practice.

Position:
Sit in easy pose, hands on knees. Apply neck lock. Make a beak with the lips and drink in air through the mouth. Hold the air in as long as possible

as you churn your stomach round and round. When you must exhale, do so through the mouth without pressure.

Do the exercise a total of three times at one sitting. Then drink two quarts of water and avoid hot, spicy foods for the rest of the day.

Comments:
This kriya eliminates all digestive problems including chronic excess acidity. Since many other diseases, such as colds and flu, start with the problem of digestion and elimination, this kriya works toward general health as well. Get in the habit of walking a mile or so to keep your body strong and healthy, so as to massage the organs of digestion and elimination. During the evening, take a walk after your meal. This will stimulate your digestive system, so that when you sleep, your body can be totally at rest.

DISINFECTANT
Dry lemon juice and turn it into a powder. Sprinkle in the kitchen, on books and clothes racks. All insects will disappear.

DRUG DAMAGE
Drink ginger tea often. (*See Nervous System*)

EAR PROBLEMS
- Pour a few drops of garlic juice inside affected ear or ears.
- Pour 3 drops of onion juice in the ear.

EMOTIONAL PROBLEMS
- For depression, drink a glass of cold water and splash the face with cold water five times.
- To stop a crying baby, feed him/her diluted apple juice.
- To make the mind healthy or heal any types of psychosis, do brisk walking for 11 minutes per day and dance.

Exercise for Depression

Position:
Sit with a straight spine in easy pose. Arms are extended straight out in front of you, parallel to the floor. Close your right hand into a fist. Wrap your left fingers around it. The bases of the palms touch. The thumbs are close together and are pulled straight up. The eyes are focused on the thumbs.

Breath:
Now inhale for 5 seconds (do not hold the breath in); exhale for 5 seconds; hold the breath out for 15 seconds. Continue with this breath pattern.

Start with 3-5 minutes and work up to 11 minutes. Build up the time slowly. In time, you can work up to holding the breath out for one full minute. However, take care not to hold the breath out so long as to make yourself dizzy or nauseous.

Comments:
This meditation is an antidote to depression. You will find that, properly done, it totally recharges you. It will give you the capacity to deal well with life.

🌿 Exercise for Mental Harmony and To Balance the Tattvas: Kirtan Kriya

Our five fingers correspond to the five tattvas (elements) of which everything in this universe is made. Prana is the expression of the five elements in harmonious action. This simple exercise balances the five elements, thereby bringing the mind, body, emotions, and spirit into harmony.

Position:
Sit in easy pose, spine straight, elbows straight, wrists resting on your knees. You will be pressing your thumb to alternating fingers with each sound. Keep your eyes closed.

Mantra:
Chant in an even rhythm for 11 minutes: **Sa–Ta–Na–Ma**

a. *Sa*: Press the thumb to the index finger. (Jupiter/Water element/*Existence*)

b. *Ta*: Press the thumb to the middle finger. (Saturn/Fire element/*Life*)

c. *Na*: Press the thumb to the ring finger. (Sun/Air element/*Death*)

d. *Ma*: Press the thumb to the baby finger. (Mercury/Ether element/*Rebirth*)

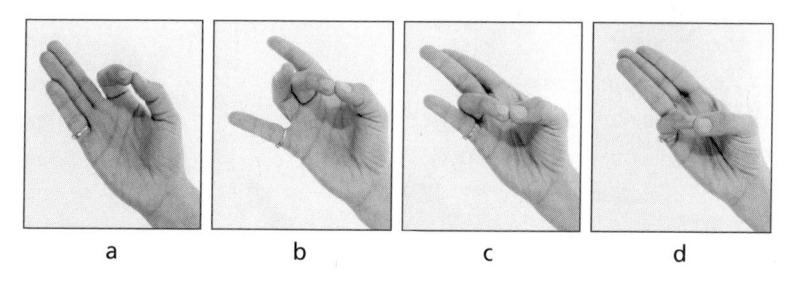

a b c d

End:
Inhale deeply, then shake the hands vigorously above the head. Finally, exhale, relax the arms onto your lap and sit calmly to absorb the benefits of this meditation.

Exercise for Insanity and To Still a Restless Mind

Position:
Sit in easy pose with a straight spine. Relax the arms and hands in any meditative posture. Focus on the tip of the nose. Open the mouth as wide as possible. Touch the tongue to the upper palate. Breathe normally through the nose. Start with 3-5 minutes of practice, building with time to 11 and then 31 minutes if desired.

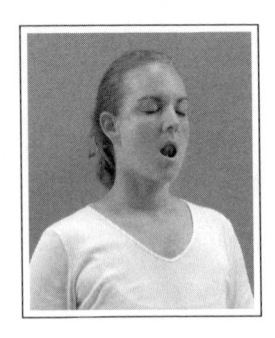

Comments:
This meditation gives immediate relief to any wavering, spaced-out mind. If psychiatric help is not available, try this meditation. Practicing this kriya allows one to still the most restless mind.

ENERGY
- Drink lemon juice with honey and water.
- To center your energy, combine and drink:
  1 banana
  2 teaspoons of raisins
  plain yogurt
  water or apple juice
- Increase energy by eating sweet potatoes. Ginger also increases energy.

EYES
- To maintain healthy eyes, ears and throat: in the morning, after showering, run cold water on the frontal lobe for 60 seconds.
- Whenever you have eye trouble—wash them with cold salted or saline water.
- Walk barefooted on cold grass in the morning. It will improve eyesight, increase vitality and prevent hair from turning gray.
- For eyes, ears and nose, eat water chestnuts.
- Carrots, spinach, and kale are excellent sources of beta carotene, which help the eye function well.

Exercise for Healthy Eyes

Position:
Sit in a comfortable and relaxed position, with eyes closed. Place the ball of the forefinger of each hand on the closed lid of the corresponding eye so that it rests directly over the pupil. Hold this position while you take deep breaths, retaining each as long as possible before exhaling.

While holding the breath, visualize your head and shoulders surrounded by a brilliant white cloud of energy.

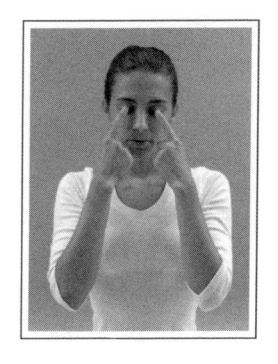

As you exhale, feel this energy run down your arms and out the tips of your index fingers into your eyes. Be careful not to press upon your eyes. Just touch your finger tips lightly to the closed lids so that the eyeball has free movement at all times.

Comments:
Practice this simple exercise for a minimum of 3 minutes once per day. You will channel healing prana to your eyes, and through them to the nervous system, causing you to benefit spiritually and physically. It will heal and improve your eyesight, and with months of practice, help you to get rid of glasses. In time, your eyes muscles will be strengthened, and the sensitivity of the optic nerves will be increased.

Exercise To Improve Eyesight

Sit in easy pose, head and neck straight. Place palms together in prayer pose, fingers pointing up, forearms at chest level and parallel to the floor. Without bending your neck, look with both eyes at your thumbs. Do long, deep breathing for 6-11 minutes.

Comments: Regular practice of this kriya improves eyesight and helps prevent eye trouble.

FIBROSIS
Drink pear juice and black pepper.

GENERAL HEALTH
- Healthy drink: *ginger juice, cardamom powder, grapefruit juice.*
- Build the whole body with cucumber juice.
- If you use the computer for long hours, drink pear juice, pineapple juice and black pepper daily. It will renew your electromagnetic field.
- To rebuild the body of a very sick person, they must eat a cup of yogurt with saffron 3 times a day and rice cooked with garlic and milk once a day.

HAIR
- Proper hair care can aid you in a variety of ways. In order to wash and dry your hair properly, devote 2-3 hours to the process. Directly after washing, wrap a towel around your head and let your hair remain wet for a while. This will prevent skull and hair problems from occurring. When it is time to dry your hair, dry it in the sun. This will provide your system with vitamins. Finally, before you go to sleep at night, comb your hair downward. This will give you a good, sound sleep.
- Baldness and graying hair: This condition is usually part of the aging process. It is very difficult to do something about baldness coming from hereditary causes. Baldness and graying can be caused by anxiety, insomnia, worries, stress, excessive sexual activity or emotional trauma. They can also be the result of too much smoking or drug abuse. Eating almonds and taking herbs such as gotu kola can help. Walk barefoot on cold grass in the morning. It will prevent your hair from turning gray, as well as improve your eyesight and increase vitality.
- Gotu kola helps stimulate hair growth.
- Rosemary is a well-known herbal remedy for healthy hair growth. You can mix with almond oil and massage it into scalp to stimulate hair growth by increasing circulation.

- Make sure that you eat a healthy diet with plenty of fresh vegetables and fruits, limiting animal fats. Too much fat and sugar in the diet can be responsible for greasy hair. Take a good multivitamin and mineral supplement so that you may get a sufficient supply of the vitamins necessary for hair growth.
- Avoid over exposure to the sun, blow drying and harsh hair care treatment and products in order to limit damage to your hair. Shampoo more often if hair is oily. Give yourself a regular scalp massage using herbs in an oil base.
- Drink a few cups daily of herbal tea that contains such ingredients as rosemary, nettle, and horsetail.

HANGOVER

Add a little salt and cumin seed to lemon juice and drink. The hangover will stop; lemon is an anti-alcohol agent.

HEADACHES

- Eat rice cooked with lots of turmeric.
- Ginkgo improves circulation to the brain.
- Eat homemade yogurt cooked with black pepper.
- Ginger has the capacity to reduce pain. Also, sliced onion, boiled on a medium heat for 20 minutes, and taken as a tea helps headaches.
- For hay fever: By eating yogurt before the pollen season, one can build up their immune system.

Exercise for Headaches

Lie down on your back, arms by your sides, palms down. Raise your head off the floor and do long, deep breathing. Continue for 1-3 minutes.

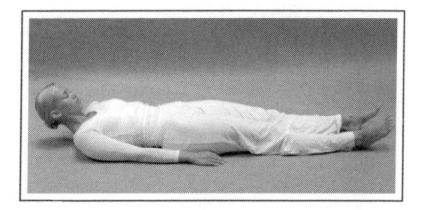

Exercise for Migraines

Sit in easy pose. The hands are in gyan mudra, with the thumbtips touching index fingertips. Extend the arms straight at a 70° angle out and up from the sides. With closed eyes, look to your hairline. Hold the posture with normal breathing for at least 11 minutes.

Then relax the hands down onto the knees and chant, in a monotone, *"We are the love"* for 1-2 minutes.

Comments:
This meditation is good for headaches, especially migraines. Pain in the back and behind the shoulders while doing this is a sign of weak blood circulation.

HEMORRHOIDS
Add calcium to your diet.

HERPES
- Chickweed herb or tea.
- Tea tree oil and vitamin E.
- Odorless Kyolic garlic (aged garlic extract) *The suggested recommended dosage is 4 capsules AM and PM, with each meal.*
- L-lysine/Acyclovir

INFERTILITY FOR MEN/WOMEN
Add garlic juice to a glass of warm milk and drink at night before retiring. It will strengthen the nerves in the ovaries and reproductive system.

INSECT BITES
Rub lemon juice on the spot for 10 to 15 minutes.

INSOMNIA

- Make a juice out of lettuce and drink. It is not only a powerful relaxant but it will put you right to sleep.
- Make lettuce soup with milk to aid with sleeping problems, since lettuce contains .01% opium.
- Reduce the salt content of the body; it will induce sleep quickly.
- Valerian helps sleeping. Also, by boiling cabbage and drinking a tea out of the juice, one can prevent insomnia.
- Drink juice of lettuce and cabbage boiled for 5 minutes or juiced. If you boil it, chop finely.

IMMUNE SYSTEM

To increase the immune system and stimulate the metabolism, take a brisk 15-minute walk in the morning.

REISHI has been popular for 2,000 years in the far East. It was rated number one on ancient Chinese lists of superior medicines, and was believed to give eternal youth and longevity. It is used to treat a variety of disorders and to promote vitality. Reishi is used to control high blood pressure and heart disease, to control and lower cholesterol, to build resistance to diseases, and to treat fatigue and viral infections. It also known to have anti-tumor properties valuable in treating cancer.

ASTRAGALUS acts as a tonic to protect the immune system. It aids adrenal gland function and digestion. Increases metabolism, produces spontaneous sweating, promotes healing and provides energy to combat fatigue. It increases stamina. Good for colds, flu, and immune-deficiency–related problems, including AIDS, cancer, and tumors. Effective for chronic lung weakness.

KIDNEYS

- Drink a mixture of ginger and lemon juice in warm water in the morning and at night.
- Ten drops of gin in water takes care of the kidneys.

- To stop kidney stones, drink pear juice and black pepper.
- Parsley juice is excellent for kidneys.
- Cranberry juice is also good for kidneys.

Exercise for the Kidneys, Liver and Adrenals: Cobra Pose

Cobra pose keeps the spine supple and healthy. Arching the spine improves circulation in the back region and tones the nerves, resulting in better communication between the brain and body. This posture has a strong effect on all organs related to the sex, navel, heart, and throat chakras. It harmonizes the appetite, alleviates constipation and is beneficial for all the abdominal organs, especialy the liver and kidneys. The adrenal glands, situated on top of the kidneys, are massaged and stimulated to work more efficiently. This posture also tones the ovaries and uterus and helps alleviate menstrual and other gynecological disorders. People with peptic ulcers, hernias or hyperthyroidism must be very careful and may need expert guidance.

Position:
Lying on your stomach, bring your hands in line with the shoulders. On the inhale, enlongate through the feet and pelvis, press from your hands and sequentially rise up and forward from the head, shoulders, then ribs. Reach skyward to create a long, even arch with the heart reaching up and out of the lower back. Continue with long deep breathing for 1-3 minutes. To end, inhale deeply, then exhale as you very slowly come down vertebra by vertebra. Push back into baby pose *(see page 203)* to reverse the spinal stretch.

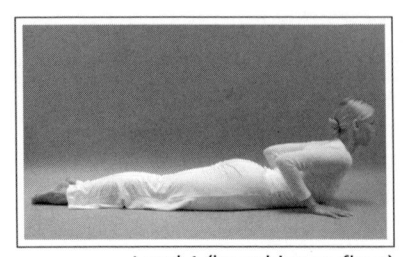

Level 1 (keep hips on floor)   Level 2

LABOR
- Start drinking turmeric in hot milk for an easy and smooth delivery and a healthy body.
- Reduce the intake of common salt as the due date approaches. A low salt content promotes smoother muscle contractions.

LIVER
- Cleanse the liver with daikon radish.
- Drink warm water with lemon.
- Do the Sitali Pranayam breathing exercise *(page 139)*.

Exercise To Cleanse the Liver

Position:
Sit in easy pose, the right arm behind your back, left arm up at 60°, fingers stretched straight up, elbow straight. Maintain the posture as you swing left and right.

Continue for 1-3 minutes.

Contraindications: Do not perform this exercise in cases of severe liver disorders.

(See also Women's Health: Menopause and Chapter 13: Healing Heart Disease)

LUNGS

- The betacarotene in carrots, oranges, and dark green vegetables such as spinach, is an antidote to lung cancer.
- If you use the computer, do not type with the finger tips. To avoid lung problems and tuberculosis, type with the finger pads. The tips act as an antenna. The five areas of the brain are electromagnetically controlled by the fingers. The thumb controls the id, the ego, and corresponds to the central part of the brain.

MEMORY

- Oysters have been known to improve mental function. They are a good source of zinc.
- Gotu kola is also excellent. (*See also Brain*)

MENOPAUSE

See Women's Health

NOSEBLEEDS

- Drink acidophilus.
- Mix 1 part eucalyptus oil to 9 parts of almond oil. Drop in nose. Bend head back 90 degrees and shout out.
- Take 5 drops of sandalwood oil, 15 drops of honey and a little ginger juice and drop into the nose.

MUSCULO-SKELETAL

- For injury and swelling, massage area with garlic oil.
- Aches in the joints come from deposits of extra acid. To treat and prevent, take lemon juice with lukewarm water.

NERVOUS SYSTEM

- Lemons contain magnesium, which will take care of your nervous and circulatory system.
- Your nervous system will benefit greatly from drinking a juice of cucumber, celery and parsley.

Exercise To Repair Nerves Due to Drug Damage

Position:

Get onto your hands and knees. Begin flexing the spine up and down, inhale as the spine goes down and exhale as it goes up (Cat-Cow pose). The neck is arched back on the inhale. Continue for 3 minutes.

Comments:

To repair nerve damage due to misuse of drugs, do this exercise once a day for 40 days.

Also, drink Golden Milk daily during this time. To make Golden Milk, boil 1/8 teaspoon turmeric in 1/4 cup water for about 8 minutes, until it forms a thick paste. If too much water boils away, add a little more. Meanwhile, bring 8 ounces of milk to a boil with 2 tablespoons of raw almond oil. As soon as it boils, remove from the heat. Combine the two mixtures and add honey to taste.

Exercise To Repair the Sympathetic Nervous System

Sit in easy pose with a straight spine. Touch the tip of the ring finger of each hand to the corresponding thumb (ravi mudra). Extend both arms parallel to the floor with the palms down. Spread the fingers wide. Put the sides of the tips of the index fingers together. Raise the arms slightly so the index fingernails are at the level of the eyes. Keep the eyes relaxedly open. Look over the index fingertips at the horizon. Just hold this position completely still.

Continue for up to 11 minutes, but no longer.

Comments:
Otherwise known as the *Meditation for Human Quality,* this kriya balances and repairs the sympathetic nervous system. It also helps the heart, and gives resistance to tension and high pressure environments. Its greatest result is to connect you with the inner sense of being human by enhancing the qualities of endurance, creativity and compassion.

PANCREAS

You can fight pancreatic cancer and keep your pancreas in good working order by eating tomatoes and watermelon. They both have lycopene.

PNEUMONIA

Add 4 drops of garlic juice in lukewarm water and drink. Also massage the rib cage with garlic oil.

POISON

To remove poison from the body, take parsley and turmeric at 8 AM and 4 PM.

PROSTATE

To maintain prostate health, take saw palmetto berry and pygeum. Men who fear prostate cancer are advised to consume more tomato-based products. *(See Frog Pose, page 195)*

PYORRHEA (INFLAMMATION OF GUMS)

- Wash mouth AM and PM with golden seal and warm water.
- Also, use a cotton swab to rub lemon juice on gums without touching teeth. They will become strong again.
- Brush teeth with salt powder and alum, and fill cavities with garlic or a garlic oil-soaked cotton ball to kill bacteria.

SCIATICA

Anything that harms or weakens the nervous system, such as anxiety, stress and fear, can cause or exacerbate sciatica. In addition, injury to the disks in the lower back can contribute to sciatica. Indeed, the sciatic nerve originates in the lower back. Therefore, treatment must address the lower back region. Other physical causes may include constipation *(see page 199)*, gynecological disorders such as uterine fibroids, prostate disease, kidney and bladder disease, and insomnia.

In general, those who suffer from sciatica need to avoid sitting or standing in one position for extended periods of time, and should increase their level of flexibility. It is important to stretch the front and back of the legs, as well as the Iliopsoas muscles, the waist, hips and back. Acupuncture, "Non Force Directional" Chiropractics (NFDT) and very gentle foot reflexology can be very helpful in treating sciatic pain. In almost all cases, increasing the level of physical activity through yoga, walking, and, as previously stated, stretching will help alleviate the symptoms of sciatica.

Treatment should also emphasize deep relaxation. Relaxing and increasing the strength of the parasympathetic nervous system will prevent the nerve from inflaming and getting pinched. Meditation is crucial here. Before chanting, find a comfortable sitting position. Also, avoid long-term arm postures that require raising the arms above the head. You may need to shift positions a few times during your meditative routine. Just do the best you can. Stick with it, even if you eventually have to stand up and walk while chanting.

Sciatica sufferers who are not very flexible, have injuries, osteoporosis or disk involvement should seek qualified guidance to develop a beneficial routine. To avoid additional injury, consult with your doctor before beginning a stretching, yoga or exercise regimen. The following are exercise recommendations for those in relatively good shape and health:

- Walk for at least thirty minutes each day.
- Swim in a warm pool, but not during cold weather.
- Sit in a hot spa after exercise or during severe flair ups. This will relax your muscles and skeletal structure.
- Avoid over exposure to the cold, as this can aggravate the condition.
- Sufferers who have not been injured and are not pregnant will benefit from the *Daily Exercises* and *Five Tibetans* in the back of this book, as well as *Frog Pose (page 195)* and the exercise in the section on Diabetes, *page 201*. Approach all of these exercises with gentleness and common sense. Begin with a few repetitions. Do not over do it or push through pain.

In addition to a regular routine of exercise and stretching, adopt some or all of the following practices and natural remedies:

- Foot Bath *(see page 73)*
- Apply ice and hot water bottles to the affected area alternating between the ice and the heat. Electrical heating pads need to be avoided.
- Get a good night's sleep *(see section on Insomnia, page 213)*. To facilitate a good night's sleep, do Left Nostril Breath by plugging the right nostril with your index finger and inhaling and exhaling through the left. Left Nostril Breath should be done before retiring at night or while you are in bed. Continue until you feel like falling asleep. Also, as you work on your stress levels through chanting your sleep will improve.

- Harmonyum treatments are extremely effective for sciatic pain, as well as stress and insomnia. If lying on your abdomen is painful, you may want to try lying on your side with several pillows under your head and between your knees.
- Turmeric, taken in pill, powder or tea form, is an excellent anti-inflammatory. This makes it beneficial for both sciatic and arthritic conditions. Take 1/4 teaspoon in water and milk two times per day for 3 days, then decrease the dose to 1/8 teaspoon two times per day for an additional 3 days. Avoid taking turmeric with blood thinners, during menstruation or pregnancy, and if you suffer from ulcers, menorrhagia or other bleeding disorders.
- Ginger tea is also an excellent anti-inflammatory, and is safe for the conditions that preclude turmeric usage. Boil 3, 1/8 inch slices in 3 cups water for 10 minutes. Drink 1 cup two times per day. Add milk if the taste is too strong.

SKIN
- Rub a small amount of garlic juice over the acne and pimples. It will not only cure them, it will heal up the skin spot.
- Massage the face with lemon juice and glycerin water.
- Apply 1/2 spoon of vinegar and 1/2 spoon of honey to affected area. Wash off after one hour.
- Apply lemon juice to the itching area; it will vanish.
- Take chickweed as an herb or tea.
- Tea tree oil and vitamin E.
- Odorless Kyolic garlic (aged garlic extract) *The suggested recommended dosage is 4 capsules AM and PM, with each meal.*

SMOKING
By regularly eating oatmeal and oat bran, one can help cut down on nicotine cravings.

STOMACH
Add bananas and ginger to your diet. Ginger works on the spinal nerves and fights nausea. Bananas are good for indigestion problems. Aloe vera juice is also good for the stomach.

STROKES

Green tea has been known to protect against the build-up of arterial plaque, which can lead to strokes.

SPLEEN

To heal spleen trouble: Add the juice of a lemon to lukewarm water and drink AM and PM.

THROAT

- Add garlic juice to vinegar with water. Gargle and drink.
- Put 3 garlic cloves in vinegar for at least one hour and chew. The trouble will be healed.

A Healthy Throat Chakra

When our throat chakra works properly, it redirects some of the healing, constructive and vitalizing forces of the human body to other chakras, so this creative power can manifest in building up harmony and strength of the body. A healthy and properly active throat chakra can help awaken all the other chakras that may be dormant. This will strengthen the psychic body. Also, a well-functioning throat chakra causes the thyroid and parathyroid glands to improve in their functioning, thereby resulting in improved physical health and a larger and stronger aura. A healthy throat chakra gives a strong heart and youth to the body. It protects the body from foreign bacteria. It rejuvenates the body, thereby delaying the aging process. The thyroid controls the rate at which your body can burn oxygen and this renews its cells. When the throat chakra works properly, it leads to a vitalizing cellular regeneration and a renewed enthusiasm for life.

Exercise To Heal the Throat Chakra and Strengthen the Aura

First bring your conscious attention to the throat area to help the thyroid in its work. Bring a sense of love and caring into the thyroid gland, urging it to perform its function for the welfare of the whole body. The throat chakra knows better than we do what needs to be done.

Position:
Sit in a comfortable meditative position (easy pose or sitting in a chair with feet apart). Remember to keep the spine straight and the neck lengthened.

Take three long, deep breaths.

Place the golden triangle, shown at right (thumb, index and middle fingertips touching), or the right index finger alone on the throat chakra where the Adam's apple is located. Take a deep breath and hold as long as comfortable, then remove your finger and exhale. You may feel a warming sensation in your throat or in the skin of the right finger.

Repeat three times. Feel the warmth of your throat radiate through your whole body.

Meditation: Seed Sound for the Throat Chakra—THO

Remain in a meditative position, either with the legs folded in easy pose, or sitting in a chair with the feet slightly separated and flat on the ground. Keep the spine straight. Raise the arms straight above the head, pressed against the ears, palms touching.

Turn your attention to the thyroid gland in the throat center. As you vibrate this mantra, visualize bright light radiating from your throat center. *(See Seed Sounds on the Healing Fire CD)*

Inhale, and on the exhale vibrate the following on one breath. Repeat 7 times.

THO... (pronounced zzzoh...)

ULCERS
- For ulcers take parsley and turmeric with warm water 15 minutes before eating. It purifies the blood.
- Cabbage juice is best in the prevention of ulcers. Anti-ulcer compounds have been found in cabbage juice and aloe vera juice.

WEIGHT
- To regulate your weight (if overweight or underweight) take either:
   2 Tablespoons of apple cider vinegar in warm water. Sweeten to taste with honey. Drink daily, preferably in the morning before eating.
   OR
   Take juice of half lemon and mix with a glass of fresh squeezed grapefruit juice. Drink three or more times a day.
- Combine: 5 zucchini, 4 celery sticks, fresh parsley, a few mint leaves and black pepper. Steam 15 minutes, puree in a blender and add cheese if desired.

WOMEN'S HEALTH
GENERAL HEALTH
- Eat 1 banana in the morning and 1 teaspoon of raisins at sunset. Bananas are a complete food with the exception of containing no vitamin C. It balances potassium and magnesium which promotes the absorption and retention of calcium, thereby taking care of the bones and preventing arthritis. Raisins, when taken in the evening, prevent low energy.
- A good diet is a necessity, supported by ample exercise and rest, a positive mental attitude, a spiritual discipline, fulfilling work, and a simple lifestyle.
- Okra is good for trouble with menstruation, breasts or cramps. It is also good for calcium and magnesium deficiency.

MENOPAUSE
The first thing a woman can do to ease the effects of menopause is get plenty of exercise.

Next, be sure to do 31 minutes of 1-minute breath daily. One-minute breath involves breathing in for 20 seconds, holding for 20 seconds and exhaling for 20 seconds. If you are unable to complete 31 minutes initially, begin with 3 minutes and build up.

An appropriate diet is crucial during menopause. Avoid overly spicy foods as well as overcooked and fried foods. Your stomach and digestive system do not work the way they once did. Respect this systemic change, otherwise the internal changes you are experiencing will be externalized. Beneficial foods include parsley, sweet potatoes, raisins, water chestnuts, and beets. For example, cooked beets with a little turmeric (for the joints) is excellent. Pears will help prevent the skin problems that can occur with hormonal changes. One raw onion a day can prevent cancer. And, one banana daily can help keep you young. Mangos are a great post-meal treat that also help to keep you young, and can, in the long run, prevent you from having a negative experience during menopause. One day each week, eat food without salt. Replace your salt intake with lemon to help replenish your reserves of vitamin C. Dong quai and red clover are very good for menopause.

Be kind to your kidneys now. Clear them by drinking 1 ounce of yogurt, blended with 6-8 ounces of water and, if you wish, a pinch of salt. In addition, drink celery juice.

If your body becomes overburdened with mucus, or if you have a leaky uterus or other fluid imbalances, drink sage tea.

PREMENSTRUAL SYNDROME

- For menstrual cramps, eat okra.
- For PMS, combine and blend:
  small handful of almonds
  2 oz ginger juice
  1 banana
  1 teaspoon raisins
  apple juice
- PMS sufferers should eat corn flakes, because it reduces fatigue, depression, and even anger.

Exercise for the Prevention and Alleviation of PMS

Position:
In a standing position with knees and heels together, feet flat on the floor and angled out to the sides for balance, raise your arms straight overhead, close to the ears, with palms forward (figure a). The thumbs can be locked together. Keeping the legs straight, bend back from the base of the spine 20°. The head, spine, and arms in an unbroken curve, the arms in line with the ears.

Hold the posture with long, deep breaths for two minutes.

From this position, very slowly bend over as far as possible, keeping the arms straight and close to the ears (figure b). Inhale, hold the breath in as long as possible and pump the navel point. Then exhale and do the same on the held exhale.

Continue this process for 2 minutes.

Comments:
These two exercises help prevent premenstrual syndrome, which is characterized by bodily discomfort, a feeling of insecurity, and very emotional behavior just before the onset of the menstrual period. These exercises are also helpful in preventing the onset of menopause.

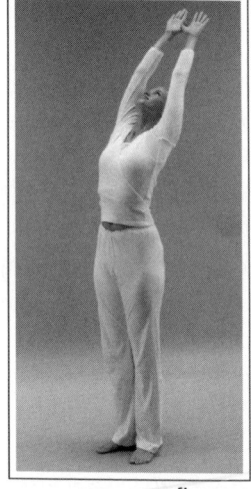

figure a

figure b

🍃 Camel Pose

Contraindications: <u>Do not</u> practice this posture if you have peptic or duodenal ulcers, abdominal hernia, severe back ailments or an enlarged thyroid.

This posture massages and stretches the colon and abdominal organs, and improves digestion. It tones the female organs and is especially recommended for women who have a tendency to miscarry. For this purpose, it is important to prepare the body well before conception. This exercise is used in yoga therapy for menstrual disorders, prolapse, asthma, and various bronchial and thyroid conditions. Stretching the stomach and intestines tonifies the digestive and reproductive systems and treats constipation. The front of the neck is fully stretched toning all organs and glands of the region, especially the thyroid.

Position:
Sitting on your heels, lean back and place your hands behind your feet. Squeeze the buttocks to support the lower back, press the hips forward, lift and open the chest, drop the head back without collapsing the cervical vertebrae. Walk your hands to your heels.

Time:
Breathe long and deep for 1–3 minutes.

To end:
VERY GENTLY come to a vertical spine starting with the head. Then relax in *Baby Pose*.

YEAST/FUNGAL INFECTIONS

Yeast proliferation in the body is an extremely common problem today. This is due to the fact that several factors of modern society create the conditions in which yeast thrives. *Candida albicans*, commonly known as yeast, lives in a healthy intestinal tract. Under normal conditions, good intestinal bacteria kill the yeast, thereby keeping its population low. Under abnormal conditions, the production of yeast is such that the good intestinal bacteria cannot keep up with it. An overabundance of yeast in the body is the result.

People with O blood types, diabetes and immune diseases are at greater risk of being affected by yeast overgrowth. Several factors, however, contribute to yeast proliferation. First, a diet high in sugar and yeast breads feeds the yeast, causing it to overgrow. Secondly, substances such as antibiotics and mercury in dental fillings can kill off the good bacteria in the body, leaving it susceptible to heightened levels of yeast. Thirdly, several medications and treatments predispose the intestines to yeast growth. These include oral contraceptives, corticosteroids and chemotherapy. Finally, an impaired immune system allows yeast to proliferate.

If left unchecked, yeast is able to send out long roots that burrow into the intestinal lining and allow contaminants and undigested food to exit the intestines and enter the blood stream. This can lead to a system-wide spread of yeast that may appear almost anywhere, especially the mouth, skin, ears, and underarms. Yeast may also travel from the anus to the genitals. A variety of symptoms are associated with yeast overgrowth such as itching, gas, bloating, constipation, diarrhea and skin rash. When an overabundance of yeast becomes a chronic problem and it has spread from the intestines to other areas of the body it may also lead to fevers, fatigue, acne, dandruff, arthritis, headaches, poor memory and concentration, sinus infections, food allergies, heartburn, depression and much more. Systemic yeast infection has been suspected as a key player in autoimmune diseases. It is common for women to be affected by vaginal yeast infections, however in chronic or recurrent cases, couples must be treated together to avoid cross and/or recurrent contamination. It is best to avoid sexual intercourse during the length of the infection.

Treatment of yeast overgrowth is a multi-layered process:
1. AVOID FOODS THAT FEED YEAST
Because yeast feeds on sugar, it will create sugar cravings. Those who have yeast overgrowth must strictly avoid any and all sugars, as well as food that process like sugar in the body. These foods include fruit, honey, bread, yeast-containing products, alcohol and fermented foods. Practice the *Exercise for Addiction, page 181*, as it is excellent for subduing difficult cravings.

2. ENCOURAGE RE-GROWTH OF THE GOOD BACTERIA
Supplementation of the good bacteria is critical for the prevention of yeast overgrowth when taking medications, as well as for treating a present infection. For best results, consult your doctor when taking pharmaceutical medications. You may also consult a homeopathic physician, a licensed herbalist or doctor of Chinese medicine. It is possible to obtain one product that contains many or all of the various strains of necessary bacteria. Eat plain yogurt as well. The acidophilus it contains is helpful in replenishing beneficial bacteria. In most cases, however, yogurt alone is insufficient to clear the infection.

In addition to eating yogurt, douches and enemas with a ratio of 2 tablespoons of plain yogurt to 3 cups purified water are very efficient methods for bringing the good bacteria to the precise location affected. Completely fill the enema or douche container with the liquid mixture. For acute infections repeat one to three times over the course of one week. For chronic infections repeat once per week for 5 weeks. Discontinue both enemas and douching when menstruating.

3. PROMOTE DETOXIFICATION OF THE INTESTINES & LIVER
Because the origin of yeast is the intestines, it is imperative that you avoid constipation *(see section on Constipation)* and choose food options that are sugar free.

Meditation to Get Disease Out, page 141 and *Daily Exercises/The Five Tibetans* in the next chapter are excellent for promoting detoxification. *Inner Sun: Immune System Booster, page 138* and *Meditation to Improve the Function of the Spleen and Liver: Sitali Pranayam, page 139* are possible recommendations, while the *Exercise to Cleanse the Blood, page 140* is helpful for chronic cases.

It is imperative that you clean your environment of molds and fungus that may live in the walls, floor and soil of your home and work environment. For plant-based mold and fungus problems consult the book *Natural Pest Control* by Andrew Lopez.

4. FORTIFY THE IMMUNE SYSTEM
- Getting plenty of rest and exercise will encourage detoxification and improve the immune system.
- Reishi mushroom (*Ganoderma Senensis*) 500 mg: twice daily is excellent for strengthening the immune system.
- Nettle and pau d'arco tea strengthens and cleanses.
- Fresh lemon water cleanses the liver.
- Dandelion leaf and root tea cleanses the liver. You may also eat or juice the fresh leaf.
- Sun healing (*see The Healing Fire of Heaven*)
- Harmonyum healing system (*see Chapter 16*)

5. KILL THE YEAST
- Caprylic acid 350 mg: 1-2 capsules, 2 times daily without food fights candida.
- Oil of oregano capsules kills candida. Follow the directions on the bottle.
- Garlic taken fresh or in pill form. See the section on garlic, *page 118*, for more information on the healing properties of garlic and its uses.
- Olive leaf is a traditional anti-fungal remedy. Follow the directions on the bottle.

NOTE: In difficult cases it is helpful to see a medical doctor, as well as a licensed herbalist for further guidance. While there are several other highly effective natural remedies, they are best taken under the supervision of an herbalist.

A FINAL NOTE ON BACTERIA, YEAST AND PARASITES

While treating these problems with physical medicine is absolutely necessary, it is also important that you strengthen your electromagnetic field. Those who suffer from chronic cases often become frustrated as infections return even after meticulous adherence to diet, herbs and medications. Remember that these are opportunistic living organisms that can only survive in the body when it is in a weakened state. The strength of the body is directly related to the level of energy in your aura or electromagnetic field, which is affected mostly by your thought patterns. These organisms cannot effectively thrive in an environment whose vibration is strong. Although there may be good physical reasons for these infections, those who have a strong aura will not be as affected with chronic and hard-to-treat infections as those whose energetic defenses are weakened. This book will help you accomplish both a strong mind and body!

SURGERY

PROGRAM FOR PRE-SURGERY

Before you undergo any surgical procedure, take care to fortify your body. Vitamins A and C, taken in combination with selenium and zinc, are recommended to help reduce both the risk and intensity of tissue damage due to surgery. Deep blue and red fruits, such as blueberries and raspberries, contain antioxidants that are also helpful in this process. Echinacea, Siberian ginseng, golden seal, gentian and astragalus will strengthen your immune system and ward off the infections that can occur during surgery.

It is equally important to relax the mind before any invasive procedure. Visualize a perfect outcome. The day of surgery, chant with the Rootlight CD *Triple Mantra* for a minimum of 11 minutes in the morning or a maximum of 31 minutes. If possible, right before surgery, whisper *Triple Mantra* eleven times for the light to create a protective, healing shield around you.

Finally, try to make your hospital room a pleasant environment. Soothing images, along with healing and classical music, such as the *Ra Ma Da Sa* CD, Bach, and Mozart, will calm the body and mind.

PROGRAM FOR POST-SURGERY

Liquids are essential. Ginger tea will prevent post-surgical nausea and promote circulation. Drinking this tea is especially beneficial after gynecological procedures. Along with ginger tea, take in plenty of broth and juices. Miso soup will help to replenish the intestinal flora that can be diminished by traditional medications. Intestinal flora helps with proper digestion and produces B vitamins that help our bodies cope with stress. If possible, take these natural remedies while in the hospital.

The body now needs to direct all of its energy into recovery. Eat lightly after surgery so as not to tax the system. Liquid and soft foods are recommended, as they are easier on the digestive system. Bromeliad, a protease found in pineapple, will also aid the body in regulating digestion and reducing inflammation.

Vitamin C promotes healing. Eat and drink plenty of it now. Apply aloe vera to scars.

After surgery, speed up the healing process by listening as often as you can to the *Ra Ma Da Sa* or *Lumen de Lumine* CDs. *Ra Ma Da Sa* is like a rare diamond that connects you with the pure healing energy of the universe. It purifies the aura and consolidates mental projection to focus towards your health.

WHAT TO AVOID

Avoid all herbs and medicines that move and/or thin the blood. Included in this category are ginkgo, red clover, alfalfa and aspirin. Such substances inhibit proper clotting function.

Pre- & Post-Surgery Vitamin Program

Vitamins		Minerals	
Vitamin A	20,000 IU	Boron	2-3 mg
(or drink a lot of carrot juice)		Bromeliad	200-400 mg
Beta carotene	15,000 IU	Calcium	800-1,200 mg
Vitamin C	4-6 grams	Chromium	200 mcg
Vitamin D	400 IU	Iodine	100-200 mcg
Vitamin E	200 IU	Iron	20 mcg
Vitamin K	300 mcg	Lactobacillus	2 billion microorganisms
Thiamine	50 mg		
Riboflavin	25-100 mg	L-amino acid	1,000 mg
Niacin	25 mg	L-arginine	
Pantothenic acid	1,000 mg	L-lysine	500-100mg
Pyridoxine	50 mg	Magnesium	500-800 mcg
Cobalamine	200 mcg	Manganese	10 mg
Biotin	300 mcg	Molybdenum	800 mcg
Inositol	1,000 mg	Potassium	2-3 grams
Bioflavonoids	500 mg	Selenium	200 mcg
		Sulfur	400-800 mg
		Vanadium	150-300 mcg
Reishi (great after surgery)		Zinc	60-100 mg
		Iron	

TRIPLE MANTRA	MEANING
Ad Guray Nameh	*Hail to the Primal Light*
Jugad Guray Nameh	*Hail to the Light throughout the ages*
Sat Guray Nameh	*Hail to the True Light*
Siri Guru Devay Nameh	*Hail to the Transparent Light*

Ad Such — *It was true in the beginning*
Jugad Such — *True through the ages*
Heh<u>bee</u> Such — *And true even now*
Nanaka O-See <u>Bee</u> Such — *Nanak shall ever be true*

Ad Such
Jugad Such
Heh<u>beh</u> Such
Nanaka O-See <u>Beh</u> Such

RA MA DA SA	MEANING
Ra	*Sun*
Ma	*Moon*
Da	*Receiver of Saa*
Sa	*Totality*
Sa	*Totality*
Say	*Spirit, energy*
So	*Manifestation*
Hung	*Experience of Thou*

LUMINE DE LUMINE	MEANING
Lumine de Lumine	*Light of Light*
Deum de Deo	*God of God*
Lumine de Lumine	*God by the way of Light*
Deum Verum de Deo Vero	*Light by the way of God*
Lumine de Lumine	*Light of Light*

CHAPTER NINETEEN

DAILY EXERCISE FOR OVERALL HEALTH

KUNDALINI YOGA

THESE YOGIC SETS are designed to help maintain the spinal column, as well as the muscles and joints in a healthy and supple state. They stimulate the glandular system and strengthen the nervous system, thereby bringing balance to many physiological abnormalities, such as hyperthyroid or hypothyroid, faulty insulin secretions, and other hormonal imbalances.

Make proper breathing and use of the breath of primary importance. Breathing supplies fresh oxygen to our system while strengthening the lungs. These exercises will allow you to release your creativity, while helping you develop self-confidence, self-awareness and self-control.

The condition and constitution of our body reflects our state of mind. It expresses our cares, joys, our past and present. Our attitude toward life is mapped out in our muscles, tissue, posture and level of flexibility. People hold on to their worries in frowns and stiff necks. They store their sorrows in aches and pains; their anger is constrained in clenched teeth. Disappointments are hidden in rounded shoulders; and mental confusion is mirrored by hypertension, digestive upset, headache and insomnia. Pain, physical discomfort and distress are a tremendous energy drain and the body compensates for this by reallocating mental and spiritual energy to help the person to continue to function with it. Anxiety, depression and an inability to act are symptoms of the eventual energetic taxing of the mind.

The above symptoms can be relieved through conscious application of relaxation techniques to help you release the physical tension in your body. As your muscles resume homeostasis and you regain flexibility of your spine, you will be able to quickly experience a calmness and clarity of mind, which is your birthright.

These four exercises will give you the ability to totally relax during work, play and rest. They will help you let go of tension as it arises, so you may continue to function throughout the day. Your level of relaxation becomes a decision you make because you will have learned to take complete control over your internal state.

Keep the eyes closed throughout this and all of the exercises, so that you may better connect with your body and feel the rhythm of the movement without visual distractions.

Step I: Exercise for Strengthening the Heart

The first exercise relaxes your heart and the surrounding area. It stimulates the nerves that go from the tips of the fingers, through the hands and arms into the chest, meeting at the heart center. By properly holding the position for a set time, the heart muscle literally relaxes, the lungs expand and there is a general cleansing of the entire upper torso by the stimulated activity of the lymphatic system. The shoulder and neck muscles are isometrically flexed, so that a wave of relaxation flows into these muscles when putting the arms down. This exercise is excellent for everyone with a heart! It immediately makes you feel light and at ease, as tension is released from your entire upper body!

The arms may shake slightly and there may be a tingling sensation in the fingers. This is normal. The shaking comes from the release of tension buildup. The tingling is increased nerve activity in the hands.

Do your best to concentrate on your breathing rather than any discomfort you may feel in your arms or shoulders. Your concentration and maintaining straight arms are the keys to this exercise. As time goes on, and with practice, the exercise becomes easier and easier.

To Start:

Begin by sitting on the floor with your legs crossed and your back completely straight. Alternatively, you may sit in a chair with both feet flat on the floor and spine completely straight. Close the eyes.

Position:

Raise the arms to the side at a 60° angle, keeping the elbows straight with the palms facing up; fingers straight and side-by-side. Begin by taking long, slow deep breaths. Breathe through the nose only.

Time:

Hold for a minimum of one minute and a maximum of three minutes. If you find it impossible to hold for the minimum, start with twenty seconds and work up in twenty-second intervals each day until you have completed three minutes.

When you reach the three minute time period, inhale deeply, hold the breath for ten seconds, then exhale and relax the arms down, resting the hands on the lap. Sit still for at least one more minute with your eyes closed, feeling the calming effect of the exercise.

Let your thoughts come and go, but regardless of the difficulty, resolve to complete your time goal without bringing the arms up and down during the exercise. This is essential for you to actually experience the results.

Step II: Exercise for Toning the Organs

Many people store chronic tension in their abdominal area. The term "my stomach is in knots" refers to the constant holding or tightening of the abdominal muscles. This tension hinders or stagnates all of the abdominal organs, including the stomach, intestine, pancreas and liver, thus decreasing physical vitality and general health. A person without abdominal tension is not as prone to sluggishness, constipation, ulcers and other "stomach-worry" ailments.

The second exercise, releases abdominal stress. It gives you an immediate boost of energy throughout your body that lasts well into the day. It stimulates your thyroid, allows you to breathe deeper and increases your energy level.

Benefits: This posture may be utilized to realign the spine. It eliminates rounded shoulders and relieves backache. It massages and stretches the colon and abdominal organs and improves digestion. It tones the female organs and is especially recommended for women who have a tendency to miscarry. It is used in yoga therapy for the management of menstrual disorders, prolapsed asthma and various bronchial and thyroid conditions. Stretching the stomach and intestines tonifies the digestive and reproductive systems and treats constipation. The backward bend loosens up the vertebrae and stimulates the spinal nerves, relieving backache, lumbago, rounded back and drooping shoulders. The front of the neck is fully stimulated, toning all organs and glands of the region, especially the thyroid.

Position:
Lie on your back and relax for a moment. Bend the knees and draw the heels towards the buttocks, while keeping the feet flat and parallel on the floor. Then grab your ankles and holding on to them; slowly raise the hips, arching the lower spine, lifting the navel towards the sky and squeezing the buttocks.

As you lift up, slowly inhale the breath through your nose. Hold the breath as you gently stretch up, lifting as high as it is comfortable, then slowly release the position as you exhale through the nose.

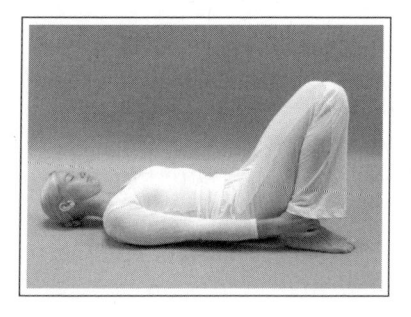

Repetitions:

Slowly repeat this up-and-down movement for a minimum of twelve or a maximum of 26 repetitions, synchronizing the breathing with the movement of the hips. Complete this exercise by holding the last repetition up, inhale and hold the breath for ten seconds. Then relax down, stretching the legs out, feeling the energizing effect of the exercise.

Exercise Tips:

If you can't grab your ankles, keep the knees bent as much as possible and let the arms be at your side with the hands as close as possible to the feet. Lift the buttocks, using the arms to help push you up.

People with a history of low back pain or neck injuries should check with their doctor before beginning. Try to let your breathing do the work. Inhale while bringing the hips up and exhale while letting them down. This exercise will automatically cause you to breathe deeply. Rest on your back for two minutes after the exercise and enjoy its vitalizing effect!

Step III: The Neck Roll Exercise

All the nerves connecting the different organs and limbs of the body pass through the neck. Therefore the muscles of the neck and shoulders accumulate tension, especially after prolonged work at a desk. This exercise relaxes the bridge that joins the brain and spinal chord—the neck. The neck is designed to rotate. If yours doesn't, then you are not getting the proper amount of blood and nerve flow to the brain, because tense neck muscles restrict the blood flow and often calcium deposits or degraded discs block nerve function. Also, nerve impulses from the brain to the rest of the body become impaired. Your nerves allow you to feel life; if the neck is loose and flexible you'll feel more alive and better able to respond successfully to life's challenges. This exercise releases tension, heaviness and stiffness in the head, neck and shoulder region.

Position:
Sit in any comfortable position with the spine straight, feet flat on the floor if sitting in a chair. The eyes are closed.

Gently and slowly drop the right ear down to the right shoulder. Let the head roll back, chin reaching up so as not to compress the cervical vertebrae, then gently roll to the opposite shoulder. Bring the chin all the way around and down by sweeping the chin across the chest from shoulder to shoulder. Continue in the same direction twelve times moving slowly, then switch directions and complete twelve rolls.

Move in synchronization with the breath. Inhale as the head goes back with the chin up. Exhale as the chin points toward the chest. Complete the neck roll by returning the head to center. Feel its relaxing effect for a few minutes. Let your breathing be relaxed.

Step IV: Exercise for Nerve Strength

This pose strengthens the nerves and muscles of the arms and legs. The spinal nerves are toned and circulation is stimulated, especially in the upper spine between the shoulder blades.

The next time you feel short-tempered or impatient and are tempted to take your frustrations out on someone else, do this exercise first. It promotes an immediate balancing effect of your entire nervous system; makes your breathing long, slow and deep; and relaxes isometrically most of the major muscle groups in your body. It gives you an instant outlet for frustration, while it builds your patience. This exercise is as much for the people around you as for yourself.

Position:
Drop to your hands and your knees. Keeping your hands and feet on the floor, lift your hips straight up so that you form a 60° triangle. Drop your head down so that the neck can relax as you hold this position. Hands and feet are spread approximately 24 inches apart.

Close your eyes. Balancing your weight equally on your palms and feet, try to keep both your hands and feet flat on the floor, while maintaining straight knees. Additionally, try to press the head through the arms without bringing the chin to the chest. It's a test!

Time:
Begin long, slow breathing through the nose and continue for a minimum of one minute. Work up to a maximum of three minutes. For many, maintaining this position for just one minute is difficult. You can work up to this by increasing the time you hold this posture by fifteen seconds each day.

Breathing deeply will greatly assist you in maintaining this posture. You must breathe through the nose only because it prevents hyperventilation.

After you have completed your time goal and breathed through the shaking and discomfort, inhale deeply, hold for ten seconds, exhale and relax. Sit in any easy sitting position for at least two more minutes, keeping the spine straight and just be still. Be aware of your breathing and keep the eyes closed to heighten your attention internally.

Exercise Tips:
Enjoying your exercises is far more important than the length of time or number of repetitions you complete. Your body responds more favorably to exercises done with joy than those done with just a sense of discipline. Feel what's happening in your body as you hold the positions. Do not give in to discomfort and let your common sense guide you as your willpower holds you.

The key to successfully completing all the exercises is reliance upon the strength of your breathing. Long deep breathing requires that you first draw the breath into the lower lungs by pushing the abdominal area out as you begin to inhale. As the lungs increase in size, they take more room in the abdomen, requiring the abdomen to expand. After the lower lungs have been filled, the upper lungs can be filled as the chest rises. Exhalation occurs as the lungs decrease in size, thus allowing the chest and then the abdomen to flatten.

Done! Four simple, but very powerful exercises. Their combined effort will not only immediately calm you and give a sustained energy lift, but if done for the full forty days, that calmness will be in everything you do, bringing you greater enjoyment, vitality and success. Keep it up!

THE FIVE TIBETANS

In less than 15 minutes a day, these simple exercises can boost your energy and give your whole body a workout!

Tibetan #1

Stand up straight with your arms outstretched to the sides. (figure 1a) Fingers are together; palms are open and facing downward. Holding this arm position, spin a full circle in a clockwise direction. (If you were to turn your head to the right, that is the direction in which you want to spin.)

Repeat the spin 21 times without a break.

When you finish spinning, stand with your feet together and your hands on your hips (figure 1b). Take a full, deep breath, inhaling through the nose. Exhale through the mouth with your lips pursed in an O. Repeat the inhale and exhale, completing two full breaths before moving on to Tibetan #2.

figure 1a

You may experience some dizziness when you first practice this exercise. Be careful, and don't push it. This exercise strengthens the vestibular apparatus, the balance mechanism residing in the inner ear. With regular practice the dizziness will stop, and the spin will become easy and fluid, even at very fast speeds. This is the same motion practiced by Islamic dervishes, Sufi mystics who twirl at rapid speeds for long periods of time. These mystics are known as "whirling dervishes."

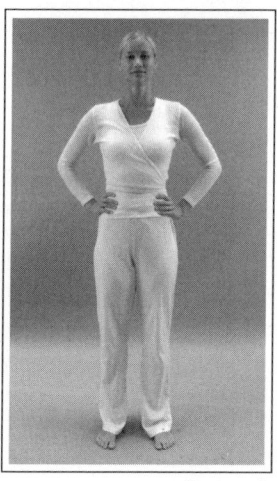

figure 1b

Daily Exercise for Overall Health 243

🌿 Tibetan #2

Lie on your back on a mat or rug. Your legs are fully extended, ankles flexed and touching. Arms are by your sides with the palms flat on the floor (figure 2a). Inhale through the nose, lift your legs to a 90° angle and lift your head, tucking your chin into your chest (figure 2b). This is all done in one smooth motion. Your feet reach toward the sky; your lower back should remain flat on the ground.

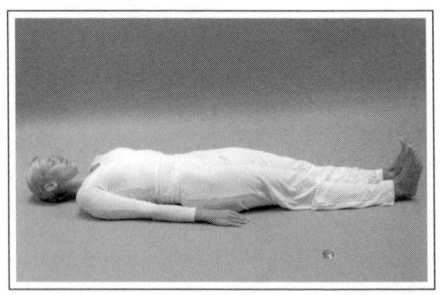

figure 2a

Exhale through either your nose or mouth, bringing your legs and head down to the starting position—completely flat on the ground. Repeat the

figure 2b

entire motion 21 times, inhaling as you raise your legs and head, exhaling as you bring them down. Modification: if you experience lower back pain or have a history with lower back problems, support your lumbar spine by placing your palms face down underneath your hips.

When you are finished, stand with your feet together and hands on hips (figure 1b). Take two full, deep breaths, inhaling through the nose and exhaling through the mouth, with your lips pursed in an O. Continue to the next exercise.

Benefits:
This posture strengthens the abdominal muscles and massages the organs. It strengthens the digestive system, lower back, pelvic and perineal muscles, and helps correct prolapse.

🌿 Tibetan #3

Contraindications: People with severe back ailments, such as lumbago, should not attempt this posture without expert guidance. Those suffering from enlarged thyroid should also be careful.

Kneel with the balls of your feet resting on the ground. Your knees are about four inches apart. Place your palms against the backs of your thighs just below the buttocks. Your spine is erect, with your chin tucked into your chest (figure 3a).

Inhale through the nose, arching back from the waist. Lift and open the chest. Drop your head as far back as you comfortably can (figure 3b). Your hands will support you as you lean back. Then exhale through either the nose or mouth, as you return to the starting position. Repeat the entire motion 21 times in a steady, unbroken rhythm. When you finish, stand with your feet together and your hands on your hips (figure 1b). Take two full, deep breaths, inhaling through the nose and exhaling through the mouth, with your lips pursed in an O.

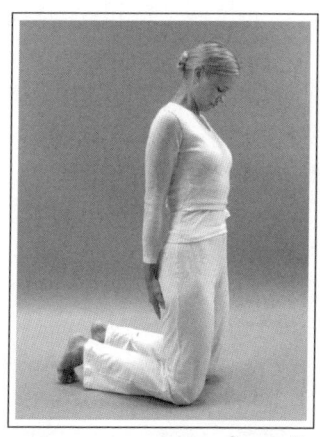

figure 3a

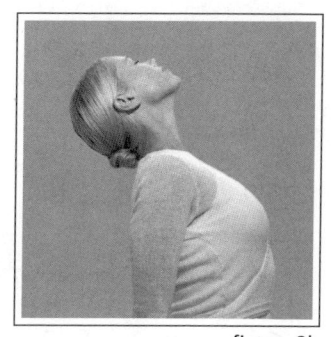

figure 3b

Benefits:
This posture is beneficial for the digestive system and reproductive systems. It stretches the stomach and intestine, alleviating constipation. The backward bend loosens up the vertebrae and stimulates the spinal nerves, relieving backache, lumbago, rounded back and drooping shoulders. The front of the neck is fully stretched, toning the organs in this region and regulating the thyroid gland.

Tibetan #4

Contraindications: People with high blood pressure, heart disease, stomach ulcers or weak wrists should be careful doing this exercise.

Sit up straight with your legs outstretched in front of you. Place the palms of your hands flat on the ground beside your hips. Positioning of the hands is very important; they must be placed exactly alongside the hips. Tuck your chin into your chest (figure 4a).

Inhaling through the nose, raise your hips as you bend your knees, bringing the soles of your feet flat to the ground and dropping your head all the way back (figure 4b). You will come into a position in which the trunk is parallel to the ground while the arms and legs are perpendicular. Exhale through either the nose or mouth as you come down to the starting position. Repeat this motion 21 times in a steady, unbroken rhythm. Do not let your feet slide. The feet should stay in the same place through this whole exercise. Also, the arms should not bend; the movement is instead accomplished by pivoting at the shoulders.

figure 4a   figure 4b

When you are finished, stand with feet together and hands on hips (figure 1b). Take two full, deep breaths, inhaling through the nose and exhaling through the mouth, with your lips pursed in an O.

Benefits:
This posture is good for the nervous, digestive, respiratory, cardiovascular and glandular system. In women, it influences all the hormonal secretions and relieves various gynecological disorders. It also tones the lumbar region of the spine and the achilles tendons.

Tibetan #5

Begin this exercise by supporting yourself on the palms of your hands and the balls of your feet. Both the arms and the legs are about two feet apart. Your head is up and back (figure 5a). Keeping your arms and legs straight, inhale through the nose as you raise your buttocks and tuck your chin into your chest, bringing your body up into a perfect triangle (figure 5b). Exhale through either your nose or mouth as you swing back down to the starting position. Except for the palms of your hands and the balls of your feet, your body remains off the ground during the entire exercise, and your arms and legs do not bend at all. Repeat the entire motion 21 times in a smooth, unbroken rhythm.

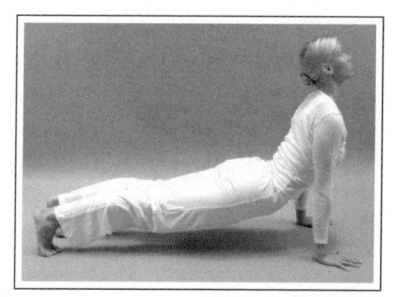

figure 5a

figure 5b

Upon finishing, stand with your feet together and hands on hips (figure 1b). Take two full deep breaths, inhaling through the nose and exhaling through the mouth, with your lips pursed in an O.

When you have finished performing all five exercises, lie down on your back and relax for several minutes. Let the breath be gentle and easy. Notice any new sensations in your body.

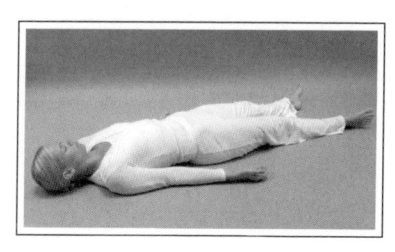

Benefits:

This posture can relocate slipped discs, remove backache and keep the spine supple and healthy. A stiff spine interferes with all nervous impulses sent from the brain to the body and vice-versa. By arching the spine, thus improving circulation in the back region and toning the nerves, better

Daily Exercise for Overall Health 247

communication results between the brain and body. This posture tones the ovaries and uterus and helps alleviate menstrual and other gynecological disorders. It harmonizes the appetite, alleviates constipation and is beneficial for all the abdominal organs, especially the liver and kidneys. The adrenal glands, situated on top of the kidneys, are also massaged and stimulated to work more efficiently. The cortisone level is maintained and the thyroid gland is regulated. This posture has a strong effect on all organs related to the sex, navel, heart, and throat chakras.

CHAPTER TWENTY

THE THREE LINES OF DEFENSE

EVERY PERSON, like God, is a trinity that is expressed by the head, chest and body. The head, which corresponds to the Fire of creation, is the seat of both the primitive substance of the nervous system and the intellect. It is the house of divine fire. It corresponds to the letter Shin in Kabbalah. It governs the will and nervous system. The head, or fire in human creation, represents the mental world. It is the world of thought that we depend upon to understand life. The head is represented in our hands by the head line, which reveals the kind of mentality we possess. The mind, which is responsible for producing the head line, works through the brain. That line shows the activity of the brain—our command center. The capacity to shape our future to our liking is found in the mind and revealed by this line. When the brain is healthy, we acquire the ability to focus the mind and reach our goal. The gifts of mental concentration and self-control, so necessary to overcome the challenges of life, are in this line. The immune system, which is one of our main lines of defense against illness, is affected by the head line. Any break, island, cross or imperfection in the line can display a lack of concentration, a weak intellect, or fixed ideas. This leads to the inability to overcome stress. Therefore, a severe imperfection in our head line can affect our nervous system and make us vulnerable to the detrimental effects of stress. Such imperfection can be repaired by the use of the principle of sound. In other words, the molecular frequency of the brain can be significantly improved by the proper use of sound, giving both a strong nervous system and healthy mind.

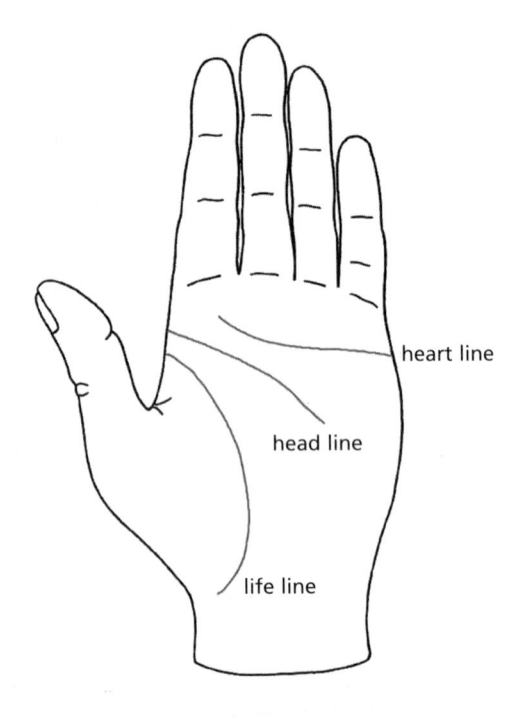

[Diagram of a hand showing the heart line, head line, and life line]

A strong immune system can be obtained by practicing yoga and meditation daily. Also, forgive yourself and others of any wrongdoing that may have been done to you in the past. Blessing the past, both the good and the bad, will transform it into something creative in your life, rather than holding you in the resentment and pain of the experience. It is the process of our thoughts, emotions, reactions to experiences, and our breathing, eating, and exercise habits that influence the formation of the lines of your hands. These signs will accurately and quickly reveal to you what a medical professional, psychologist or counselor may take hours, days, months or years to diagnose. These signs also act as pointers, so you can take action to strengthen the weakness before a serious illness sets in. Following is a suggested meditation to help heal the head line.

Meditation To Heal a Deficient Head Line: Ganpati Kriya

Our five fingers correspond to the five tattvas (elements) of which everything in this universe is made. Prana is the expression of the five elements in harmonious action.

The palms are the face of one's astral body. The astral body is between the mental and physical bodies. Therefore, anything that is to happen on the material plane must first go through the astral plane. A person can change his or her destiny by first creating change on the astral level.

Pressing the thumb to each fingertip applies the science through which each can rewrite his or her destiny. It balances the five elements, thereby bringing the mind, body, emotions, and spirit into harmony.

Ganpati Kriya (pronounced gun-puti) is a very sacred kriya. Ganpati means Ganesha, the elephant god who rode on the back of a rat that could go anywhere. It is also called the impossible-possible kriya, whereby all negativity from the past and present will be redeemed. Ganpati is sometimes called Mangalam, the God of Happiness.

This meditation deals with *samskaras*, *karma*, and *dharam*. It will take away all samskaras, all the negative karmas that you carry from past lives and have to pay for now. The sufferings we have are only because of past debt and past credit.

It also takes away the karma you create from what you do in your day-to-day life. It creates the way for *dharam*—the good you do today that will be rewarded tomorrow.

Mudra:

Sit in easy pose, spine straight, elbows straight, wrists resting on your knees. You will be pressing your thumb to alternating fingers with each sound. Keep your eyes closed.

Chant in an even rhythm to the following simple tune for 11 minutes:

(musical notation) Sa Ta Na Ma Ra Ma Da Sa Sa Say So Hung

Mudra: *(see Kirtan Kriya page 145)*

Sa Press the thumb to the index finger.

Ta Press the thumb to the middle finger.

Na Press the thumb to the ring finger.

Ma Press the thumb to the baby finger.

Continue finger pattern through RA-MA-DA-SA SA-SAY-SO-HUNG

End:

Inhale deeply, then move and rotate your body as if going through physical spasms. Every muscle must be stretched, squeezed, and moved, from the muscles in your face, head and neck, down to your toes. The idea is to circulate the prana to every part of your body. The breath is held approximately 35 seconds. Repeat this procedure, with the breath held in, a total of 4 times. Finally, inhale, sit calmly and concentrate on the tip of your nose for 20 seconds. Then relax.

Meaning of Mantra:

Sa–Ta–Na–Ma	Existence–Life–Death–Rebirth
Ra–Ma–Da–Sa	Sun–Moon–Earth–Infinity
Sa–Say–So–Hung	Infinity–I am thou

A recording of this mantra is also found on the *Blissful Spirit* CD.

HEART LINE

The chest symbolizes the Air of creation and corresponds to the Hebrew letter *Aleph*. It contains the lungs and heart, and is the seat of the respiratory and circulatory system. This is the house of the universal vital essence; it governs the blood and life. The chest is the seat of our emotions and sentiments, and further, it pumps the life blood throughout the body. The chest is, as well, the seat of the electromagnetic field*—another main line of defense. Therefore, it exerts a more refined influence upon us. The chest and magnetic field are represented in our hands by the heart line. This line shows the activity of the heart, a main sustaining device, which pumps and controls our blood stream. The state of our health is determined by the quality and quantity of our blood. Therefore, a strong physical heart will not only render one very magnetic, but also it will give one both good health and a sympathetic nature. A weak heart will generate a lack of warmth and weaken the magnetic field. Also, it will take away the energetic quality of the affection one gives. Any break, cross or imperfection in this line reveals a weak heart, a lack of self control or weak affection. Such problems can be healed by the use of slow, conscious breathing.

In the case of finding one single line in the position occupied by both the heart and head lines, one must remember that since the lines are controlled by the brain and not the heart, the head line will always be present, for it represents the brain from which all lines emanate.

---

*In regards to the electromagnetic field, all living things have a force field. It is our ability to maintain and nurture our energy and balance the frequency of our energy with the people with whom we interact. That determines our health and happiness.

Meditation To Heal a Deficient Heart Line: Three-Point Breath To Maintain and Improve Health

This breath will bring the entire nervous and glandular system into balance. The beauty of life is based on the breath. It is the link between God and you.

Position:
- Sit in a meditative position with the spine straight.
- Hands are in prayer pose (palms pressed together, fingers pointing upwards, placed at the level of the sternum).
- Eyes are closed and focused between the mid-brow point.

Breath:
Inhale for 20 counts, hold 20 and exhale 20. If you cannot do each part for 20 counts, start with 10 counts for each and gradually build up to 20.

Repeat breath cycle for 11 minutes.

LIFE LINE

The abdomen, which symbolizes the Water of creation, contains the stomach, liver and intestines. It governs the lymph and flesh, and corresponds to the letter Mem in Kabbalah. The activity in the abdomen is shown in the hand by the life force line. This line indicates one's physical health and vitality. It represents our third line of defense—the digestive system. It reveals the abundance of strength that we accumulate and from which we operate. Any break, cross or imperfection in this line can be a threat to both our health and life on earth. Such a problem can be corrected by the practice of yoga and exercise, proper diet and the use of herbs. It cannot be stressed enough how important it is to maintain a healthy digestive system. This can be achieved by proper eating habits, and by refraining from eating when you are under stress, emotional, or in a hurry. All food we eat must preferably be cooked or served by someone who not only loves cooking, but also has a love for us.

REGARDING THE LINES:
- A broken, wavy, uncertain, chained or islanded line weaken the power of that line.
- A break in a line indicates troubles, obstacles, changes or illness.
- A star on a line is a challenging sign.
- When a line turns back and starts toward the source after a break, this is not good.
- A dot on a line indicates disorder.
- A deep-cut cross on the line indicates an obstacle.
- Pale lines indicate weakness of health and want of energy.
- Red lines indicate hopefulness of disposition or rash temperament.
- Broken lines denote failure of energy and vitality.
- Small and branched lines are indicative of troubles.

If you have a deficient life line, you need to make the above improvements and additions to your lifestyle. Do the following meditation for healing.

Meditation To Heal a Deficient Life Line: Vatsar Dhouti Kriya

This kriya should only be done on an empty stomach. Don't do it more than twice a day. It should also be the last of your daily morning or evening meditation practice.

Process:
- Sit in easy pose, hands on knees. Apply neck lock, with the back of the neck straight and the chin pulled in.
- Make a beak of the mouth and drink in air through the beak. Hold the air in as long as possible as you churn your stomach round and round. When you must exhale, do so through the mouth without pressure.
- Do the exercise a total of three times at one sitting, then drink two quarts of water. Avoid hot, spicy foods for the rest of the day.

Comments:
This kriya eliminates all digestive problems including chronic excess acidity. Since many other diseases, such as colds and flu, start with problems of digestion and elimination, this kriya works toward general health as well.

Develop the habit of walking a mile or so a day to keep your body strong and healthy, and to massage the organs of digestion and elimination. During the evening, take a walk after your meal. This will stimulate your digestive system, so that when you sleep, your body can be totally at rest.

CHAPTER TWENTY-ONE

TRANSITION

GENERALLY, AFTER THE LOSS of a dear one, the question about the purpose of life and death surfaces quite strongly. We start to question the reason of existence. We often want to resolve the mystery of where our loved ones go after death.

The truth is, since the time of our first incarnation from our fall from paradise as individual cells, we have had numerous earthly experiences in different physical bodies as different personalities. Throughout these experiences, our inner self has been the same, and through the cycle of earthly existences, the separate lessons and experiences of each lifetime have accumulated as added wisdom.

The final goal of this process is the perfection of selfhood to the point where earthly experiences are no longer repeated because study and growth, as well as consistent efforts at reintegration, have brought that person again to divinity. Then, we become a pillar in the temple of God and go out no more.

Death in this world is birth in the hereafter, or astral world. Although the physical body disintegrates to dust after death, life always goes on. The astral body arrives in the heavenly sphere with the soul. After the same process of birth, maturity and death, the astral body dies in the astral world. The only thing left is the divine parcel, which is the soul with the essence of its former personality and experience. Memory of our former life on earth gets buried in our subconscious mind.

One of the reasons that we do not readily recall former lives on this earth is simply due to the fact that the physical brain is new at birth and is a clean slate, without impression from either the senses or the mind within. The cycle of life can metaphorically be described by the sun's procession from dawn to dusk. The sun rises at dawn, reaches its zenith at noon, and sets at night. Sunset in one place is sunrise in another. The same logic can be applied to man. Man is born and grows to maturity, then the body declines until death.

At the moment of departure from earth, there is often a struggle, shown externally in the agony of death. The silver chord, which is the bond between the spirit and the physical body, breaks during the fainting fit.

The silver chord connects our soul with the physical body at three important locations. The first location, spiritually referred to as the Father, is in the vicinity of the pineal gland. This is the seat of the will. The will manifests in our physical selves through the breath and sleep.

The second location, spiritually referred to as the Son, is at the heart. This is the center of love. Love manifests in our physical selves through the circulatory and nervous systems. It governs the etheric body as it works to assimilate the life force operating through the blood and nerves.

The third location, spiritually referred to as the Holy Spirit, is at the base of the spinal column. The final nerve outlet, located at the rectum, provides a base for the silver chord. This is the center of activity. Activity manifests in our physical selves through the processes of assimilation and elimination.

When the time has come for a soul to leave the earth, the silver chord is severed from its three points of attachment. Simultaneously, activity occurring in the brain causes a break between the subtle body and the nervous system.

During the first phase of soul departure, certain endocrine glands inject the blood with a mortal substance that slows the heart. The silver cord attachment to the heart begins to loosen. Eventually, it breaks altogether and life departs, via the vagus nerve, through the fontanel located at the top of the head. During this process the individual experiences the coma state that precedes death. This coma state is reflected in the decreasing activity of the brain. Once it has reached the fontanel, the vital energy, or life force, exerts its power to tear the thin etheric membrane. The energy of life effectively leaves the body.

Generally, the separation of the physical, or material body and the astral body occurs slowly as the individual enters into a space of ultimate relaxation. This process is not always conscious. As the physical body becomes lighter and lighter, the individual feels a sense of great peace. Physical eyesight progressively gives way to a spiritual vision that allows the individual to view his own departure. Moreover, the astral body assumes the shape and contour of the physical body and the individual is given the last opportunity to reexperience his life on Earth. In some cases, the astral body is visible during departure, appearing as a luminous form that stays near the physical body. At times it is even seen near the grave of the newly departed.

For the less evolved individual, the physical body has a stronger magnetism than the soul. During decomposition, the astral body of such individuals remains with the physical body for a long period of time, as opposed to promptly joining the soul on its journey. These people can stay suspended in the coma state that occurs after death for months or years without any awareness of their own departure. Sometimes, attachment, greed, lust and insecurity make a human earth-heavy.

To avoid getting stuck on the Earth after death, we must balance the amount of earth and ether in us. Those who are ruled by the lower self have too much earth energy. It is very difficult for their spirits to leave the Earth after death. For example, they may have a beautiful house that they don't want to let go of when they pass on, so often they become the ghost that haunts certain sites. It is important to emphasize that the soul's awareness of its own departure is determined by the individual's level of evolution. Those who are more evolved will quickly proceed to the higher astral world.

Judgment occurs within the first three minutes of death. You are your own judge and jury. There are only two choices: you can either condemn or forgive yourself. If you choose forgiveness, you will be liberated. Exaltation is possible only when you acknowledge and accept that the experiences that caused you guilt, pain and suffering were God's will.

The three principles man is made up of are the physical body, the astral body, and the eternal spiritual principle. These are also affected at death.

The first principle, the physical body, disintegrates into its elemental constituents. The corpse of body and flesh returns to the earth or to some other modality of the physical plane that has given up its elements to allow the spirit to exist in it. Since the body consists of the five elements, normally three days after death, the soul leaves, and the body goes back to the 5 elements of earth, air, fire, water, and ether. The cells separate and return to the mineral kingdom. Those cells and substances that have been employed in human evolution will eventually find themselves returning to help nourish other life.

After death, the second principle, or the astral body, divides itself into two parts: the lower, which will remain on the physical plane, is diffused throughout the life of the universe and helps in decomposing the corpse, if need be.

The higher part of the astral body or plastic envelope which is influenced by astrological patterns, carries the spiritual principle or spirit to the realm where it is harmonized by the sum total of its karma. The higher part of the astral body will evolve on to the higher astral plane, enfolding the spirit in its astral evolution. The amount of astral matter, or size of higher astral body, the spirit is able to bring with it corresponds to the quality of aspirations held by the spirit during its incarnation. That is why it is so important to do good, to help, serve, and uplift others while one is on earth. A spirit who held lofty aspirations is able to take a greater portion of astral matter. Of course, at the moment of departure, the spirit attempts to draw in as much astral energy as possible. Spiritual help arrives in the form of angels and loved ones. They provide both comfort and guidance to the newly departed soul. Ancestors wait to receive the soul returning to them on the astral plane, just as relatives wait to receive the child who is delivered into the earthly plane. It is important to note that individuals are able to stay close to the earth during the initial days following their departure in order to both advise their loved ones and ease their pain. This is accomplished through dreams and/or intuition.

As the spirit begins its journey, it goes through a period of distress, during which its current consciousness seeks to rid itself of all memory of the physical organs to which it was once connected. The length of the unrest depends upon the help given to the spirit on both the physical and astral planes. When the spirit is released from unrest, it realizes that, while more truly alive than when on earth, it can no longer access the material plane through communication. Feelings become the spirit's only link between the two worlds.

Those who have been liberated and purified from the influences of the material world have the chance to meditate on their mistakes and repent. It is through repentance that they are blessed and cleansed of all their misdeeds. Those who have done a lot of service work can continue to do so from the astral world.

The spirit journey is not complete, however. It now makes every effort to attain the second astral death that will hasten its evolution. Whether or not an astral death can be achieved depends on the level of morality attained by the spirit. Indeed, the entire astral odyssey is marked by judgments, questions and tests as the spirit is compelled to battle the astral beings that seek to challenge it. When the spirit is successful, the lower astral body is cast off, atom by atom, and the body of glory replaces the astral body. As the lower astral body dies, the tenuous aspects of the material body undergo a process of disintegration in the hereafter. Then, the inner self is compelled by law to reincarnate in a physical body in order to equalize its karma. Evolution continues.

The spiritual principle or spirit is the permanent part of a human and of all mankind. Full awareness of this is Christ-consciousness.

A new physical incarnation often gives an opportunity of hastening forward a tardy evolution. As a result of millions of incarnations, man starts searching for a way out of the cycle of life and death. Then the cycle of the rebirth of the self begins again. Humanity is imprisoned within a circular course. The only way to break out of this is for us to start to set aside the personal ego and all I-centeredness, so that we may open the door to the higher state of consciousness, one in which all the glory of God's wisdom comes to light again. People waste their lives running after money, power, fame, glory and sensual pleasures. We forget that everything is temporary. The things we strive for are nothing but shadows. They come out of nothingness and return to nothingness. Most things rise, shine and fade away. Everything we try to hold onto slips away and is replaced by something else. Nothing of eternity can be found in this world. *Everything changes. Nothing is permanent.*

In fact, on the seventeenth day after departure, the soul must cross the magnetic field of the earth. Those souls who cannot cross the magnetic field are earthbound. That is why it is so important to pray, meditate or chant mantras while you are alive, because a meditative or prayerful mind can make the crossing much easier. More importantly, the mantra that you chant while you are alive will surround you with an aura of light and beautiful music, and carry you across the magnetic field with a clear consciousness, on your way to the higher astral world.

While it may appear that the human body is merely the sum total of its physical representation, the truth is that the human system is a composite of three bodies: the physical, astral and mental. The essence of our being does not reside with the physical self, but rather with the internal spark of God which gives us the strength to subjugate our ego and turn away from the I-centered behavior that strives for arbitrary, material success and the fulfillment of vain glorious pursuits.

The astral body is the animating force. Just as the newborn is connected to his mother via the umbilical cord, the physical body is connected to the astral body via a silver cord. Life can only be initiated after this connection between the physical and astral bodies has been firmly established. When the umbilical cord is severed after birth, the human being begins another cycle on Earth. It is in the physical body, then, that both the astral body and the soul are able to function on this plane of reality. The physical body has become the vehicle, not the point.

At the moment of death, the silver cord is severed, just as the umbilical cord is severed at the moment of birth, and the individual again enters into a new existence. For those who commit suicide, this process is one of great anguish. They remain invisibly bound to the physical body they thought they had left behind until the day appointed for natural death arrives. During this time, they experience tremendous moral suffering. Tormented by physical thirst and hunger, they watch as the organs they have recklessly discarded begin to decompose. Moreover, they enter into an unceasing battle with the larvae of the lower astral body, which come, determined to claim their spoil. Closely tied to the Earth, though unaware of this condition, suicide spirits can consume the minds of weak individuals and mediums. Many occultists attribute madness to such spirits.

Upon the moment of natural death, a suicide spirit returns to his ancestors and is immediately reincarnated in an inferior physical body that is often deformed in some way. Suicide increases the karmic obligations of the soul. The struggle the suicide spirit believed he had successfully abandoned is resumed in the next life cycle, when the burdens incurred by the suicide act, must be dealt with. The conscious enactment of black magic rituals and criminal behavior will add to the punishment meted out during the reincarnation of the suicide spirit.

Again as mentioned earlier, the visible, physical world is the shadow of the often invisible, astral world. Our souls alternate between these two worlds during various states of incarnation. During death in the visible sphere, the physical body decomposes and its elements remain in this sphere. We are then born into the hereafter. In due time, our human system experiences death in the hereafter as well. The elements that comprise the invisible body disintegrate and the self is born into the visible world once again. This is the process of reincarnation.

The hereafter must not be mistaken for the kingdom of God. The kingdom of God exists beyond the boundary of the circular, continual course of life and death. It is only when we free ourselves from the wheel of birth and rebirth, through the resolution of karma, that we are able to return to our eternal home. Full realization of the internal spark of God, our true self, is the only means to achieve this desired end.

A MANTRA OF LIGHT FOR DEPARTING ONES: LUMEN DE LUMINE

Lumen de Lumine is the symbol of the ineffable presence of the supreme principle. Chanting or listening to *Lumen de Lumine* will create a communion between you and the beneficent and benevolent hosts of the superior astral world. It will connect you to the most powerful and protective egregore of the Kabbalists of Light. It is the mantra of physical protection against the ill will of other people. It is a prayer of the strongest potency that will keep misfortune away and bring peace, love, and mercy into the lives of those who chant or listen to it. There is a great hierarchy of celestial and terrestrial beings between heaven and earth. By chanting or listening to *Lumen de Lumine*, you are establishing a spiritual communion with these beings, but most important, you are connecting with the luminous ones who dwell in the sun.

Lumen de Lumine will bring out the spiritual light of the soul and make you receptive to its healing force. Working with it will spiritualize your thoughts, thereby giving you more understanding of the truth. *Lumen de Lumine* is at the root of the Christian Doctrine, which is a vital part of Kabbalists of Light. *Lumen de Lumine* is the only part recovered from the Nicene Creed. The ancient Nicene lived in the town of Nicaea near Constantinople, now known as Istanbul. A creed is a formula for the expression of the faith that one holds or professes, and *faith is wisdom in action*.

Lumen de Lumine is the prayer, the energy and the pattern of Christ—the generally misunderstood divine element in all humanity. If it manifests accurately in the individual, it becomes the personal Christ within that individual. Christ manifested Himself in Moses, Buddha, Krishna, Jesus and Guru Nanak. He infiltrates all lands and all ages.

Christ is the illumined master, in whom the divine and the human are so perfectly synchronized that the powers of the cosmic operate through him and in accord with the laws of nature. He is the embodiment of the logos principle, the perfect human. He is the ideal human, the pattern for all humans to follow and emulate, and to follow in his steps is the solution to the world's troubles, therefore redemptive. Christ is the universal, spiritual, living, and conscious power principle, identical in its nature with the logos (word of God made flesh) with which the highest spiritual attributes of each person becomes ultimately united.

The light that flows from the sun, which produces tremendous transformation in the universe and brings with it great benefits for all creatures, is the light of Christ. Christ is the spirit of the sun, the cosmic principle without beginning and end. The sun leads to universality of all people of all faiths. *Lumen de Lumine*, or Light of Light, invokes the beneficial Christic force, the spiritual and positive energies of the Sun, the fountain of light.

Extensive use over the ages by the Kabbalists of light has empowered it on the collective psyche. As a result it surrounds those who chant or listen to it with a blanket of light. It opens the heart and brings serenity. Time has proven that holy blessings come to those who are in its company.

Lumen de Lumine	*Light of Light*
Deum de Deo	*God of God*
Lumen de Lumine	*God by the way of Light*
Deum Verum de Deo Vero	*Light by the way of God*
Lumen de Lumine	*Light of Light*

Everything is temporary.
The things we are striving for
are nothing but shadows.
They come out of nothingness and
return to nothingness.
Most things rise, shine and fade away.
Everything we try to hold onto slips
away and is replaced by something else.
Nothing of eternity can be found in this world.
Everything changes. Nothing is permanent.

CONCLUSION

LEARNING TO HEAL OURSELVES actually brings us into direct contact with spiritual life and the source of all blessings, opening the channels to the divine good as it exists within us and throughout the universe. In reality, no one can cure you but yourself, and the only way to generate a permanent cure is through self-healing. Self-healing is only possible when you recognize and remove the negative mental attitudes and speech patterns that are at the root of all health troubles. God has no decree that we should suffer. It is the unhealthy way we think, feel, speak and act that brings about our physical suffering, for what is within you is reflected without. *Self-healing simply means our becoming acquainted with the healing laws of the universe and living in accordance with them, so that the damage caused by living out of harmony with the laws can be undone.* This, in turn, will cause us to become filled and infused with the Christ consciousness, so that we may be able to work in the light and become one with the light until all darkness disappears from our lives. It leads us to be at peace with ourselves and our environment.

It is also important to take special care of our physical body by keeping it clean, comfortable, and nourished with the right food, thus providing all the vital nutrients for the normal functioning of our cells. Another important step is the necessity of regular medical check-ups to insure that our physical bodies are functioning properly and to detect minor health problems when they can be easily treated.

This book will ease your karmic burdens, connect you with the benevolent frequencies of the universe, and bring God's bounty into your life. Above all, the divine spiritual wisdom herein revealed will become your best protection against illness and disease. By adopting the healing principles of the great spiritual masters and wisemen who discovered, experimented with and then shared this timeless and priceless knowledge with the world, we may unearth many truths about ourselves and experience self-healing. Nothing else will give you the divine consciousness that comes from self-healing. You will begin to experience a deep, real and lasting satisfaction within yourself and greater understanding and compassion for the world. Working with these truths will assist you in eradicating thoughts of limitation and disease in your mind, so that you can achieve your goals and heal yourself completely. As you read and work with the principles revealed in *The Divine Doctor*, the beneficial and healing energy of the universe will pour through you. As a result, you will become a clear channel for divine good and reach a higher level of attunement with the universe. This, in turn, will give you creative power that you can use to accomplish your desires with wisdom, so you may manifest your highest destiny.

Raise your awareness, become acquainted with the healing truths revealed in this book, and realize that you must bring the harmony of these laws right through your simplest actions. As a result, you will draw to yourself the continuous grace and healing energy of the universe, as well as like-minded and nurturing people. Above all, by learning the laws of these sacred teachings, developing your spiritual nature and putting God first, you attract the good graces of the universe, causing self-healing to occur. Always remember that the most vital aspect of healing is our daily communion with the God of our hearts, for it is through self-healing that w come to know whe we are and our true place in the Universe. May you ever dwell in the Love, Peace and Light of God and your own divinity.

ABOUT THE AUTHOR

Joseph Michael Levry's work is an invitation to discover the intense and pure inner life of a brilliant mystic and Master teacher who, at the dawn of the 21st century, is bringing a renewal to spirituality. A tireless and dedicated teacher, writer, and lecturer, Mr. Levry, who is also known by his spiritual name Gurunam, has traveled extensively and continuously in the United States, Europe, and Asia for almost three decades. By adopting such a rigorous travel schedule both here and abroad, Gurunam has been able to introduce many to the divine spiritual wisdom as well as tune the frequency of the countries he visits to a higher level of vibration. With the current shift in global consciousness that will culminate in the year 2012, he has decided to teach more intensively in the U.S. and Europe. To this end, he travels nine months out of the year, focusing on New York, Los Angeles, Sweden, Germany, Switzerland, Israel, the UK, and France. Whether traveling, or at home in New York or Los Angeles, Gurunam corresponds with thousands of people of every race and religion, guiding them through the process of self-healing and the realization of meaningful careers, healthy relationships, and life-long dreams.

Since the age of 12, Gurunam has been trained in the esoteric arts and sciences and initiated into many spiritual orders, through which he learned the science of Kabbalah. In his books and lectures, he illuminates Kabbalistic symbols that were once kept secret within the doctrines of Judaism, Christianity, and other religions. Time and time again, he has earned the trust of even the most skeptical through his precise diagnosis of physical ailments, and unique ability to see and analyze the energy field. After 30 years of study, research, and teaching, Gurunam has created a unique synthesis of the powerful teachings of Kabbalah and Kundalini yoga that helps people avoid adversity and improve their lives, the proof of which is revealed in the testimonials of those he has worked with. Believing that nothing is done by chance, and that one can rewrite his or her destiny through the knowledge and application of this divine spiritual wisdom, Gurunam is able to reach all who come to him with a willingness to actively initiate and participate in their own healing.

Having experienced a high level of spiritual realization that made God a reality in his life, Gurunam places a strong emphasis on the fundamental oneness of all religions and the divine spiritual wisdom that comes from the one and only source. For there are many ways but One Supreme Way. There are many truths but One Supreme Truth. God is one, and His Name is Truth. If you ignore the Truth, you will be ignored. Gurunam leads a Kabbalistic, research oriented life, imparting his knowledge without hesitation to a chosen set of students as well as all worthy individuals who cross his path. Many spiritual traditions have lost their knowledge of the science of the soul and the spiritual technology necessary to develop higher consciousness in man. The teachings that flow from Universal

Kabbalah can improve one's life, restore one's health, solve the many problems of one's existence, and lead one to happiness; and that is why they are authentic.

Gurunam's universal style of Kabbalah does not focus on the traditional requirements of an Orthodox lifestyle and the study of ancient texts. Rather, Gurunam espouses and teaches Universal Kabbalah, which is free of the religious aspect of Judaism, Christianity, and Sikhism, yet promotes a Godly and conscientious lifestyle. Whereas traditional Kabbalah emphasizes mysticism as a part of devoted Judaism, Gurunam's teachings focus on the merger of Kundalini yoga and Kabbalah for personal improvement and spiritual happiness. It is targeted to people of all faiths, as well as those with no specific faith. The ultimate goal of Universal Kabbalah is to unite East and West through the magic of sacred music. Sacred music is food for the soul; in it the underlying unity of all life is revealed. It has positive effects on the soul, and the making of spiritual music encompasses ancient science and a vast body of philosophical teachings. Working with Sacred music is akin to meditating on the divine truths that exist on a higher plane of reality. When we engage with sacred sounds, the depths of our being awaken fully to life. In practice, Universal Kabbalah is based on the proper use of the Word. In fact, the whole meditative life of the Universal Kabbalist is built upon the mystery of the Word. Universal Kabbalists believe in the power and efficacy of the WORD which went forth at the creation of the world, and which is now "lost" to the majority of humans. That WORD is supreme. Since the fall of man, it has become our only hope. By practicing with the WORD humans can get to infinity without interpretation or understanding. Devotees do not need to learn Hebrew in order to partake of the divine spiritual wisdom. What is emphasized is the importance of seeing God in oneself, in others, and in every sacred teaching. Gurunam believes that to confine oneself to a particular belief system and deny all others puts us at risk of missing the vastness that is the knowledge of reality. In other words, much good eludes those who restrict themselves, for God is much too vast and tremendous to be limited to one belief or another. God is everywhere, indestructible, indivisible, fearless, unborn, forever, within everything, invisible, immortal, unimaginable, unnamable, formless, unfathomable, destroyer of all, beyond birth and death, more than love itself, beyond all color, all form and karma, beyond all doubt, again God is too vast to be limited to one belief or another.

The combination of Kundalini yoga and Kabbalah produces the ultimate spiritual science, providing the necessary tools for healthy, effective living. The majority of men and women who study Universal Kabbalah have chosen the path of becoming both yogis and Kabbalists. Through the application of both spiritual disciplines, they have come to realize that there is a natural kinship between them. In working with both, they have attuned themselves to the unseen powers and forces of nature, as well as the universal laws that flow in, around, and throughout all of life. The spiritual technology of Universal Kabbalah has shown them how to work in accordance with these laws in order to achieve great success and contentment in their worldly experiences. Together, these men and women have formed an invisible empire of agents of light contributing to the positive evolution of humankind. Universal Kabbalah is expanding quickly in America and other parts of the world. Gurunam has established a healing center in New York, Universal Force Healing Center, of which he is the CEO. True to his vision, Universal Force Healing Center is a non-profit organization dedicated to philanthropic activities that serve humankind, as well as healing individuals by uplifting them from the sufferings of life. In turn, of course, these individuals are then better able to positively contribute to society in both large and small ways. The institution is not only committed to intellectual and spiritual development but is also dedicated to providing a healing sanctuary for the average man or woman. Moreover, Universal Force Healing Center is creating a research team devoted to natural and holistic healing in New York City. Universal Force Healing Center is truly one of a kind in the U.S., where the science of yoga, Harmonyum, sound and mudra therapy, as well as meditation based on the purity of life are helping to diagnose and heal people from chronic cases of physical, emotional, and/or mental disturbance. Moreover, it is committed to the prevention of further troubles. Universal Force Healing Center operates according to the philosophy that spiritual diagnosis and treatment is of the utmost value and efficacy. Its team includes highly qualified yogis and Kabbalists who are well-versed in many diagnostic and healing modalities.

In addition to establishing Universal Force Healing Center, Gurunam is also the president of Rootlight, Inc., a publishing, production, and consulting company that produces sacred music and books that reflect the sacred teachings. In his various CDs and books Gurunam, like traditionalists, presents Universal Kabbalah as a way to know the unknown and see the unseen forces that govern our lives. Moreover, he offers a wealth of Kabbalah and Kundalini Yoga exercises and meditations that allows one to strengthen the nervous system, balance the glandular system, renew the blood, merge with the higher worlds, and improve life. He has also developed Harmonyum, a transcendental healing system born out of Universal Kabbalah. The "Harmonyum Healing System" activates the original seed and awakens the threefold soul, born of the threefold spirit, from the threefold body into self consciousness and self knowledge.

Gurunam maintains that the divine spiritual wisdom contained in Universal Kabbalah creates, within Man that which is known as Mysterium Conjunctionis of the Alchemists, symbolized by the Star of David that unites the upper heavenly triangle with the lower earthly triangle. Only through the true spiritual marriage of the upper and lower triangles can the sacred wisdom cause the spirit to spiritualize matter, transforming one into pure spiritual gold.

ROOTLIGHT PUBLICATIONS
HEALING BEYOND MEDICINE SERIES

Books:

Alchemy of Love Relationships
A practical guide to creating successful relationships through the application of spiritual principles from Kabbalah and Kundalini yoga. The application of these principles will completely change your approach to life and relationships. This is an invaluable book for a richer and more fulfilling love relationship.

The Divine Doctor: Healing Beyond Medicine
This book gives you the key to hundreds of mysteries in medicine and healing which are completely unknown within ordinary medical practices, thereby giving you access to timeless healing technologies that are the birthright of humankind. *The Divine Doctor* reveals the precise methods for working with the spiritual body to achieve self-healing and maintain vibrant health. It will also guide you through these techniques, so that you may recover more quickly from illness and become healthy. *The Divine Doctor* is for all yogis, Kabbalists, doctors, serious health practitioners and anyone who desires to achieve self-healing and help others heal through the application of profound meditations and practical techniques. By reading and practicing these sacred teachings, you will nurture your energy, expand your consciousness, purify your mind, and renew yourself.

The Healing Fire of Heaven: Mastering the Invisible Sunlight Fluid for Healing and Spiritual Growth *(Previously titled The Splendor of the Sun)*
This book will show you practical ways of connecting with the sun in order to capture its many benefits and blessings. Working with the sun is one of the highest, most potent and effective spiritual systems you can come across on this earth. Working with the sun will cause your soul to become active and your spiritual powers to become operative, showing clear visible signs in your mind, spirit and physical body. On a physical level, working with the Sun sparks a complete metamorphosis and renewal of the cells and tissues in the body—all the unhealthy cells and energies are replaced, resulting in health, vitality, complete balance and intelligence.

Lifting the Veil: The Divine Code
Lifting the Veil allows you to penetrate the high mysteries of the Kabbalah by presenting this timeless wisdom in a practical, workable and understandable way. In this book, you will find a time-proven formula to experience a life of grace and joy. Included are over 30 different meditations and simple exercises to enhance your health, balance the mind, body and spirit, and develop intuition.

Advanced Self-study Course (Levels 1–4)
The Sacred Teachings of Kabbalah with Kundalini Yoga
Kabbalah and Kundalini yoga are two ancient and powerful sciences for spiritual growth, and for understanding one's self in relation to the universe. This course is a compelling and extremely practical masterpiece of Universal Kabbalah. The sacred teachings of Kabbalah have been presented in a practical, doable and

understandable way. You will be given some of the most effective meditations and prayers that Kabbalah and Kundalini yoga have to offer. The essence of Kabbalah, that was previously hidden and confusingly presented in various books, has been decoded and put into a form that is effective and powerful in its application. By working with this course, all the dormant qualities and virtues in you are brought to full life, resulting in improved health and well-being on all levels. Then your spiritual knowledge, presence and words will start healing and uplifting others.

Sacred Music Series CDs:

BLISSFUL SPIRIT — Har Gobinday/Ganpati Mantra/Wahe Guru/Ong
These sound vibrations eliminate mental impurities and cause the spirit to blossom, while bestowing divine grace and radiance.

GREEN HOUSE — Har Gobinday (II)/Har Haray Haree Wahe Guru (III)/ Ad Such/*Calm Heart*
These sound vibrations extend the power of projection and protection in the personality. They help open the door to opportunities and attract blessings.

HEALING FIRE — Ong/Prayer of Light/12 Seed Sounds
These sound vibrations give youth, beauty and spiritual illumination. They work on the glandular system and organs. A regular practice of listening to this CD or chanting along with it promotes good health and helps develop intuitive intelligence.

HEAVEN'S TOUCH—Guru Ram Das/Sat Narayan/*Mystical Ivory Coast*
These sound vibrations bring grace, blessings and internal peace. The sound current on the first track synchronizes your energy and expands the aura. It is also for emergency saving grace and spiritual guiding light. The second sound current cleanses the emotions, creates internal peace and allows you to project outer peace. The third track moves you into a meditative space with rhythm.

LUMEN DE LUMINE—For opening the heart and touching the soul
This sound vibration surrounds those who chant or listen to it with a blanket of light. Just listen to it and it will purify and strengthen your aura. Play it in a room and it will clear the energy in a short time. Go to sleep with it and you will wake up revitalized. When faced with challenges, play it continuously; it will eat the darkness out of your life.

MYSTIC LIGHT—RaMa Ram Ram/Hallelu-ya/Lumine De Lumine (II)/ Har Haray Haree/*Sophia*
The sound vibrations on *Mystic Light* revitalize the energy flow within the body and make the aura strong, bright and beautiful. They not only affect the two brain hemispheres and bring you into balance, but they also draw down the protective light and grace of heaven. They give you light, healing, and strength.

OM HOUSE—Activating the Primal Force Within
The sacred sound OM/AUM on *Om House* is mystically vibrated in the most potent and correct way—ONG/AUNG—in order to heal, empower and rejuvenate the chanter or listener. It creates the healing space. This sound is thought to have spe-

cial universal powers for the creation of worldly things. The divine word OM, which is nothing more than AUM, is pregnant with mysterious power. OM stimulates the psychic centers, and is known to have certain therapeutic value.

RA MA DA SA—To heal and/or maintain balance and health
This sound vibration cuts across time and space and brings healing. It maintains, strengthens and improves your health. It can generate beneficial energy in hospital rooms and places of recovery. It will also create a peaceful and productive environment in the workplace. Families can benefit from its harmonizing effects on the home, children and even pets.

SOUL TRANCE — Wahe Guru (II)/Har/*Love, Peace, Light to All (SaReGaMa)*
These sound vibrations help awaken the soul, so you may manifest your higher destiny. They help give clarity, stability, and harmony.

SOUNDS OF THE ETHER — Ad Such/I AM That I AM/Aim/Hari Har/ *The Fire of Prayer*
The sound vibrations on this CD open the door to opportunity, good fortune and the realization of one's dreams and ambitions. When you chant and/or listen to them, you are calling upon the divine helping hand to assist you in attracting true happiness. As a result, you will be blessed with a fulfilling and successful earthly life.

THE SEAL OF HIGHER DESTINY — Eck Ong Kar Sat Nam Siri Wahe Guru (two versions)
This is a Naam that projects the mind beyond the realm of everyday earthly consciousness into the infinity of the cosmos and awakens the soul to one's higher destiny. As all things are included within it, this mantra allows you to understand the greatness of He who spoke and brought the Universe into being. It brightens your energy, wipes out karma, and increases your sense of personal relatedness to the infinite identity.

TRIPLE MANTRA—For protection and to clear obstacles
This sound vibration clears all types of psychic and physical obstacles in one's daily life. It will strengthen your magnetic field and keep negativity away, and it is a powerful protection against car, plane or other accidents. This mantra cuts through all opposing vibrations, thoughts, words and actions.

◆

To obtain our full, updated list of publications and offerings, such as books and meditation/mantra CDs, please contact Rootlight, Inc. by phone, mail, e-mail or visit our web site. In addition, contact us if you would also like more information on Universal Kabbalah workshops, Kundalini yoga and meditation intensives or Harmonyum Healing Certification.

Please visit us at www.rootlight.com for more selections.

Rootlight Order Form

Title	Each	Qty.	Subtotal
BOOKS			
Alchemy of Love Relationships	$25	x ____	= ____
The Divine Doctor	$25	x ____	= ____
Lifting the Veil	$23	x ____	= ____
The Healing Fire of Heaven	$23	x ____	= ____
ADVANCED SELF-STUDY COURSE			
Level 1	$390	x ____	= ____
Level 2	$390	x ____	= ____
Level 3	$390	x ____	= ____
Level 4	$390	x ____	= ____
CDS			
Blissful Spirit	$19	x ____	= ____
Green House	$19	x ____	= ____
Healing Fire	$19	x ____	= ____
Heaven's Touch	$19	x ____	= ____
Lumen de Lumine	$19	x ____	= ____
Mystic Light	$19	x ____	= ____
OM House	$19	x ____	= ____
Ra Ma Da Sa	$19	x ____	= ____
Soul Trance	$19	x ____	= ____
Sounds of the Ether	$19	x ____	= ____
The Seal of Higher Destiny	$19	x ____	= ____
Triple Mantra	$19	x ____	= ____

SUBTOTAL ____

Shipping in USA:
add $5.50 for 1st item,
$.50 each additional item.

Shipping/Handling ____
N.Y. residents add 8.65% sales tax ____
TOTAL DUE ____

Prices subject to change (11/05)

PLEASE CONTINUE ORDER ON OTHER SIDE OF FORM>>>

PAYMENT INFORMATION: (Please print clearly)
Payment enclosed: ❑ Check ❑ Money Order *Made payable to:* Rootlight, Inc.

Please charge order to my credit card: ❑ Visa ❑ Mastercard

NAME AS SHOWN ON CARD: _____

CREDIT CARD NUMBER _____

EXPIRATION DATE MM/DD/YYYY _____

SIGNATURE _____

BILLING ADDRESS _____

CITY _____ STATE _____ ZIP _____

SHIPPING INFORMATION

NAME _____

ADDRESS _____

CITY _____ STATE _____ ZIP _____

PHONE (if we have questions about your order) _____

E-MAIL _____

Thank you for your order!

ROOTLIGHT, INC.
15 Park Avenue Suite 7C, New York, NY 10016
TOLL FREE IN U.S.: (888) 852-2100   FAX: (212) 685-1710
rootlightorder@aol.com   rootlight@earthlink.net
www.rootlight.com

UNIVERSAL FORCE HEALING CENTER

7 WEST 24TH STREET
NEW YORK, NY 10010
T 917.606.1730
www.universalforceyoga.com

universal kabbalah studies • daily yoga classes • corporate and private yoga programs • children's yoga • workshops • harmonyum healing • holistic healing & massage • retreats • yoga teacher training • and more!